Judges

Oagile Bethuel Key Dingake

INDIA · SINGAPORE · MALAYSIA

Notion Press

Old No. 38, New No. 6
McNichols Road, Chetpet
Chennai - 600 031

First Published by Notion Press 2020
Copyright © Oagile Bethuel Key Dingake 2020
All Rights Reserved.

ISBN 978-1-64828-865-4

Dedication

This book is dedicated to my wife and our children, whose love and support have always sustained me.

I owe a heavy debt of gratitude to them.

Contents

Foreword

A judiciary that is independent and impartial is the bedrock of democracy and the rule of law. The life blood of any judiciary is the confidence and trust the public repose in it. As is often said the judiciary is the last line of defence against any encroachment on rights and freedoms under the law.

This book discusses the work of judges, highlighting, judicial values that are essential for earning and retaining public confidence in the judiciary. These values include: independence, impartiality, integrity, propriety, equality, competence and diligence. These core values were agreed at a meeting of the Judicial Integrity Group held in Bangalore, India, in February 2001, resulting in what is now commonly referred to as 'Bangalore Principles of Judicial Conduct'. Two years later, in 2003, the United Nations Human Rights Commission (UNHRC) endorsed the above principles, considered amongst common and civil law jurisdictions as the authoritative statement on the values that should inform judicial conduct.

The book also discusses wide ranging topics of daily interest to judges such as fact finding, accountability, judgment writing, judicial case management and sentencing. The book is packed with practical tips on how judges should approach their work.

In an era where simplicity and brevity often eludes legal literature, this book is written in breathtakingly simple language and is free of jargon. It is also not cluttered with references or footnotes. Judge Dingake was able to write with amazing simplicity that does not however oversimplify the subject.

These days judges' and the judgments they write are hardly out of news. What they decide often excites happiness and anger in equal measure. Judges are only accountable to the constitution and should not deliver judgments to please anyone. They must absorb condemnation and praise with grace and humility.

In this book Judge Dingake makes many invaluable practical tips, including the following critical ones:

- That a judge should serve with humility.

- That a judge's primary role is to preside and should not be chased from the judgment seat without justifiable cause.

- That a judge's role is to keep the ring and not to enter the fight.

- That whilst a presiding judge may discuss legal principles in particular factual settings, in general terms, the ultimate duty to decide lies with the presiding judge.

- That a trial is not an opportunity to demean the dignity of any person.

- That judges should always be alive to the possibility of subconscious bias.

I am certain that this book would be extremely useful to judges, lawyers, law students, scholars, political scientists and members of the public who are interested in how judges approach their work, their guiding values and principles and the decisional tools they employ. It will particularly fascinate lawyers who may be interested in the judicial process from a jurisprudential perspective.

We have in this book, an articulation of the fundamental principles that must guide modern judiciaries of all nations; a book of immense value to the general public and all those concerned with nurturing and building judiciaries of unimpeachable integrity.

I am grateful to Judge Dingake for inviting me to write this foreword to this very thought provoking book. I recommend it strongly to all Judges across all jurisdictions and members of the public.

*** Professor Elizabeth Crawford Spencer***

Acting Dean of College of Business, Law & Governance,
James Cook University, Australia

Acknowledgements

This book would not have been completed and published without the support and assistance of a number of people. I am especially indebted to my sister Lady Justice Sunkutu for editing and proof reading the manuscript; my friends Beryl Shumirai Akumu and Alice Nantaba who also assisted greatly in proof reading the manuscript. I also wish to express my sincere gratitude to my friend, Dr Melinda Sutherland for her invaluable and helpful comments on some ideas propounded in this book.

The Acting Dean of College of Business, Law and Governance at James Cook University, Australia, Professor Elizabeth Crawford Spencer was kind to provide a foreword to this book. I thank her most sincerely.

Nobody has been more important to me in pursuit of publishing this book than members of my family. Their love and support are always guaranteed in whatever I do. I thank them most sincerely.

Preface

The fundamental role of the judiciary as an independent branch of the State, in accordance with the principles of separation of powers and the rule of law is recognised by many international legal instruments including the United Nations Basic Principles on the Independence of the Judiciary of 1985.

The aforesaid Principles obliges the judiciary to decide matters before them impartially, on the basis of facts, and in accordance with the law, without any restrictions, improper influences, inducements, pressures, threats or interferences, direct or indirect from any person or authority.

An indispensable element of the judicial guardianship of the constitution within the framework of democracy is that the judge and the judiciary, as an institution, enjoy manifest independence. The other branches of the State should not, under any circumstances, influence judicial outcomes.

The judges, in the performance of their duties, must be impartial. Impartiality means that the judge should treat the parties before him equally, providing them with equal opportunity to say their side of the story. Impartiality means a judge has no personal interest in the outcome of the case.

The notion of separation of powers comes into play in matters of judicial appointments and selection. Quite often perceptions of judicial independence are influenced by the way in which judges are selected.

International standards require that a necessary condition of an independent judiciary is that it must enjoy security of tenure and should not be subject to politically motivated removals. International standards have established clear criteria for removal of judges. It requires among other things that removal processes should be fair. The mandate of the judiciary in a democratic State is to guarantee the very existence of the rule of law. When disciplinary proceedings against a judge are initiated, public confidence in the functioning of the judiciary is at stake.

The judge's role is to keep the ring and not to enter the fight. Quite often sparks fly in court, often impugning the knowledge, independence or impartiality of the judge. However, in preparing judgement the judge should cast all these aside and remain faithful to facts and law. It is also important for judges to always keep in mind that trials are not opportunities to demean the dignity of any of the participants – but an occasion for the dispassionate findings of fact and application of the law.

Every judge is a product of his time. It is through this prism that his objectivity must be assessed and critiqued. The purpose of objectivity is to be dispassionate as one can possibly be; it is not to rid the judge of the circumstances that produced him. The objectivity required of a judge is not always easy, but it is attainable.

The values of any civilised society based on the rule of law and democracy depends to a greater extent on the faithful performance of judicial duty. Today's judge is required to give effect to the values of a pluralistic society that cherishes democracy, human rights, tolerance and diversity.

The primary function of a judge is to dispense justice. It has always been a revered principle of liberty and freedom that judges are no respecters of persons but the law; and that they should always stand between the subject and any attempted encroachment on his liberty by the executive, ever vigilant to ensure that any governmental action is justified,

This book is about judges; how they are appointed and removed; their work, and the basic values that every judge must subscribe to. It discusses varied topics that are important to the work of every judge such as: principles of judicial conduct, fact finding, how to approach issues of credibility of witnesses, judgment writing, judicial case management and sentencing.

OAGILE BETHUEL KEY DINGAKE,

Port Moresby, Papua New Guinea

*15*th *August 2019*

Chapter One

INTRODUCTION

The Bangalore Principles of Judicial Conduct provides that there are six core judicial values. These are: independence, impartiality, personal integrity, propriety, equality, competence and diligence. As the United Nations Office on Drugs and Crime commentary on the said principles observes, a judiciary of undisputed integrity is indispensable to a democratic society. Consequently, the judiciary in any country that proclaims to be a true democracy should always be the last line of defence against unjustified encroachments on the rights and freedoms of individuals.

Whether a judiciary in a democracy can be trusted to protect rights and freedoms of individuals is a function of many factors. The manner in which judges are appointed impacts on both the personal and institutional independence of the judges and the judiciary as an institution respectively. It also impacts on the integrity of the judiciary. The independence of the judiciary does not mean it is not accountable. The judiciary, in executing its functions is accountable through the constitution to the people, but the accountability mechanisms must not be such as to undermine the independence of the courts.

This book is about all the above, including judicial craft. It is born out of my more than fifteen years on the bench, as judge of all tiers of the Superior Courts, and also as judge of an International Criminal Court. The book discusses, in as candid a manner as possible, various aspects of judgeship; their appointment and removal, the values of independence and impartiality, ethics, theoretical positions on law and life, qualities and attributes, judgement writing, case management, fact finding, and sentencing those convicted of crimes. It discusses all these in the context of separation of powers and the need for mutual respect amongst the three branches of the state, namely the executive, legislature and the judiciary.

Judicial craft or the art of judging, essentially refers to how judges go about doing their job, in a manner that is not only fair but seen to be fair, consistent with their duty to do right to all people without fear or favour, affection or ill – will. It encompasses many elements such as command and mastery of the language of the court and effective communication.

In many ways judicial craft is what Aristotle described as practical wisdom. This comes more with experience. It is often a function of practical engagement with the law. It includes the way in which, amongst others, judges wade through a maze of procedural rules, law and facts to decide a matter. Through judicial craft, judges often find greater meaning and fulfillment in their professional lives. The art of writing judgements and making findings of facts are in my mind, some of the most important aspects of judicial craft.

Judges have extensive powers over the affairs of their fellow human beings; they are the ultimate guardians of the constitution, and the rights embodied therein, and lastly, but certainly not the least, judges are the last line of defence when rights are in jeopardy. At the work place, judges have a special role to promote an environment of harmony and fairness. Judges also have the power to set aside, or cancel, decisions of other branches of government; if they believe that they are contrary to the law and or constitution. By fearlessly upholding the constitution, and the rule of law, judges contribute to an orderly development of society.

Co-equal branch of the state

The judiciary is a co-equal branch of the state, together with the executive, and the legislature. Its primary mandate is to interpret the law and protect the rights of persons. It must at all times demonstrate mutual respect to other branches, but never should it shirk its responsibility to say what the law is. At the same time, it should not be over enthusiastic to accept to adjudicate matters that belong to the other branches.

The principle of mutual respect is important because, amongst other reasons, the judiciary has no purse or sword to enforce its decisions, and for this reason it relies on the good will and sense of constitutional duty of other branches to have its judgements enforced. It is the mutual respect and fidelity to the law that would earn it public confidence that it needs for its authority. Public confidence does not mean that judges should engage in popularity contests.

Judges should be indifferent to popularity

It is in fact the business of the judges to be indifferent to popularity. Public confidence demands that judges must act in accordance with their professional standards and obey the law. Public confidence is enhanced by transparent processes and reasoned judgements. The requirement to provide reasons is good judicial practice. The Court's decision must be analytically sound and rationally defensible.

Although most constitutions attempt to enumerate and separate the powers of the three branches of the state, quite often the respective lanes or spheres of influence are not always clear. This notwithstanding, the courts should always be vigilant that they don't encroach into the other lanes of other branches. It is very important to understand and appreciate that the appearance of encroachment may just be as bad as actually overstepping the constitutional boundaries.

Judges wield enormous powers that they must use with extreme care. Court rulings impose official and practical consequences on litigants, some life changing. In court they must exude impartiality, independence and common courtesy. In court they should always ensure that everyone plays by the rules.

Increasingly, it is accepted that judges are not merely umpires, but for lack of a better phraseology, lawmakers of a special type. I discuss this controversial proposition in one of the chapters of the book. It is an idea in which judicial opinion is still divided. It is an idea with respect to which I do not equivocate. The interpretative power of the courts is a source of law.

Protection of human rights

At the international level, judges are important in ensuring that rogue states do not ride, roughshod, over the rights of people with impunity. They also have a duty to bring offenders, no matter what their positions or stations are, in society, to account to the law and before the judges who are sworn to administer justice. I do not know of any other profession that is mandated, by the people, to ensure order, stability and peace; other than judges. People look to the judges to vindicate their grievances and to do justice to all and sundry; whether rich or poor. It is, indeed, true to say that, ideally, every judge must be the very personification of justice.

This book is intended to be simple, and free of legal jargon, so that even people who do not have a legal background may appreciate it or, if nothing else, at least learn something about what judgeship entails.

Before I proceed any further, I find it necessary to point out that the type of judges a country has, may well, determine the fortunes and development direction of the country. As studies have repeatedly confirmed, the rule of law is a significant determinant of human progress; impacting on all indicators of development and human welfare. Somewhere in the pages of this book, I interrogate the role of a judge in a democracy; beyond just the routine determination of the disputes that serve before judges.

I also bring out the fact that in difficult questions, impacting on the democratic ethos of a nation, it is only a judge who does not take his/her mandate seriously; that will not worry about the ultimate impact of his/her decision on the democratic and human rights trajectory of the country. The role that judges play in a democracy has seen people increasingly turn to the judiciary to determine difficult questions touching on the democratic legitimacy of a government of the day.

In 2017, whilst I was busy writing this book, the judiciary in Kenya annulled the August 2017 Kenyan presidential elections. This decision was a first in Africa, and it unsurprisingly, unleashed mountains of praise; and a torrent of criticism in equal measure. The decision also resulted in many scholars posing interesting questions; relating to whether the judiciary overreached, or had the separation of powers been blurred?

Some scholars have claimed that the decision of the Supreme Court of Kenya, in annulling the presidential elections as it did, was politically motivated; and remotely connected to law. These scholars also claimed that the court had departed from the established normative framework, that was supposed to guide its work, and had, thereby, endangered its legitimacy. Some commentators even faulted the Supreme Court of Kenya for being too activist.

Speaking for myself, the fact that there was more than one dissenting judgment, in the 2017 Kenyan Presidential election case, demonstrates this was, by no means, an easy case. No lawyer or judge can say that there was only one permissible or, indeed, correct answer.

I imagine that even Professor Ronald Dworkin, (1931-2013) the proponent of the theory that every legal problem has only one answer, would have conceded that in the case of the 2017 Kenyan presidential election case, there was, possibly, more than one correct answer. I am compelled to say, in passing, that in my more than 15 years of serving as a judge, in several jurisdictions, I can positively attest to the fact that it occurs, quite often, that a legal problem may have more than one answer.

The exposition alluded to above suggests that in hard cases, such as the Kenyan case referred to above, judges have a choice to make. They may be confronted with a choice that restricts, or expands, the boundaries of democracy. In exercising this choice, some judges may be more activist, whilst others may be more restrained. This is normal; and can also be a function of the personality of an individual judge.

A question that arises, in relation to the choices that judges have to make, is 'did the judges in the Kenyan case merely state the law or did they create a new legal norm?' It seems, to me, that this question must be answered in the affirmative. I say so because in embracing the qualitative approach, they did create a legal norm; and by annulling the elections, on the basis of a process that they held to be faulty, the Kenyan judges created law. This should be sufficient to put paid to the notion that judges do not make law.

Here, I add my voice to those of many legal luminaries that have held the view that it is fictitious to suggest that judges do not make law.

Strictly speaking, there is no need to make law in a large number of cases. However, in difficult and novel cases, judges may find themselves creating new norms. To give an example of this, the High Court, in Botswana, recently abolished the civil wrong of adultery, which would ordinarily give rise to a claim for compensation. By that landmark decision, the High Court suggested that the common practice of seeking compensation for the civil wrong of adultery was no longer consistent with the contemporary morals of the society in Botswana. If that decision is not appealed against, and reversed, the High Court will have created a new legal norm.

A friend of mine, who is also a judge, reacted with deep concern at the decision; asking how the court could sanction adultery. The judge went on to ask, rhetorically but with palpable concern, whether this was the beginning of the end of the world, as we know it. On the other hand, some judges praised the decision; arguing that it was unacceptable that a third party must be drawn into the picture, when a spouse, as an adult, consented to engaging in conduct that is considered to be adulterous. Having garnered various opinions on the Botswana High Court's decision, concerning adultery, I considered the decision progressive and long overdue. The legal reasoning was in my mind palpably sound. It is not the only possible decision that could be reached. Other judges may reach the opposite decision.

In June 2019, the High Court in Botswana revisited the question whether the offence of sodomy is constitutional. A panel of three judges concluded that it was unconstitutional. It was their view that the law has no business following people in their bedrooms and policing what they were doing. Its correctness even among the judges is a matter of debate. I have read the monumental decision and found its reasoning difficult to fault. Again, as in the adultery case earlier discussed the judges created a new norm.

I revert to the decision of the Supreme Court of Kenya again, to conclude the discussion that judges do generate new legal norms from time to time. Before the Supreme Court, in Kenya, pronounced its presidential election verdict in 2017, the law was as stated by that same court in a 2013 case; in which the same parties, as those in the 2017 case, fought it out in court, as to who had won the 2013 Kenyan presidential election. For those who may not be aware of the facts, in the 2013 case, the Kenyan Supreme Court did not annul the elections. Instead, it seemed to have been persuaded to adopt the substantive effect test; which led to the court concluding that the irregularities, if any, which the Petitioners complained of, could not have affected the results of the elections.

After the 2017 judgment, the law, in Kenya, is what the Supreme Court ruling says it is. Essentially, the meaning of the law has changed; and a new legal norm has been created; not by parliament, but by judges. This is the reason why some scholars say that the law that is in the statute books, as passed by parliament, is but potential law; whose true meaning is dependent upon the circumstances of each case, and as may be interpreted by a judge. As many in the legal profession may well know, judges sometimes differ as to the meaning to be given to a single word, or section in a statute. While differences in opinion and interpretation of statutes are perfectly acceptable, judges must avoid giving expression, or lending the authority of their exalted office, to undemocratic fundamental values. Judges should always be mindful of the possibility of abusing judicial power; as it is not only the executive or the legislature that are capable of abusing power, but even the judiciary can do so.

In general, the potential abuse of power by the executive and the legislature is kept in check by the judiciary. Flowing from this, the question that is often asked is 'who, then, should keep the judiciary within the boundaries of its constitutional mandate?'

My view is that this question has not always been satisfactorily answered and, in my mind at least, there is, to date, no effective constitutional mechanism to police the possibility of abuse of judicial power. It is, therefore, absolutely imperative for judges to ensure that judicial power is exercised responsibly and reasonably. Judges should always be conscious of the fact that they are not above the constitution; and should not exercise their power in a manner that has a negative impact on constitutional democracy.

Judges should not overreach

Judges should also, always, be extremely careful to ensure that they do not overreach, and find themselves being unjustifiable participants in the political spaces, because if these were to be so, then the authority of the courts would be politicized and undermined; and the courts would serve no useful purpose in a democratic society. Courts must ensure that public confidence in the judiciary is maintained because once it is eroded, as a result of judges overreaching, then the rule of law will ultimately suffer; and the democratic project subverted.

The brief anecdotes on the Kenyan presidential election case and the adultery case in Botswana underscore the importance of judges in any society. Of all aspects of judgeship, and perhaps more fascinating for me, are the judges' backgrounds, broadly, and their individual ideological outlook. Many judges whom I have met, and interacted with over the years, do not think one can even start to talk about 'the ideology of a judge' because, in their minds, they associate ideology with politics, even partisan politics.

In doing so, my colleagues overlook the stark fact that every judge has a way of looking at social phenomena, in a way that is shaped by his/her upbringing and experiences. It is this unique way of looking at things differently, whether because of some different cultural background, or some other reason, that may loosely be said to be the ideology of a judge. I touch on this element further along in this book.

Reflecting on judges and their work, which brought this book into being, has been an intellectually draining exercise, but one that I have found to be extremely rewarding; especially since I do this from the privileged position of being a judge myself. I think it is fair to say that very few people would deny the fact that a life on the bench is a rare honour and privilege. Some authorities, who are religiously inclined, have poignantly observed that judgeship is an attribute of God. I confidently say that this is an assertion which is not, at all, surprising; given that judges have the power of life and death over their fellow human beings. Some with religious inclinations issue a reminder that even God, who created human beings, does not sit in judgment over peoples' deeds until their death; and only then does He determine their fate, namely, whether they should be sent to heaven or to death, for eternity.

I am aware that there are many religious judges; who would readily associate with the interface between law and religion. However, it needs to be said that the religious position of a judge should never prejudice a litigant; and/or create a perception of bias, or any form of injustice. It would be invidious for a judge to disclose his, or her, religious inclination in court; especially in a manner that suggests, to the litigant, that because they do not share the religion of the judge, then the litigant may be disadvantaged by a decision that the judge will make. Although it may be said that there is a religious aspect to the work of a judge, since witnesses have to either take a religious oath, or be affirmed, before giving evidence in court, spiritual allegiance is, generally, not a requirement for the holding of judicial office.

If, however, for religious reasons, a judge may feel a conflict of interest in a particular case, then they should recuse themselves, or refrain, from hearing and determining that matter. This being said, the prohibition of a judge from showing his or her religious inclinations in court, which may be perceived, rightly or wrongly, as being prejudicial to a litigant or a person on trial for a crime, does not bar a judge from taking part, even in public, in religious functions of the faith to which the particular judge belongs. It is very important to note that in public spaces and meetings of judges, sensitivity is sometimes needed in order not to give the impression that those who do not subscribe to a particular religion are coerced to conform.

Religious inclinations notwithstanding, it is of cardinal importance that judges, in a secular state, should always be open minded; in order to accommodate peoples' diverse world outlooks and beliefs. Judges must understand, as a matter of necessity, that both believers and non- believers are equal in the eyes of the law and, as such, all deserve equal recognition. Judges should never give the impression that a disadvantage may accrue to any person on account of his or her world outlook.

The primary responsibility and function of judges, which many of us would rather avoid, is to take decisions; and dispense justice. It has always been a revered principle of liberty and freedom that judges are no respecters of persons, but the law, and that they should always stand between a subject and any attempted encroachments on his liberty, by the executive. Judges should be ever vigilant to ensure that any governmental action is justified.

The concept of justice has always been a permanent feature of human existence. In modern times, the concept of justice is represented by the Roman goddess *Justitia* or 'Lady Justice'. She is normally portrayed as a blindfolded woman with a sword in one hand, and the scales of justice in the other. This is the symbol that has the pride of place atop the High Court in the Central Business District (CBD) in Gaborone, Botswana, and can actually be seen on the letter heads, or stationery, of many courts across the globe. The symbolism portrays the idea that justice is blind and it knows no colour, status or creed; because no one is above the law. The clear and unequivocal message, of the symbolism of Lady Justice, is that the evidence tendered in court must be weighed carefully and the issues determined dispassionately.

Judges are called "your Honour", 'the Honourable Mr. /Mrs. Justice so and so'. They wear flowing, and often colourful, robes that set them apart from the rest of the people. This attire adds to the mystique of one being a judge. The mystique is heightened by the manner in which the judges are addressed, namely, 'My Lord', or 'My Lady', or 'your Honour'. The mystique thickens, further, by the elevated bench upon which the judges sit, in court rooms, and the wigs which they wear. Their entry into court is often preceded by a big bang, accompanied by a court official announcing: "All stand/rise please. This court of justice is now in session". Following the announcement, the judge takes a bow, followed by others who are in the courtroom. A reader who is unfamiliar with court decorum may wonder why such, seemingly peculiar, practices are observed. The simple answer is that it is because the legal/judicial profession is steeped in old common law traditions.

I can bear personal testimony to the fact that some old common law traditions are still thriving in modern times. For instance, when I joined the Supreme and National Courts of Papua New Guinea, in 2018, I was taken aback by the fact that judges are still required to have their wigs on; when they preside over a case. However, my surprise has been watered down by the fact that I have since come to learn that this practice also obtains in some jurisdictions closer to my home country of Botswana, such as Zambia, where judges preside while wearing wigs. A judicial colleague of mine, from that country, informed me that the practice of judges wearing wigs, while presiding, appears to sit quite well with most judges and, as such, is unlikely to be discarded any time soon.

Judges and wigs

In some jurisdictions, judges no longer wear wigs in an attempt to make the courts look 'normal' and 'user friendly'. In Botswana, debate in that direction has not yet started. I do not mean to stir up the hornet's nest but, speaking for myself, I believe that the time to discard the colonial robes has long passed. However, and in contrast to my view, there are many judges who consider that robes and the wigs serve to define judgeship; and to reinforce judicial authority. They contend that just as every profession is entitled to map out its identity by wearing uniforms, or observing practices that define the particular profession, even judgeship should, by the same token, retain a certain identity. Some stalwarts have even asserted that there is an entire book in the Bible, which is titled 'Judges', a fact which shows that the profession is a long standing one; which existed even in biblical times. As such, it is perfectly entitled to remain steeped in old common law traditions. As I see it, it may well be that the majority, in many jurisdictions, will prefer that the robes and wigs be kept.

Given the importance of judges in any given society, it makes sense to think long and hard on the qualities that any nation requires of its judges. A survey of legal texts, and writings, demonstrates that scholars have always sought to pinpoint what are the desirable qualities of a judge. I address this aspect in some detail in the later pages of this book. For now, I may foreshadow the discussion on the qualities of a judge by quoting, without elaboration, Socrates a Greek philosopher who, in the Fourth Century BC, said that there are four qualities required of a judge; "to hear courteously, to answer wisely, to consider soberly and to decide impartially".

Finding the truth can be tricky

Judges are called upon, on a daily basis, to decide where the truth in a dispute lies. Invariably, they are faced with two contradictory versions of a case and, at the end of a trial; judges are not allowed to say that they cannot make up their mind as to which version is true; and neither can they toss a coin to determine where the truth lies. I think most judges will disclose that, on occasion, they get the sense that, in truth, all they can do, as a presiding judge, is to ascertain which of the litigants before them is telling less lies than the other.

After all, judges are not prophets; but mere mortals like the rest of humanity.

In determining who, among the witnesses that appear before the courts, is telling the truth is not a function of eloquence, or confidence, as it often appears to be. My experience is that the most eloquent and confident witnesses are the ones who are less likely to be telling the truth.

For those who may wonder as to how judges determine who is, or is not telling the truth in court, I can right away tell them that judges don't wield any magical lie detector. They use a number of tools, and most often instinct and common sense, to tell which version of the facts is most probable. To this I can add that work experience also plays a part in the skill of separating lies from truths. My general observation is that judges who have served on the bench longer tend, over the years, to muster the art of picking out a fabricated version of events. However, I hasten to point out that judges can, and often do, get it wrong; and they must always be alive to this possibility.

It is common knowledge that judges, the world over, have wrongfully convicted people. Many people may remember the sad tale of the 'Birmingham Six'; where six men were wrongfully convicted of killing twenty-one people, and injuring many others, on the 21st of November 1974; in what was called the 'Birmingham Pub Bombings', in the United Kingdom. The men spent sixteen years in prison; before their convictions were quashed. They suffered punishment for a crime that they did not commit; and it is hard to imagine what effect that gross injustice had, not only on the men, but also on their families and friends. While the injustice that was occasioned to those men can never be undone, the lesson to be learned is that that unfortunate incident should be a humbling one for judges, and one which they must try and avoid, at all costs, in the carrying out of their judicial functions.

A judge must have the wisdom and knowledge to, authoritatively, find which version of a story is correct; and must state the reasons for his/her conclusion. An eminent trial judge once observed, sarcastically, that: "who says I decide in favour of truth against falsehood? Every day, on the table before me, there is a bundle of lies poured out by each one of the two sides; and I choose in favour of the one who has spoken lesser lies." Discounting the sarcasm, all I can say is that the good judge was entitled to his opinion, based on his personal court experiences. However, when all is said and done, it is imperative that a judge must be knowledgeable. This is so because for a judge to answer wisely, he or she must muster the facts and the law. A judge must have an analytical mind; and must not be gullible.

Impartiality

One key attribute of judges is that they must be impartial. It is of the utmost importance that, in carrying out their duties, judges should not only be impartial, but must be seen to be impartial. Patrick Devlin is reported to have said: "I put impartiality before the appearance of it simply because without the reality, the appearance would not endure".

Returning to present times, it seems quite plain, to me, that within the context of service to the community, the appearance is more important of the two. It is often said that a judge who gives the right judgment, while appearing not to do so, may be thrice blessed in heaven; but is of no use, at all, on earth. The doors of justice must be kept open for everybody who knocks. Judges must hear anyone who comes to them complaining of an injustice; and if they find that an injustice has, indeed, been committed, then they must give a remedy against whosoever is guilty of that injustice; and must do so without fear or favour.

The court room is a sacred place

The court room, the space within which the judges dispense justice, is a revered place. In many respects, a court room is like a temple of justice; and when a judge enters the court room, there is a real feeling that one is entering a place of worship. This sense fills the mind of a judge with a sense of heightened duty and, for as long as the controversy between the parties remains unresolved, the mind of a judge remains engaged. It is only after the judge has delivered a judgment, which accords with the dictates of justice, that he/she may feel a sense of relaxation, or relief. On a lighter note, a story is often told of a judge who used to have his daily bath, and put on clean clothes, just before leaving for the court and, before taking up his seat on the dais, would remove his shoes; for he believed that he was entering a temple.

In my mind, there is no other profession which puts the intellectual wits of a person to the severest test, than judgeship. This is because in order to navigate complex factual and legal issues, presented by litigation, judges must have clarity of thought that should translate into clarity of expression. A judge who is not clear in his, or her mind, about the facts and the law cannot achieve clarity of expression in his/her decisions. Judgments are the raw materials that speak to the judge's intellectual abilities. It used to be thought that judgments were not intended for non-lawyers. However, in today's world, judges try to write in simple language; so that litigants and the public may understand what the judgement is conveying.

Given the importance of judges, and the skills that they possess, one often wonders why judges, in most parts of the world, are not given to writing books or articles. There is, I venture to suggest, a pressing need for judges to write, in order to deploy their skills into more widespread communication with the public, and not just focus on judgments. In my mind, as the powers of the courts to review governmental actions keep on increasing, alongside the right of the people to know what the judges consider untenable, it has become necessary for judges to engage more intellectually. This would promote the rule of law; in the broader society. I am of the firm view that writing promotes the intellectual integrity of the calling of judges.

Those of us who are privileged to serve society as judges must never forget that ours is not a job, but a lifestyle. Another reason why I believe it is important for judges to communicate with society, through writing and not just judgements, is because judges have an obligation to maintain their institutional independence. They can best do that by explaining, to the public, what they are doing; and how they seek to uphold the rule of law; including stating, in simple terms, what in general terms is permissible or not permissible in law.

My career experiences from the bar and teaching law and, thereafter, on the bench, has taught me that law can be a force; both for good and bad. In the right hands, used with sensitivity and with the aim of achieving justice, the law can transform lives for the better. It can bring down the walls of prejudice that deny many people justice. But the law has limits; and its potential should never be exaggerated.

History is littered with many examples in which law has assisted oppressed nations, and individuals, to achieve freedom. Equally true is the fact that, in many instances, the law and judges have both been complicit in the oppression of many communities. In some instances, servants of the law have done the unthinkable. Some judges, particularly Chief Justices, in some jurisdictions in Southern Africa and other parts of the world, have colluded and conspired with the executive to undermine and subvert the independence of the judiciary.

It is also important to note that the law is fraught with the illusion that there is a bright red light; which serves as a clear boundary between law and politics. The distinction is there in the majority, but not necessarily all, of the cases. To this end, it is often asserted that the lack of understanding of the law, by a politician, makes a politician technically deficient; while the lack of political experience, in a lawyer, makes that lawyer not a purer person, but merely a worse lawyer. This assertion is, in my view, not entirely without merit.

In the pages of this book, I have written about the debate on whether judges make law and the much talked about, but little understood, concept of judicial activism. Nowadays, the assertion that judges make law, although still not universally accepted, is no longer seriously denied by many judges and lawyers. Through the process of interpretation, judges consciously, or unconsciously, infuse their philosophy and world outlook into what is termed judge-made law.

It is a well-known fact that the common law is all but judge made. Judges must, however, be cautious in the course of legislating; because they neither have the license to do as they please; and nor do they have the right to elevate their opinions to the status of law. The making of law, by judges, must be necessitated by the existence of certain conditions; such as the law being vague or uncertain. If a judge is arbitrary and elevates his, or her, personal opinion to the status of law; or is otherwise afflicted by over exuberance, resulting in the undermining of the law in the course of carrying out their duties, then the judge risks not only their individual reputation, but that of the judiciary, as a whole.

In contemporary society, most countries have a written constitution and judges are the custodians of the constitution; and the values that it represents. It is, therefore, the duty of every judge to strive for judicial excellence. In my experience, it helps to cultivate a habit of reading. The work of a judge condemns him, or her, to being a permanent student. A judge must know the law broadly. Indeed judges are presumed to know the law; although some lawyers claim encounters with judges who are clueless on the law. As can be expected, the same claim has been laid against some lawyers, by the courts before which they appear; but this book is mainly about judges, so I shall say no more on this accusation.

It is a fact that professions undergo some transformation, with the passage of time, and judiciaries have not been spared in that regard. These days, judges are no longer confined to civil and criminal work only. We live in a world in which science and technology now run our lives, and so it advisable for judges to read broadly on science and technology; among other subjects. Reading broadly, and not necessarily law at all times, has countless benefits; which include the ability to sharpen the mind; to enable one to unpack complicated legal arguments. Reading also improves one's vocabulary and, almost inevitably, one's ability to communicate. It should be remembered that one of the most important skills that a judge must possess, in abundance, is the ability to communicate. This aspect of a judge's work shall be elaborated later on when the subject of judgment writing is dealt with.

Technology

It is an indisputable fact that, nowadays, technology is important to a judge's work. Judges must, of necessity, have basic computer skills; which must include being able to use basic computer applications and to conduct online research. They must be able to send and receive electronic mail (emails). Travelling across Africa, I have noticed that this is not necessarily the case; as some judges seem to have an aversion or, perhaps a calculated apathy, to technological advancement. It is, therefore, important for judiciaries to train judges and, indeed, other adjudicators, to upgrade their computer literacy; in order to make them more efficient. In many countries, the courts are increasingly becoming paperless; with electronic records being the norm. The result of this is that, in many jurisdictions, the problem of missing dockets is no longer as common as before.

Type of judges

On a general note, it is fair to say that judges are not cut off the same cloth. It must have been John D. Voelker J, (1903-1991) a judge and author, who said the following about judges:

> *"Judges… may be divided roughly into four classes; judges with neither head nor heart-they are to be avoided at all costs; judges with the head, but no heart- they are almost as bad; then judges with the heart but no head- risky but better than the first two; and finally, those judges who possess both a head and a heart."*

A judge must have the humility to know that much as he, or she, may want to do justice to all, they cannot change the world. To this end, a judge must have reasonable, and realistic, expectations of what is achievable through the law. It is important that, at the end of the day, it must be said of a judge, by the community in which that judge served, that he acquitted himself with dignity and honour; and that he was truly independent, and impartial, in the service of justice. Let it also be said that the judge was a good listener and that, although not all of his or her decisions were liked by everyone, the judge understood that his job was to decide matters that served before him impartially. Quite crucially, it must be said that in deciding matters, the judge was fair and decisive. A judge's job is to make a decision; one way or the other. He or she cannot say that "I cannot decide or I don't know what the facts are; and neither do I know what the law provides". When pronouncing a decision, a judge should be least bothered by whether it will receive the applause, or condemnation, of many; because such considerations are irrelevant. What matters is that a judge makes a decision; and does so with impartiality and to the best of his ability.

Lastly, the work of a judge is tedious and requires absolute focus. Judges work long hours each day, and many have no weekends; or even holidays. Much time has to be spent reading, absorbing and analyzing written material. A trial judge has to read pleadings, and other written materials, often running into hundreds of pages. The judge then has to listen to the parties for hours and, quite often, for days; depending on the number of witnesses and the complexity of the issues in a case. What follows, thereafter, is the process of writing judgements; which is an equally tedious and laborious exercise.

Judgeship requires truly committed people. The toil, sweat and blood that are part and parcel of judgeship often leave relationships, which are forged before appointment to the bench, in ruin or neglected. Unfortunate as this may be, that is the reality of judgeship. It is a profession that demands a lot of personal sacrifice; which includes inadequate time for friends, social activities and even quality family time. Like I mentioned before, it is often said that judgeship is not a job, but a way of life; and a difficult one at that.

Chapter Two

THEORETICAL REFLECTIONS ON JUDGESHIP

In this chapter, I discuss the importance of being practical, independent and impartial and for judges to be servants and not the "overlords" of the constitution. All these values ensure that a judge obeys the fundamental values of the constitution – its morality – and not the morality of the judge. I further discuss in some detail the value of dissenting judgements and that in so far as they may speak to the "brilliance" of the future they should not be suppressed. Generally, judges, when dealing with real controversies before them, are not interested in academic arguments in court. In the main, if not wholly, the interest of judges is focused on resolving real, not imagined, controversy between the parties.

Occasionally, in the loneliness of a judge's chambers, some theoretical questions pop up; and certain concepts have to be revisited. A judge's best companion, at least in most of the commonwealth jurisdictions, should be the Oxford English Dictionary or some other suitable legal dictionary like the Black's Law Dictionary; in which the meanings of words, concepts and phrases are explained.

The reason why judges should always have dictionaries, and related legal literature, on hand, is because they work with words almost every day; and it is the meaning of words that determines the conclusions which judges reach in matters serving before them. Personally, I regard judges as intellectual leaders of their communities and they should, therefore, take care not to turn law reports, which capture the reasons for conclusions reached in any particular case, into intellectual graveyards.

The ultimate purpose of law

Other than knowledge of words and phrases, judges must have an idea of the ultimate purpose of law. I am wedded to the idea propounded by Justice Benjamin Cardozo (1870-1938), former justice of the Supreme Court of the United States of America, and renowned author of a book titled 'The Nature of the Judicial Process'; who pertinently observed that the ultimate objective of law is the welfare of society. Law should be viewed as a means to an end; the end being justice. I do not believe that the law must operate like a robot or, indeed, a mechanical calculator. If it does that, then it will not be useful for addressing different controversies, under varying circumstances, that underpin human existence.

The Law regulates relationships between the state and its citizens. It prescribes conduct, or behaviour, and consequences for those who default or breach the agreed code of conduct. Law is supposed to reflect the values of society. It is an essential, and fundamental, function of the judges to be steeped into the values which the society holds dear. These values are usually reflected in the highest law of the land; that being the constitution. The constitution is the soul of the nation; and the values it subscribes to are sacrosanct. Judges are the professionals who are entrusted to make the constitution tick; so that it can be relevant to people's lives in a concrete way.

Judges are duty bound to determine disputes, that serve before them, not by reference to their own subjective views, but going by the dictates of the constitution. I, therefore, make bold to assert that in a constitutional democracy, only one morality matters; and that is the morality of the constitution. A judge's individual morality is irrelevant because his, or her, duty is to try to extract, and apply, the morality of the constitution; with utmost objectivity. The judge must, actively, refrain from imposing his, or her, own views on society. Essentially, judges who hold religious or secular views on society must not impose those views on the broader society; which has enacted the constitution to govern their lives. This requirement makes strenuous demands on a judge.

A judge is a servant of the constitution

A judge must understand that he, or she, is a servant of the constitution; and not the controlling authority. It is a well-known fact that every judge is a product of their time and operates in a particular environment. However, no judge must allow their existential reality, or the circumstances under which they live, to subvert the constitution. If truth be said, the objectivity required of a judge is not easy. On many occasions, and much as they may try to be objective, judges process thoughts through their own minds; and see things through their own eyes. Sometimes, judges may think that they are objective, but a reasonable, well informed, bystander may think they are not. Much as objectivity is a requirement for judges, it must be appreciated that they do not operate in a vacuum. Judges are human beings, who are part of the society; and, quite often, they reflect the common prejudices of the society which they are part of.

However, if judges are truly faithful to the constitution, they are bound to implement its letter, values and spirit. A constitution is, in most constitutional democracies, the mother of all laws. Put differently, any provision of statute, which is inconsistent with the constitution, is invalid to the extent of the inconsistency. This being said, a constitution is not a document that is cast in stone; and incapable of growth. It is, in fact, an organic document that is meant to serve not only the present, but also future generations. The constitution is meant to apply to varying conditions; which the development of our societies entails.

It is often said that a Bill of Rights is very much like any sacred text, such as the Bible, Koran or whatever other book is held sacred. Any true believer in the Bill of Rights appreciates it as the primary, and ultimate, source of law and ethics; which regulates one's life immutably. Believers and their leaders, on the other hand, tend to interpret sacred texts differently. Such texts are often open to diverse interpretations; because of the words used and context under which the interpretation takes place. More often than not, the texts are open to abuse. Even the devil can cite scripture for his (or her) own purpose. Drawing on this analogy, it would be sad if the constitution, usually an instrument designed to protect the people, could mean whatever judges, arbitrarily, said it meant; thereby defeating the very purpose of its design.

Properly construed, a constitution is supposed to create legal certainty, not uncertainty. It is supposed to create respect for the law, and the judicature, not disrespect. Fortunately, this is a feat which the constitution usually achieves, if judges respect its spirit and are objective in interpreting it. It is important to note that, increasingly, judges are confronted with litigation that requires them to apply the letter and spirit of the constitution. In some controversial constitutional cases, that involve the rights of the Lesbian, Gay, Bi-sexual, Trans-gender and Intersex (LGBTI) community, some judges find it difficult to cast aside their own personal or religious views; in order to fearlessly apply the constitution, without ill-will and prejudice, as they should. In such instances, some judges have either recused themselves, or considered recusing themselves, because they cannot bring themselves to preside over cases in which their personal or religious convictions are opposed. I think that this stand point may be problematic; because upon appointment, a judge must cast aside personal prejudices, and become an impartial arbiter of facts and law.

Morality and the Constitution

Arguably, a good example of an instance in which judges seemed to confuse their morality with that of the constitution was in the case of Obergefell vs Hodges. This case concerned same-sex marriage in the United States of America (USA). A number of petitioners, comprising fourteen individuals, who were same sex couples, and two individuals whose same sex partners had passed away, were joined to the case. The petitioners challenged State officials' refusals to allow them to marry; arguing that that was a violation of the equal protection and due process laws under the 14th Amendment to the United States Constitution. The issue came before the Supreme Court of the United States; on appeal.

On 26 June 2015, the 5-4 majority of the Court, in an opinion by Justice Kennedy, held that the 14th amendment required a state to license a marriage between two people of the same sex; and to recognize their marriage. The Court reasoned that the fundamental liberties protected by the 14th amendment extended to certain personal choices that were central to individual identity and beliefs. The majority of the judges held that the courts must exercise reasoned judgment; in identifying the interests of a person, so fundamental, that the state must accord them its respect. Significantly, the right to marry had already been recognized, as protected, under the constitution in previous cases.

The result of the Obergefell decision is that same-sex couples may now exercise the right to marry, in all states in the United States of America, and there is no lawful basis for any state, in that country, to refuse to recognize a lawful same-sex marriage performed in another state; on the ground of its same-sex character. The four dissenting judges all issued separate opinions. Chief Justice Robert's dissent focused on attacking the majority's substantive due process argument;

including attacking the Court's own precedent upon which the majority reasoning was based. Justice Robert's view was that the issue was one best left to the popular will. On his part, Justice Scalia's dissent stated, boldly, that the Supreme Court was a "threat to American democracy." Justices Thomas and Alito's dissents were similarly framed, criticizing the majority's opinion as undermining the democratic process; through which it believed the issue should have been resolved.

In my mind, this is a case in which the majority upheld the constitutional injunction to equal protection of the law. The dissenting justices, essentially, wanted to pass the buck to the law making authority; ostensibly on the basis that they were better placed to reflect the will of the people. However, it is a well-known fact that the majority is not always democratic, or pro-rights. Political expediency can drive the people's representatives to cast aside the rights of the minority. The majority has been heavily criticized by the dissenting opinions; for over stepping their judicial powers and usurping the function of the legislature. In fact, Chief Justice Roberts, in his dissent, stated that, "this Court is not a legislature. Whether same-sex marriage is a good idea should be of no concern to us. Under the Constitution, judges have power to say what the law is, not what it should be. The people who ratified the Constitution authorized courts to exercise 'neither force nor will, but merely judgment'.

It is my firm belief that the views expressed by Chief Justice Roberts, with due respect, totally misconstrued his role of bringing about equality, as a judicial officer, in a constitutional democracy. The case, however, highlights the ideological tensions in many parts of the world; about the role of the judiciary in a constitutional democracy. This is a debate which, in many jurisdictions, is all too often played out at the expense of society's most vulnerable people. In navigating politically sensitive issues, the courts have to be careful both not to undermine the judiciary's institutional credibility; and also not to neglect the fundamental duty to apply the law, equally, to all who come before the court.

In the Obergefell case, it seems clear that the majority, of the judges, were determined to uphold the morality of the constitution. Scrutiny of the decision, of the majority, does not suggest that those judges, personally, support same sex marriage. They were simply being true to the constitution. As has already been alluded to, judges should not bring their personal morality, or the morality of the majority, to bear on their judgments. In any event, judges, in most jurisdictions, take oath to uphold the constitution. This oath is meant to be internalized and binding on judges.

Constitutions are not meant to protect, and safeguard, the rights and interests of individuals that judges like; and to leave, unprotected, those of the minority whose preferences and choices they dislike or, indeed, those that the majority may find to be morally objectionable. Constitutions should, and must, protect individuals from the tyranny of the state; and oppression from their fellow human beings. Individual rights, and freedoms, are not subject to the approval of the majority. They are inherent in every human being.

Judicial power should never be exercised arbitrarily

Judges often express different views as to whether public opinion has any role, to play, in the task of constitutional interpretation. It is, generally, acknowledged that public opinion may have some relevance to the enquiry. However, in itself, it is no substitute for the duty vested in the courts to interpret the constitution and to protect, promote and fulfill the rights of every person; without fear or favour. This much, at least, makes perfect sense. Quite plainly, if public opinion were to be decisive, there would be no need for constitutional adjudication, at all. Instead, a state could, well, just conduct a referendum, to determine the question of whether individuals had any rights to be protected. The bottom line is that not even parliament, which is the repository of the will of the people, has the power to determine their rights or to adjudicate over any dispute on people's rights.

The reason why most constitutions vest judicial power in the judiciary is to protect the rights of minorities, and others who cannot protect their rights adequately through the democratic process. Those who are entitled to claim this protection include the minorities whose preferences, choices or identities are not approved of by the majority. It is only when there is a willingness to protect the weakest, amongst us, that all of us can be secure that our own rights will be protected.

Judges, obviously, have many roles to play in the discharge of their duties. One cardinal role, of a judge, is to understand the morality of the constitution and give effect to it even if such morality offends the individual morality of a judge. A constitution is a living organism. Its meaning changes with time; and the judges must be loyal to its nature and character. A constitution is not a museum piece, and the judges who consider it as such do a great disservice to it. As society changes, the meaning of constitutional provisions is bound to change. The judge is the mouthpiece to announce these changes; through a rigorous reasoning process and, in so announcing, the judge is merely a servant of the law. It also needs to be said that in pronouncing on the new meaning of the law, dictated by compelling contemporary circumstances, the judge should not embark on reckless adventurism. If judges engage in reckless adventurism, they lose the protection of the law; and sacrifice the appearance of impartiality. The hallmark of a great judge is the disinterested application of the law; that is informed by meticulous findings of facts.

John Marshall, one of the greatest Chief Justices of the Supreme Court of the United States of America, once remarked that judicial power is never exercised for the purposes of giving effect to the will of the judge; as that would be a grave aberration. In truth, the greatest transformative judges have not been adventurist. They have understood that gradual, but meaningful, change is often warranted by the circumstances. As it is often said, transformative judges have moved not by fits and starts, but at the pace of a tortoise that steadily advances; though it carries the past on its back. Occasionally the Judges must take up the cudgels and be the midwives, of a better society to be born, even if they should induce the birth by carrying out a caesarian operation; and the facts and circumstances so require.

The need for change presents the judge with a dilemma; because change can have destabilizing effects. It is, therefore, important that in announcing changes, in the law, the judge must delicately negotiate the present and use its residue to build a future dispensation; mandated by the constitution itself. It is a delicate process that must not be routinely done to satisfy a judge's romantic notion of the direction of the law. It must be necessitated by the circumstances of each case.

Judges must bear in mind that law must be stable and predictable; but it cannot remain stagnant when society is changing. If it remains stagnant, when society is changing and the judges aid and abet its stagnation, then the people may, in time, decide to overturn the law; and not necessarily through constitutional means, because the law has ceased serving their interests. As Justice Aharon Barak of the Supreme Court of Israel has pointed out "stability without change is degeneration" and "change without stability is anarchy". Barak correctly adds: "The judge must ensure stability with change, and change with stability. Like the eagle in the sky that maintains its stability only when it is moving, so too is the law stable only when it is moving".

Precedent and dissenting opinions

Consistency is important to the integrity of the law. In similar cases, judges are compelled to act consistently; unless the earlier decision was plainly wrong and unsustainable.

Consistency is also important because it renders the law certain. Lawyers are better able to advise their clients, with confidence, and tell them that that was what the court had said, not on one or two occasions; but for a while. Precedent is important to the law; but not at all costs. The highest courts lay down the law and, unless the lower courts can distinguish the cases, then they are bound by the decisions of the highest courts. This is not to suggest that the highest courts cannot be wrong. They can, and have been wrong a number of times; but the discipline of the law requires that the final authority, on the law, must be the apex court. If this were not so, chaos would rule, unimpeded.

The highest courts should not consider precedent immutable. They should not allow themselves to be enslaved by precedent. Instead, they should depart from precedent; if such precedent no longer makes sense or is shown to have been wrong. I hasten to add that departures, from precedent, should only be done in exceptional circumstances. If they are a daily occurrence, the law becomes unpredictable; and its stability and integrity could be undermined.

It often happens that judges of the lower courts deliver judgments that amount or purport, in effect, to overruling the decisions of the highest court. In some cases, that is pure indiscipline, in a legal sense; but in other cases, that occurs when judges of the lower courts become, genuinely, frustrated with the inability, or reluctance, of the apex courts to infuse their jurisprudential output with requisite quality reasoning, and fidelity to the law. The apex court, that is on top of its game in providing intellectual leadership and being respectful in the manner it expresses its determination, would in turn, breed respect; and there would be little attempt, by lower courts, to seek to show that the apex court may have been wrong. Engendering respect through rigorous reasoning, based on solid analytical framework, is more enduring than hoping that a mere superior title will suffice.

A question may be asked as to how appellate courts operate. A simple explanation would be that in most jurisdictions, the highest courts, whether going by the name 'Court of Appeal' or 'Supreme Court', sit as a panel. Quite often, judges of the apex court, sitting as part of a panel, have to ponder the question as to whether, or not, they should write a dissenting opinion. Such an opinion is, basically, one that is different from that of the majority's; in any particular case that an appellate court has to determine. The root of dissenting opinions may be found in the common law tradition; which places emphasis on the independence of the individual judge to speak in his, or her, own voice; and holds the transparency of the judicial process dear. The ideal dissent is both prophetic and persuasive. An important fact about dissents is that they are often classified as merely judges' expressions of opinion, which are not essential to a decision, and are, therefore not binding.

Although some judges think that a dissenting opinion offends the principle of collegiality, and communicates the message that the court is divided, dissenting judgements should, in my view, not be suppressed. Quite often, they are not lightly done and, much as it may not always be too obvious, dissenting opinions are usually powerful, and dignified, critiques of the law. The fact that judges would reach different conclusions, on the same matter serving before them, is an eloquent exposition of the fluidity of law; which communicates the powerful message that the law is not as definitive as many would like to believe.

In the USA, immediately after the adoption of the new constitution, the then Chief Justice, Marshall, tried to enforce the idea of one judgment, thinking that it would consolidate the authority of the court. This endured for a short period of time; and then fell apart; with dissenting judgments increasing in regularity. So, instead of achieving its intended purpose, Chief Justice Marshall's plan, well-intended as it may have been on his part, actually had the opposite effect. In my native country, of Botswana, dissenting judgments are not common. However, there is nothing to suggest that there is a judicial policy to that effect; and neither is there any evidence to show that dissent is suppressed. If, by any chance it is suppressed, then that is truly ill-advised.

As I ponder the question of dissenting judgements, I believe that there is a lesson, or two, to be learned from Chief Justice Marshall's ill-fated attempt to enforce unanimity in judicial decision making. I think the biggest lesson is that forced judicial unanimity simply does not work; and it should not be encouraged at all.

In South Africa, the practice of judicial dissent pre-dates the dawn of the constitutional order of 1994; in that, long before the coming of the democratic constitutional order, judges such as Schreiner would, from time to time, pen a dissenting opinion.

After 1994, with the coming of a constitutional order to South Africa, one got the distinct impression that there was some preference for unanimity. However, with time, dissenting opinions grew. This was particularly so under the leadership of Chief Justice Pius Nkonzo Langa (1939-2013). As far as he was concerned, the beauty of dissent lay in exploding the, often unjustified, urge to conform to all sorts of pressure; be it political or otherwise. According to Justice Langa, dissent allowed those who were not inclined to political correctness, and populism, to state the law as they saw it; even if in so doing the heavens may fall. Although Justice Langa acknowledged that, sometimes, dissenters could cause discomfort and, in extreme cases, harm, he recognized that dissenters could, also, be the lone voice of reason, in the dark, and hence the importance of allowing as many views as possible to be heard.

While there is, absolutely, nothing wrong with the practice, judges should not dissent simply because they could have expressed the conclusion better than the majority, or that they prefer a different style of writing. In their nature, and properly considered, dissenting judgments can enrich jurisprudence. In fact, dissenting judgments are proof that a legal problem may have more than one 'correct' answer. However, these judgements must be written with sensitivity; and should never be allowed to degenerate into personal attacks. They should, also, not open the court to unjustifiable attacks by those who are opposed to judicial independence.

Dissenting judgements must tackle ideas boldly, and robustly, if need be; but with respect for those in agreement.

Arguments both for, and against dissenting judgments, can be divided into those having to do with the internal work of the court, that is to say, collegiality and unity, and those which are external to the court, namely authority of the court, certainty and development of law. Those opposed to dissenting judgments say that it is important that once a judgment is final, it has to be respected; regardless of the reasons for supporting it. They add that dissenting opinions cause unnecessary confusion in understanding a judgment, because such opinions reduce the persuasiveness of a judgment; such that it no longer seems to be a final decision by a court of law but a majority or minority opinion.

As one of the Justices of the US Supreme Court famously stated, "in most matters, it is more important that the applicable rule of law be settled than that it be settled right". Preserving collegiality is often cited against dissenting. According to this principle, judges have to be guided by the spirit of cooperation and collaboration; and they must fully engage in the deliberations, with the view to reaching a unanimous decision. However, it has been counter argued that the possibility of issuing dissenting opinions can foster collegiality; by reducing the risk that minority judges might develop a feeling of frustration because they are unable to make their views public.

It is often argued, by those who dislike dissenting judgments, that dissenting opinion endangers the authority, prestige and legitimacy of the court. Furthermore, that it weakens the court's credibility; and makes judgments too closely connected to particular persons. Other arguments against dissenting judgments are as follows:

- The dissenting opinion offends against secrecy of deliberations;

- The dissenting opinion overburdens the courts, as drafting the dissenting opinion takes much time;

- The dissenting opinion can potentially be misused; because some judges tend to maintain a dissenting opinion in order to gain prominence and attract public attention.

On the other hand, those who support dissenting opinions argue that they serve the important purpose of development of law, in the justice system. They opine that dissent opens up dialogue among the judges, between judges and legal scholars, between the commentators of court judgments and also with the legislator. Some of the best-known dissenting opinions rendered in a number of countries, for example, might be described as tools through which the law managed to move to a higher and more civilized stage. It is generally agreed that the dissenting opinion rendered by Justice Harlan, in 1896, in a Supreme Court racial segregation case, is the foundational basis of the seminal decision almost fifty years later, in the well-known case of *Brown v. Board of Education;* which ended racial segregation in American schools.

The importance of dissenting opinions in the US legal system has been aptly described by United States Supreme Court Chief Justice Charles Evans Hughes. In his famous quote he remarked that: "a dissent in a court of last resort is an appeal to the brooding spirit of the law, to the intelligence of a future day, when a later decision may possibly correct the error into which the dissenting judge believes the court to have been betrayed."

Similarly, a dissenting opinion by a judge may, well, provide guidance and inspiration to appellate or supreme court judges; as well as to future court judges, and lawyers, in similar cases. A fairly balanced, meaningful and well-structured dissenting opinion may provide, especially to the losing party, the assurance that his/her side of the story was taken into consideration; when deliberations were done. It gives hope to the losing side that, among the judges, there are also those who share their views; and take their arguments into consideration.

Some dissents are useful in attempting to bridge the gap between the law and society. In bridging the gap between law and society, a judge must take into account the institutional limitations of the judiciary. This means that a judge does not have an open licence to set out to bridge the gap between the law and society; but must only do so in an appropriate case. Without a dispute, such a gap cannot be bridged. More significantly, a judge cannot bridge the gap between the law and society without supporting information.

It is important to bear in mind that the potential to bridge the gap between the law and society is limited.

Certain situations are amenable to the task. For instance, the courts may develop the common law duty of care, but cannot impose a licensing regime or impose taxes. The latter is, singularly, the province of the legislature; as the primary law giver. Law making by judges, which is a function of interpretation, must be consistent with the society's values and society's perception of the role of the judiciary.

Still on the issue of dissent, it is important to note that individual opinions allow judges to maintain their intellectual integrity; by enabling them not to subscribe to a judgment whose reasoning and conclusions they do not agree with. From this perspective, the right to publish separate opinions can foster the courts' independence. In addition to this, dissenting opinion preserves judges' independence, and freedom of expression, in that the dissenting judge is able to decide by his conscience; and not by the majority. However, it must be remembered, in all of this, that a carefully drafted and circulated dissent among the bench, before the final decision is taken, can visibly improve the quality of judgments. In fact, it may not only improve the quality, but may also help in the judgment being understood better.

To disguise judges' differences of opinion as 'uniform interpretation of law' or 'achievement of coherence and consistency' in the law cannot be traded over with judicial independence. It is assumed that judges, as respected members of society who have sworn to uphold the constitution, and the rule of law, cannot abuse this powerful tool. The expectation is that they will use judicial independence effectively, judiciously and resourcefully; for the betterment and development of law.

In considering the efficacy of dissenting opinions, it must be remembered that some dissenting opinions ultimately become the law of the land; either through a change of opinion, on the part of the court, or because they produced a change in the constitution; or in the laws made by the legislature of the land. Essentially, dissenting opinions are extremely valuable to the legal profession; as they contribute much to the development of the law. From a teaching point of view, dissenting opinions are of great assistance in presenting both sides of a legal question. Furthermore, dissents instill confidence in the public.

In conclusion it could be said, without fear of contradiction, that it is useful for judges to have an idea of the overall objective of law; to understand concepts such as law and justice, and the difference between the two, if they are to use the law to achieve justice. Judges must be steeped in the values of tolerance; which allow for differences of opinion without being personal. They must also accept that, in principle, there is nothing wrong with a judge expressing dissent; for as long as it packaged professionally and delivered in a dignified manner.

Chapter Three

QUALITIES AND ATTRIBUTES OF A JUDGE

In my experience as a practicing lawyer, an academic and a judge, I have interacted with many judges; both in and outside court. From this, I have formed a clear view as to what the qualities, and attributes, of a judge should be. The first quality is humility. This reminds me of the remarks of one Chief Justice, who once said that he wanted his judges to be gentlemen (at the time the bench was overwhelmingly male); and that if they knew a little law, the better. Speaking for myself, if I were that Chief Justice I would, in addition to the traditional requirements, have wanted my judges to be humble, knowledgeable in the law, imbued with integrity, to have hearts and plenty of courage!

Humility

Why, some may ask should humility be, in my view, the first quality? Humility is an important quality; which a judge must possess. I hold this view because humility is a shield that protects judges from believing that they are, by virtue of their title and office, omnipotent. It is often, correctly, said that in the heart of a humble judge, there is no place for hatred; even for his worst self-confessed enemy. A judge must not think of himself, or herself, as a person of power; but as a servant of the people. Judges must, also, not lose sight of the fact that they are no better, or worse, characters than when they were appointed. Very significantly, they must remember that they were not born judges. They are, simply, temporary occupants of judicial positions, which they shall vacate in the course of time; to be occupied by others who, in turn, shall vacate the positions when the time comes.

The great American judge, and jurist, Learned Hand, may have been alluding to the quality of humility; when he spoke, in reference to judges, as "the spirit that is not too sure that it is right". I have met many humble judges; who, I must say, are not, necessarily, the majority. With their humility these judges lend a sense of seriousness, and fairness, to the task of adjudication. Such judges also calm the nerves in high stakes cases; with the parties going away in the belief that the judge, at least, listened and was not disruptive in the course of the hearing of a case.

Courage

In my view, another important quality that judges need is courage; and lots of it! This is particularly so in communities, or nations, in which the true role of the judiciary, as an independent arm of the state, is not yet fully appreciated. It gives me no pleasure to say this, but lack of courage abounds in many judiciaries. Some judges have been known to confess, to their colleagues, outside of formal structures, that presiding over certain matters may be career limiting! I daresay that many will have had the experience of sitting in judges' meetings, in which matters of fundamental importance were being discussed, and yet some judges hardly expressed any view, on the subject (s) under discussion, because of fear. I, personally, think that this is most unfortunate, indeed, because these 'career limiting fears' go against everything that the fundamentals of administration of justice hold dear.

In short, judges who lack courage, in their convictions, may not be an effective shield against executive encroachment; into the fundamental human rights and freedoms of the citizenry. It does not need to be emphasized that in any civilized and democratic society, it is the bounden duty of the judiciary to protect the fundamental rights and freedoms of the citizenry; at all costs. If, however, the judiciary comprises men and women who are shrinking violets in the face of the executive and the legislature, then the fundamental rights and freedoms of the citizenry lie in peril of unfettered abuse; and the relevance of the judiciary is called into question.

As Nelson Mandela (1918-2013) once said, courage is not the absence of fear; but the ability to overcome fear, and not let fear influence your decisions as a judge. Much as there is great wisdom in these words, my personal view is that to say that judges must decide without fear is easier said than done. Travelling across Africa and the world, interacting with judges, I have come to appreciate that judgeship can also be a dangerous calling. I have also come to the realization that the rule of law and the independence of the judiciary are accepted for as long as is convenient; or the status quo is not upset.

In the introductory chapter of this book, I stated that the discussions would be as candid as possible; and it is that spirit that I want to say that one unimpeachable truth, about judgeship, is that judges who are independent face many risks. They may just disappear, or have trumped up charges levelled against them; which charges are intended, if not to remove the judges, then at least to discredit them in the eyes of the innocent, and gullible, members of the public.

My interaction with judges, from all over the world, has not only broadened my mind, but has revealed some shocking truths; which I am compelled to share. For instance, it came to my knowledge that, in some parts of Africa, judges have been approached, by some emissaries of the executive, asking them to resign; failing which something would be found, against them, to force them to leave office. Yet in other parts of Africa, independent judges have expressed the fear that by being independent and fearless, they did not only risk removal; but also possible harm in many ways than one; including facing very subtle, but real danger, at the instance of the executive; or those organized by the executive. Who can forget the chilling remarks of an infuriated president, who when he lost an election petition, called judges cockroaches and threatened them with dire consequences if he should bounce back to power? Well; that president did bounce back to power and, on the face of it, he does not seem to have done anything untoward; since then. It can only be hoped that he never makes good on those threats.

Calmness

Yet another quality that judges should have is calmness. Judges need thick skins; I should go so far as to say the skins of rhinoceros, even, if they are to survive some of the perils of judgeship! The examples that have been cited above, of what can happen to independent judges, are very real. Judges must be able to withstand intimidation, harassment and even imprisonment. They must be ready to lay down their lives, for the constitution and the rule of law, if need be. In a moment of extreme pride, in my career as a servant of the law, I heard one Chief Justice proclaim, in public, that in defence of the rule of law they (judges) were ready to die; if need be. This was Chief Justice Maraga, of Kenya, in the aftermath of the watershed decision, of the Supreme Court, annulling the 2017 Presidential Elections in Kenya.

Ability to listen

In addition to the qualities, mentioned above, a judge must be gifted in the art of listening and must retain impartiality at all times. He, or she, must keep an open mind to the very end; having considered every argument and its implications. I have sat with judges who, in any given session, speak more than the lawyers and/or parties combined. This, obviously, cannot be correct. It is only a judge who listens carefully, permits debate to flow and intervenes sparingly, and even then only to clarify a point.

Impartiality should be second nature to a judge

Impartiality cannot be over emphasized. It should be second nature to a judge. Patrick Devlin (1905-1992) says; "I put impartiality before independence simply because without the reality the appearance would not endure." In truth, however, the appearance of impartiality is equally important, if not more, because, as it is often said; "The judge who gives the right judgment, while appearing not to do so, may be thrice blessed in heaven; but on earth he is of no use at all."

Having discussed some of the qualities that a judge should possess, it is also important to look at some guiding principles; upon which the functions of a judge are anchored. If questioned on which principles are the most important, I would have to say that independence and impartiality are the two sacred principles which are at the heart of the work of a judge. Judicial independence is, undoubtedly, the bedrock of any society; which is based on the rule of law. It is a fundamental guarantee of a fair trial. A judge is required to reach a decision independently; after a dispassionate assessment of the facts and application of the law as he, or she, best understands it.

It is a cardinal rule of adjudication that in taking any decision, a judge should be free of any influences from whosoever; be it relatives, family members, members of his, or her, church, members of the executive and the legislature or, indeed, judicial colleagues. As mentioned earlier on in this book, a judge may seek help from more experienced colleagues; and a hypothetical discussion may even ensue.

But, ultimately, there is only one legal mind that must decide all the relevant issues in the dispute; and that is the presiding judge.

Independence

Independence is one of the greatest virtues of a judiciary; and it must be jealously guarded and protected. To compromise the principle of independence is to threaten the orderly existence of a society that is based on the rule of law. I have had many discussions on the duties of a judge, and at different fora; and the one point on which I am consistent is that, in the execution of his/her duties, a judge must have nothing to fear and nothing to gain. To this end, no judge should do anything that his, or her, conscience tells him is wrong; and contrary to the law. No judge should deliver a judgment, so as to gain the approval of anyone, including the executive.

No judge should be driven to deliver a judgment that is contrary to law, even though public opinion should crave such a judgement. There is nothing wrong in working hard to gain promotion; but is it both unethical and unacceptable, for a judge to actively seek promotion; by delivering judgments intended to please the executive, or anyone else for that matter, knowing fully well that those judgements are wrong in law.

Just as it is very important, for a judge, to deliver informed judgements, which are based on the applicable laws and rules, it is of equal importance for judgements to be delivered expeditiously. As anyone who has litigated, in the courts, would easily testify, justice is sweetest when it is fresh. The tendency of some judges, to turn their chambers into what my bother, Moroka J, called 'ware houses', should be discouraged. Judgments must be delivered within reasonable time.

Some courts have set time-lines within which judgments must be delivered. There is absolutely nothing wrong with such a practice. But, personally, I think that it is prudent to set a flexible standard; where the time line must be dictated by the circumstances of each case. Setting a fixed time-line may be arbitrary and, where such is set, it must be regarded as a rough guideline. By way of example, it is unacceptable that an urgent application to stop a sale in execution, which is due in two weeks, should be delivered two months later; long after the sale has taken place. Unfortunately, this happens in some jurisdictions.

In a series of judicial trainings which I conducted in South Africa, Uganda and Kenya, I was shocked to learn that, in some jurisdictions, judgments could be pending for more than five years. It is my firm view that no circumstances can justify this kind of situation; as such a practice only serves to bring the courts in disrepute. I was equally shocked to learn that, in some jurisdictions, in Southern Africa, it has been common for a party, who challenges an election result, to wait until the next election cycle; on account that election petitions take too long to be heard. This is a clear travesty of justice; because election petitions, by their nature, must be prioritized. The reason for this is that any delay, in hearing and determining them, renders the petitions academic and nugatory. When I began to serve as a judge, of the National and Supreme Courts in Papua New Guinea, I was very impressed that the Chief Justice prioritized the efficient and speedy resolution of election returns; and that he insisted on regular feedback, from judges, on how the cases, concerning elections, were progressing.

The concepts of 'independence' and 'impartiality', in the context of judgeship, are very closely connected; and yet distinct. Independence relates to the freeness to take a decision that accords with the conscience and knowledge of the law, by a judge, without any undue influence from whosoever. Impartiality, on the other hand, relates to the absence of bias, ill-will or prejudice; and it has been said to be the supreme judicial virtue. As mentioned earlier, both the actual and the appearance of impartiality are important in the work of a judge. Judges should not be supporters of any cause before them; and neither should they show, or have sympathy, for one cause over another. Impartiality and its appearance can be damaged by a predilection to one argument; before hearing all the evidence and submissions.

Judges are not beholden to governments of the day

It is a golden rule, in the enterprise of judging, that judges are not beholden to governments of the day. They see governments come and go, like water; with no consequence to themselves. Judges owe no loyalty to ministers or any state officials. They are only subordinate to the constitution; and not to any other authority. Judges are lions under the throne, but in their eyes that seat is occupied not by the president, but by the supreme law, the constitution, to which they owe allegiance. It is often said, and correctly so, that judges are no respecters of persons; and that one of their primary duties is to guarantee human rights, and curb executive lawlessness; if any.

One interesting point, in the discussion on judges' loyalty to the constitution, is that it is not in all countries that judges swear allegiance to the constitution. I know of a country in which judges swear allegiance to the King. This is a departure from the true tenets of judgeship because it is wrong; in any country that subscribes to democracy and the rule of law. I, actually, know of a country where a judge was hauled over the coals; because he had apparently offended the King, in his remarks. This Judge, who is brilliant beyond measure, was finally evicted from the bench of his own country; where he had served with loyalty and distinction. This, in my view, is a very good example of the perils of being an independent judge; in some parts of the world.

It is extremely important for judges to live the values that underpin the calling of judgeship. They must know, and respect, the principle that they cannot be judges in their own cause. As lawyers often say, a monkey cannot be a judge over the affairs of the forest. What this means is that heads of courts, or even Chief Justices, cannot constitute a panel of judges to hear a matter in which their powers are being challenged. This is because doing so not only amounts to forum shopping; but is both dishonourable and unprincipled. A story is told, in some jurisdiction, of a Chief Justice who, when he was in trouble with the law, called one of the judges to come and preside over a matter in which he was involved. The judge came and did the Chief Justice' bidding; but ended up being arrested and detained.

On the matter of Chief Justices empaneling the bench, I was impressed to hear a Chief Justice, in one of the jurisdictions in which I was privileged to serve, asking judges, at a meeting, for volunteers to hear a certain matter. In my view, this kind of transparency suggests that the Chief Justice had absolutely no interest in the matter concerned; and that he trusted every judge to discharge their duties consistent with their oath of office. Aside this, I have heard the same Chief Justice say that it would be appropriate that those known to have expertise, that is implicated in the subject matter in any dispute, must volunteer to preside. I am happy to disclose that this was my experience in Papua New Guinea; and I can only say that this approach affirms the independence and impartiality of the judges. In contrast to this, however, there are many jurisdictions where a 'suitable' panel of judges will be constituted to preside over a matter. A common feature of such panels is that the members are neither the most senior, nor are they the most qualified.

In addition to the values of independence and impartiality, which are a must have for a judge, one may, legitimately, add two more values; namely integrity and loyalty. Integrity involves two different duties; the first being probity and the second being the duty of dignity and honour. The duty of probity requires that a judge refrain from improper behaviour; and not only that which is contrary to law. The duty of dignity and honour requires that a judge must show respect for individual dignity and act, strictly, within the framework of the law.

Loyalty, on the other hand, is the value of being faithful to judicial oath, i.e. to be bound by the law. It implies two things; the duty to exercise the powers entrusted to a judge, on the one hand, and, on the other, the prohibition to exceed them.

In addition to the qualities discussed above, there are other qualities, of a general nature, that are required of a judge. These are kindness, patience, integrity, hard work. Starting with kindness, I personally believe that this is one virtue that judges must possess in abundance. A judge must have a kind and loving heart. This is so because justice is, essentially, about love. It is about loving everybody as one loves himself or herself. It will be recalled that, in the preceding chapter, I spoke about the idea of judgeship being akin to priesthood. I think that justice being about love sits very comfortable with judgeship being akin to priesthood.

Kindness is a virtue that embraces humility; and that is why arrogance and judgeship do not go well together. When dealing with criminal matters, judges are required to pass sentences that fit the crime; and do not undermine societal interest. Judges must never forget that at the point of conviction and sentence, the accused does not cease to be human and so kindness and mercy are still required.

Patience

Patience is another critical virtue in the enterprise of judging. A judge must be patient; and must understand, and appreciate, that the lawyers, litigants, or any other people who appear before the courts, may be emotionally charged, hurt and disappointed; and may not be as dispassionate, in presenting their side of the story, as they should ordinarily be. A judge must remain calm and collected; even when a lawyer has no clue about the issues that brought him, or her, to court. Difficult as it may, to be in that scenario, a judge must still endeavour to guide the lawyer accordingly. It is, indeed, true, and as is often said, that most litigants, if given a choice between an average and patient judge, and an ill-tempered and impatient genius of a judge, they would prefer the former any day.

Anyone who has litigated, in court, will agree that there is nothing as frustrating as a judge who is not prepared to listen to what the people appearing before him, or her, have to say. Sometimes, a litigant simply desires to be heard and be allowed to lay their concerns bare; before a judge. Litigants want to, at least, leave the court with a sigh of relief; saying "well I don't know how I performed, but at least the judge listened to me"; and they can only get this from a listening judge.

My experience on the bench has really taught me the value of endurance. I recall a case in which my patience was tested to the limit and, to this day, I think it was a miracle that I resisted committing a lawyer to prison for contempt. At the end of the day, I went home happy that I didn't. What happened, in that particular instance, was that a matter was called for hearing, before me. The lawyers introduced themselves; as is customary. A third lawyer, who was not representing any of the parties, nonetheless, stood up and insisted that he be heard; because his client ought to have been cited, but was not. I asked that lawyer to sit down, and not take part in the proceedings, since he was not a party. He insisted that he had a right to speak, 'in the interest of fairness'. It took a while, but the lawyer eventually decided to behave. Suffice it to say that by that time, the temptation to send that lawyer to prison, for a few days or hours, at the very least, was at boiling point. But somehow, and with every ounce of strength that was in me, I mustered some patience and managed to overcome the temptation to send the errant lawyer to prison. While that lawyer, certainly, deserved some sanction for his conduct, I am happy that patience carried the day; and I didn't commit him to prison. The moral of this personal story is that judges should not always be too happy, or quick, to pull the trigger; unless it is absolutely imperative to do so.

Looking back, I guess I was able to resist the impulse to commit the lawyer to prison, for contempt, because of a prior experience that impressed me. In 2013, I was part of a team of African Judges dispatched to observe a Presidential Election in Kenya. When the matter was called up, an infuriated woman, who was not a party to the proceedings, raised her hand, from the gallery, and demanded to speak. The Chief Justice, graciously, gave her an audience. The woman went on a tirade, and spent a few minutes denouncing the Chief Justice. She suggested that he could not be impartial because, in the past, he had written, in glowing terms, about the leader of the opposition; who was a party to those proceedings. When the woman finished saying her piece, the Chief Justice calmly explained the context of his writing. He told her that, at the time, he was not constrained to express an opinion and was, in fact, entitled to express his opinion in the manner he did. He added that the situation was different; now that he was the Chief Justice. I do not know whether the lady was happy with the explanation, but that appeared to settle the objection. The Chief Justice did not make any threats, to that woman, of imprisonment for contempt. I think many would agree that, by his action, the Chief Justice of Kenya perfectly carried out a judge's duty to be patient; even in the face of a frustrating, or challenging, situation. That was a great personal lesson for me, which I put into practice years later, in the example I have given.

I have already referred to another critical value for judgeship, namely integrity, and have pointed out that it is a value that is important for the discharge of judicial functions. Judges must carry, and conduct, themselves in a manner that should earn respect for both their office; and the institution of the judiciary. A judge's conduct, and behaviour, must be such as to enhance the honour and prestige of their office. It is common knowledge that judges occupy an exalted office, in the communities in which they serve. As such, they must be people who are, upright and righteous; and must also have integrity and honour; before the title 'Honourable', which precedes their names. Judges are the pillars of the justice system and it is because of their importance to a society that is based on the rule of law, that the public are to demand irreproachable conduct from their judges.

It is a truism that confidence in any judiciary is founded on the integrity and moral uprightness of its adjudicators. A judge must not only be a 'good judge', but must also be a 'good person'. This is because in the minds of ordinary people, a judge has not only pledged to serve the ideals of justice and truth, on which the rule of law and the foundations of democracy are built, but has also promised to embody them. It follows, from the above narrative, that the personal qualities, conduct and image which a judge projects, affects those who are in the administration of justice as a whole and, therefore, the confidence that the public reposes in it.

Public confidence

Public confidence in the independence, impartiality and integrity of a judge is the most precious asset that a judiciary can have. I once asked a brother judge, in Papua New Guinea, as to why there was minimal security around judges. His answer was that "In this country, the public trusts the judges, more than any other entity, or organ, of the State". He then told me an extra-ordinary story that once, while walking, leisurely, in town, he was greeted by someone he couldn't remember. The person, who appeared quite relaxed and happy with him, told the judge who he was. He added that he had been sentenced to prison, by that very judge, but was now free; since he had completed serving his sentence. The man thanked the judge; and assured him that he had now repented, and was a good citizen. That story truly amazed me; because I could not imagine that happening in many other parts of the world.

Returning to the subject of integrity, it is because of the importance of judges, in enforcing standards of good conduct, that the public demands, from a judge, conduct that is far above what is demanded of ordinary citizens. In short, the standard of conduct, for judges, is much higher than that of society; as a whole. It is as if the judicial function, which is to sit in judgement of others, has imposed a requirement that the judge remain beyond the judgment of others.

I now turn to a subject which I have, also, already mentioned, in the earlier part of this book; that of hard work. In the judiciary, hard work is a pre-condition for success. Strictly speaking, judges have no working hours. The nature of their work requires them to work long hours on weekdays, weekends and even on holidays. They are required to read voluminous documents, before they start a trial; and to listen, and take notes, during trial. Judges must also read the law; in order to find out which law is applicable to the case that they are dealing with.

It should be mentioned that finding the applicable law may not be as easy as it may seem. It may require reading judgments of the superior courts, and even of the courts of other countries, in order to properly appreciate the law. In jurisdictions where judges sit every day, this may be a near impossible task; but it has to be done, all the same. A lazy judge is bound to be a bad judge, and to give the judiciary a bad name.

Most significantly, judges must see to it that they deliver judgments as soon as is practicably possible. A matter that was heard on an urgent basis requires that judgment be delivered urgently; as the circumstances require. Where it is reasonable, and expedient, to do so, an order may be issued; followed by a reasoned ruling, or judgment, later on. Reserving judgment must be done in exceptional and compelling cases and, even then, it helps to reserve judgments to a fixed date; rather than indefinitely. It is a grave injustice to reserve judgment for years, on end, because, in all probability, the judge may have forgotten certain essential features of the trial. It is always better to deliver judgment when the events are still fresh.

An example of what I mean would illustrate the issue better. Once, I sat in a mundane matter; in which the applicant brought an application to dispense with the requirement to file an 'Appeals Book', in the manner that the rules prescribed. In his original papers, the applicant had cited a wrong rule. When he moved the application, he sought leave to cite the correct rule. The application was not opposed; and I granted it. What this meant was that the applicant had now cited the correct rule. I reserved judgment longer than was necessary. When I came to write it, I forgot that I had granted an amendment to cite the correct rule, and proceeded to deliver a judgment based on the original papers. I dismissed the application; on the basis that the rule cited, by the applicant, was a wrong one. Fortunately, that matter was procedural and related to whether, or not, the applicant must be excused from relying on a rule which, he contended, would be more cumbersome. It was not about the violation of any right or legal duty; in which case an injustice would have been occasioned to the applicant.

Justice delayed is justice denied

While justice demands that judgements, and rulings, be delivered in a timely manner, it is also very important, indeed, that every judgement, and ruling, be accompanied by reasons. This helps the parties, involved, to understand why the court decided in the manner it did; and also allows for an unhappy party to take legal advice and, if so advised, lodge an appeal against the judgement or ruling.

It may be recalled that I emphasized, earlier on, that a judge should never lose sleep over the possibility of his, or her, decision, being reversed on appeal. I reiterate this, of necessity. Law is not an exact science; it is fluid. The ascertainment of facts is fraught with too many risks; and judges are, but human beings, who are fallible.

As with any discipline, knowledge is a critical component of any decision making. Uneven knowledge may manifest in the conclusions that the judges reach; after hearing cases. Sometimes, judges may be, unconsciously, biased or prejudiced and, unless they make an effort to discover and suppress this bias, it may explain the decision that they reached. But despite all this, no judge should spend a sleepless night; because a higher court disagreed with his, or her, decision. On occasion, a judge can learn a few valuable lessons why his, or her, decision could not be allowed to stand.

It is worth noting that appellate courts have, also, been known to reverse a correct decision; and to substitute the same with a wrong one, instead. Judges of the superior, or highest, courts are not final because they are infallible; not in the least. They are 'infallible' because they are the final doors at which one may knock for justice. If there was no system of finality, it would have been possible that a court above the now 'final' courts, could reverse the decision of the said 'final' courts; thereby resulting in never ending litigation and, of course, a denial of justice to those seeking it. Ordinarily, because the judgments of the higher courts are crafted by the most senior and experienced judges, the assumption is that their knowledge of the law is, necessarily, superior and, therefore, binding on the lower courts. It behoves the superior courts to demonstrate superiority of reasoning, and intellectual leadership, characterized by humility and collegiality; in the manner that they craft their judgments.

Higher courts must respect lower courts

One unfortunate truth, which I am compelled to point out, is that some judgements tend to be personal; and to tackle individual judges of the lower court. This is totally unethical; and should be avoided at all costs. If it was done routinely, it would, almost certainly, damage the reputation not only of the concerned judge; but the judiciary in general. The appellate courts, being the final arbiters, must always be concerned that they do not commit any error; that may occasion injustice to a litigant. This is so because once they have taken a decision; nothing else may be done about the particular case. In short, a decision made by the final courts means that all the doors of justice are shut in the face of a litigant. Judges of the higher courts must use neutral, and respectful, language in their decisions. They must also be alive to the possibility that they may, actually, be wrong in the conclusion that they reach; and that the lower court was, in fact, correct. Humility requires that such a possibility should not be ruled out. In my view, this is the reason why all courts, without exception, must embrace humility; as a value.

Good character

In addition to the qualities that have been discussed so far, an ideal judge must be of good character. This must go hand in hand with being humble, patient and affable; which have already been discussed. A judge must have the skill, or talent, to manage the lawyers and litigants who appear before him, or her. There are, obviously, times when a judge may be frustrated by a rambling lawyer; who fails to address a pertinent point head on; choosing, instead, to prevaricate and waste time.

A judge who confronts such a challenge is better off being calm, and patient, and guiding courteously. A good judge tries to set everyone at ease; even under the most difficult of circumstances. The judge must ensure that he, or she, is friendly, but firm and personable, but not personal. A good judge must ensure that the rules of procedure are followed; and everyone is given a fair hearing. Character defines a person, and a judge must have a good character; which is worthy of the office that he, or she holds.

Ability to reason well

Another quality, that judges must possess, is the ability to reason well. This is a quality that is required for judges to be able to deliver sound judgements; for the benefit of litigants. Judges must have the ability to make relevant findings of fact; and must avoid making conflicting findings of fact. A judge must find the correct law; which applies to his, or her, findings of facts. A judge must have the skill to unearth the truth; because a significant number of cases, perhaps the majority, may be determined by reference to facts alone. It happens, quite often, that once the facts are known, then law to be applied is easy to find.

In the interactions that I have had with judges, the world over, and also most of the judicial trainings which I have conducted, I have often been faced with the question as to what should constitute a good judgment. My response has, constantly, been that judgements need not be excellent academic pieces. Additionally, judges do not need to be too anxious to display knowledge and erudition. All that is required is that a judge, succinctly, address the issues in controversy; as expeditiously as possible.

Reproducing large tracts of evidence and the law is unnecessary; where same can be compressed into a few paragraphs or pages. However, in saying that judgments are not supposed to be academic pieces, I do not mean that judges must turn their courts into intellectual graveyards. I am also not suggesting, in any way, that judgements should be hollow. I give my view while being very mindful that judges have different styles of writing; with some, perhaps a little more skilled, at stringing sentences together, than others. At the end of the day, what is important is that judgements must be well reasoned; and must make sense to the parties concerned. To this I add that, in my view, it is particularly important that a judgement should make sense to the losing party; who must understand, why the decision did not go their way.

A good manager

There is another quality which is taking on more relevance now, than previously, which judges must have; and that is to be a good manager. This quality is essential if a judge is to be able to control court proceedings effectively. In the olden days, judges did not need to bother about being good managers. But we are now in the era of judicial case management; which requires judges to manage their cases; from the moment that they are registered, to disposal, in an increasing number of jurisdictions. After they receive cases, to deal with, judges need to allocate time-lines that are enforceable; for hearing and determining the matters. This requires constant monitoring, so that cases which enter the system don't circulate forever, but are determined and finalized, within reasonable time; depending on their complexity. With the countless number of cases being registered, virtually every day, the value of being a good manager cannot be over emphasized.

A good judge must control court proceedings; ensuring not only that every litigant has a fair hearing; but also that all participants, in the court process, are accorded the respect, and attention, that they deserve. It needs to be emphasized that while controlling court proceedings is a necessary part of adjudication, judges should not play God; in the process of keeping order in their courts. It is all too easy, and tempting, for judges to take the usual address of 'My Lord/Lady' to heart; to see it as signifying that they are demi-Gods and, as a result of that, to be tempted to play God. Suffice it to say that it would be, most, unfortunate for ordinary mortals, like judges, to play God; because that is not their call, at all. The function of a judge is to 'do justice to all manner of persons, without fear or favour, ill will or affection'. This duty is the very essence of the Judicial Oath; to which every judge must subscribe, before commencing his, or her, duties and functions; as a Judge.

Having outlined the qualities that a judge should possess, it is necessary to discuss the workplace, or environment, of a judge; which is where some of the qualities, that have been referred to, above need to be displayed; by judges. The workplace of judges is, of necessity, the court room. This is the public space devoted, by society, for the adjudication, and settlement, of all controversies that are justiciable. When adjudicating matters, a judge must be totally in control of the proceedings before him or her. A judge, who is not in control of the proceedings in his, or her, court, fails in their duties as judge. This is for the obvious reason that disorder, in court proceedings, will inevitably lead to a miscarriage of justice; and run the risk of a judiciary being held in low esteem, by the public at large.

There are many examples of possible distractions that a judge should not permit in the court room. As everyone who is familiar with the way courts function, or are run, will know, one golden rule is that there should always be total silence in court. It is discourteous to the authority of the court, and other participating litigants and attendants, for a phone to ring; and disrupt the proceedings. But, occasionally, a judge's phone may ring; as once happened, when I appeared before a certain judge. In that case, a phone rang during the proceedings; and the judge responded, to the ring, with indignation; appealing to the offender to step out of court. However, the phone kept on ringing; until it became clear that it was the judge's phone that was ringing. The judge apologized; and proceedings continued. I must confess that I was, secretly, quite amused by that incident; as it was a reminder that judges were human, like the rest of us, and were not exempt from certain life experiences, such as a phone ringing at the wrong time! On a serious note, however, the judge's apology, at the disruption of proceedings, showed that humility was a necessary virtue for judges to possess. An arrogant judge would, almost certainly, just have turned his phone off; and carried on as if nothing had happened; which would have been disrespectful of the people appearing before him.

It is the duty of a judge to ensure there is total silence in court. Where the audience is not willing, or able, to be quiet, then the judge should not hesitate to evict them. It is not acceptable, when court attendants are disrupting court proceedings, by talking and whispering, for a judge to sit by, passively, and do nothing about it. In such instances, a judge must, in a firm, respectful and clear voice, be able to stamp his, or her, authority on the proceedings, by calling for silence. A judge who cannot stamp his, or her, authority on the proceedings risks losing control of the proceedings; if silence is not observed. As it is often said, silence in court is truly golden, for justice cannot be administered without it.

The other equally important role of judges, in court, is how they communicate with the players, before them, in a particular case; whether those players be the parties, themselves, and/or their attorneys, and, in the case of a party without an attorney, the undefended litigant. One cannot over emphasize the importance of communication. It is the lubricant that keeps the wheels of justice turning smoothly. To say that a judge must communicate effectively, with the parties, does not mean that a judge must descend into the arena and speak even more than the litigants or their lawyers put together. A judge who talks too often, and interrupts counsel or witnesses, may be harmful to the cause of justice and the principles of fair trial. It is, after all, the parties who appear before the court, with issues to be settled, who should be heard, and not the judge; who is not a party to the proceedings; but is only the arbiter.

Communication skills are important

A judge must have good communication skills. These should include the ability not only to express himself, or herself, clearly, but also to listen, closely, to what is being said in evidence; by witnesses or by counsel. Every lawyer would agree that an inattentive judge is, surely, an undesirable judge. In jest, I must say, from experience, that once in a while, some judges who appear to be fast asleep, when lawyers are making submissions, are actually not sleeping. The evidence would be the reasons and the speed with which they deliver their ruling. As they say, the proof of the pudding is in the tasting.

During the course of proceedings, a judge must be attentive and, where possible, keep constant eye contact, especially on witnesses. It is impossible for a judge to evaluate the veracity of the testimonies, of witnesses, if the judge is not attentive. The importance of eye-contact, and body language, cannot be over-emphasized. Eye contact is indispensable in the assessment of demeanour, or outward behaviour, of witnesses. Judges must, however, be careful not to let their body-language disclose their disposition as to what is being said; whether by witnesses or counsel, in making submissions. To show one's disposition, in the course of the proceedings, is often productive of resentment, especially with the losing side; and does not promote respect for the court, itself, and the rule of law.

Still on the subject of controlling proceedings in court, the ultimate tool that may assist judges, as a last resort, to bring order and discipline, is contempt proceedings. It is not always necessary to resort to contempt committal, in order to stamp one's authority on court proceedings. A judge should only use committal for contempt, to stamp his, or her, authority; as a last resort. Every judge would do well to remember that the power to commit for contempt is not for the self-esteem of the judge, or his or her sense of self-importance; but is meant to protect the administration of justice.

A last word on the issue of staying on top of things, in court, is that under no circumstances should judges allow proceedings, before them, to descend into chaos. That can only damage the reputation of the court. At the end of the day, the role of judges in controlling proceedings in court, whether at the trial or appellate level, is to ensure the due administration of justice, by means of fair trial; or a proper and fair disposal of any appeal.

Common sense

I now turn to yet another quality of significance, for adjudicators, namely common sense. One of the principal tools of a good judge is common sense. Judges use their common understanding, their contemporary knowledge of society and the expectations of the community as part of judicial decision making. Common sense understandings, about the world and human behaviour, also form part of the tools that judges use; to interpret the meaning of matters such as reasonableness and normality of human behaviour. It is quite normal that judge's factual assumptions may be influenced by their own cultural world views.

It is often said that 'law is common sense as modified by the legislature' and that 'whilst a judge may get by if he doesn't know any law, a judge cannot get by, at all, without common sense'. Be that as it may, it is important to note that commonsense is not always accurate; and can sometimes be based on assumptions, and not facts.

Punctuality

The next issue that I discuss may not, necessarily, fall into the category of qualities that a judge should possess, but it is, certainly, a necessary attribute for every judge to have. I am referring to the matter of 'punctuality'. A judge must be punctual. In fact, punctuality must be part of the personality of a judge. The reason for this is that the time of a judge is not his, or hers. It is the public's time, and a public resource; which must be utilized efficiently. As such, it is unbefitting for a judge to start court late. Lawyers must learn, from the judge, that being on time is important in the dispensation of justice. Justice Hidayatullah, (1905-1992) who was the eleventh Chief Justice of India, is said to have, once, remarked that those who did not respect time did not respect the rule of law. Whether, or not, people may agree with these sentiments, one thing that is true, of the dispensation of justice, is that time wasted never returns.

In my early orientation days, as a judge of the Supreme Court of Papua New Guinea, I sat with the Chief Justice; on interlocutory motions. I observed that he was always on time. Once, he told me that his staff, and lawyers, knew that he was always on time. He said, to me, that his Associate, which is the equivalent of a Court Orderly, in my jurisdiction back in Botswana, knew that if he was not there, to bang on the door to announce the Chief Justice's appearance, then His Lordship would do it himself, when it was time to walk into court. In sum, the Chief Justice, of Papua New Guinea, led by example and everyone would follow suit.

While punctuality, at holding court sittings, is of the utmost importance for a judge, it must be acknowledged that there are times when it becomes a challenge to be punctual. For example, time keeping may be difficult, in some jurisdictions, where there are not enough courts, or personnel, for all judges. This means that it is important that resources are availed; to ensure that judges have court rooms and the requisite personnel; so that they can start their courts in time.

Yet another subject, which cannot, strictly, be termed 'a quality', but which cannot be separated from the functions of judgeship, is reading. Judges must invest in reading; as it is a tool that sharpens their knowledge of the law, and makes the task of adjudication, and writing judgements, easy. Reading also improves the vocabulary of judges; and improves their ability to communicate. Studying legal literature is imperative. As such, judges cannot escape the duty to read; and neither can they profess a dislike of reading; otherwise it would call into question why they became judges. I have often said that being a judge is akin to being a perpetual student since it entails having to read all the time. I retain that view to date.

The qualities which judges should possess, as outlined in this book, are by no means exhaustive. But a last quality, that I wish to discuss, briefly, is loyalty. I think it cannot be argued that loyalty is an important value in the life, and career, of a judge. Loyalty is a value of being faithful to the judicial oath; which requires a judge to be a servant of the law. Loyalty implies two things; firstly, the duty to exercise the powers entrusted in one; and secondly, the prohibition to exceed them.

In concluding the discussion on the qualities and attributes of a judge, I wish to state that developing and/ or maintaining all these values is easier said than done. As has been pointed out, judges are mere mortals; like the rest of the human populace on earth. They come from different social and educational backgrounds, and have their personal human biases and prejudices. But when all is said and done, what is important is that every judge must aspire to the highest standards of judgeship; in order to ensure that the highest quality of justice dispensation is rendered to the public. Both in the exercise of their functions and by their individual conduct, judges must ensure that the courts become the fountains of justice; and not justice in name, only, but in practice too.

Chapter Four

APPOINTMENT OF JUDGES

The manner in which judges are appointed is important in ensuring that they are independent and also qualified to do the job. A judiciary that is not appointed on the basis of merit and in a transparent and fair manner does not usually inspire confidence amongst the people. The quality of the judges, that grace a country's judiciary, sets the tone for the overall quality and independence of the judiciary.

Those who keep abreast with the happenings in any judiciary may attest that the appointment of judges has been a topical issue, in recent times. This is, mainly, because of the concern that politicians have politicized the appointment of the judges; by paying lip service to merit and, instead, appointing judges whom they believe could protect their interests.

Cadre judgeship

A judge, in Uganda, once expressed his concern at the growing phenomenon of what he called 'cadre judgeship'. He was referring to a rising tendency, particularly in Africa, where the executive authority is appointing judges whom they think can be the gate-keepers of their interests and, in the process, leaving out the best qualified, and experienced, persons who would make better judges.

In my view, the tragedy about 'cadre judgeship' is that it often leaves a trail of broken hearts, creates de-motivation, especially amongst the most senior and qualified lawyers, who deserve to be considered ahead of the beneficiary, and generally breeds contempt and disrespect of the system. 'Cadre Judgeship' also divides the bench amongst those perceived to be lackeys of the system and those perceived to be upright and independent. This is, obviously, not a conducive, or healthy, state for any judiciary to be in.

Politics may divide the judiciary

A colleague once explained to me about the division brought by appointments that seem to be based on political considerations. He explained just how dangerous, and cancerous, the situation could become. The judge spoke of mistrust in each other, by judges, and also gossip about each other. He, also, spoke about how, at tea meetings, judges would be factionalized; and how certain topics would not be discussed, or would be discontinued when the other faction perceived that it had been infiltrated. As can be imagined, those revelations made for very sad hearing, and were an eye opener as to how a judicial system can go wrong; with interference from the executive. On a positive note, though, in some countries, Law Societies have fought tooth and nail to force executive authority to abide by the constitution; and appoint candidates who are recommended by the relevant constitutional authority; instead of appointing those whom executive authority prefers.

As earlier indicated, the manner in which judges are appointed impacts on their independence. The method and safeguards in place, with regard to the appointment of judges, have deep implications for the institutional and individual independence of the judges. Giving too much power, and discretionary authority, to the executive to appoint chief justices, without the mechanism of a judicial services commission, judges of the High Court may be seen to undermine the independence of the judiciary.

Executive influence must be eliminated or kept minimal

Ideally, the legal framework governing the appointment of judges must make it difficult for the executive to appoint inexperienced, and under-qualified, candidates to the bench. An appropriate legal framework would make it harder for political appointees to be given positions on the bench. An ideal appointment process must be designed in such a manner that it can identify the best to become judges. Any appointment process must enjoy public confidence because, without it, the judiciary can hardly claim to be legitimate. This explains why most international legal instruments and declarations insist that judges should be appointed on the basis of clearly defined criteria; and by a publicly declared process that is open and transparent.

In many developed countries, the appointment of judges is on the strength of their varying degrees of experience; either as superior court judges, distinguished academics or legal practitioners, or on the basis of their experience in other relevant fields.

Closer to the jurisdiction, of Botswana, from which I hail, many countries have dedicated constitutional bodies that appoint judges. There are provisions in the constitutions of many African countries, including Kenya, Uganda, and South Africa, for the establishment of Judicial Service Commissions; which recommend, or nominate, those to be appointed as judges; by the executive. The extent to which the appointment of judges is free from political manipulation is also dependent on the independence of the Judicial Service Commission. In Botswana the constitutional provision with respect to the appointment of the Chief Justice merely provide that 'The Chief Justice shall be appointed by the President'.

One of the issues for judicial reform, intended to be resolved by the new constitution in Kenya, was the need to have a more independent, transparent and accountable judiciary. For that reason, a more inclusive, and accountable, Judicial Service Commission was established; as an independent mechanism for judicial appointments. The constitutions, of many countries, accord judges certain protections and privileges; by virtue of their office. For instance, judges enjoy security of tenure; and have their salaries charged on the Consolidated Fund. They, also, cannot have their salaries, emoluments and benefits varied; to their disadvantage. Judges are immune from any action, or suit, in respect of anything done in good faith; in the exercise of their judicial function.

The principle of the independence, of the judiciary, seeks to ensure the freedom of judges to administer justice impartially, without any fear or favour. This freedom of judges has a close relationship with judicial appointment because the appointment system has a direct bearing on the impartiality, integrity and independence of judges.

The rule of law requires an independent judiciary

An independent judiciary is an essential prerequisite of a democratic state, which is ruled in accordance with the dictates of the law. Courts are involved in critical decisions; that can shape the life of an individual and the nation. The courts can decide whether a person on life support system must be allowed to die, or whether national elections must be annulled. All this heavy responsibility requires not only an independent and impartial judiciary, but a competent one; in so far as juridical work of finding facts and applying the law is concerned.

The need for an independent, and competent, judiciary is universally recognized as essential to individual rights and freedoms. Article 14 of the International Covenant on Civil and Political Rights states that:

> *"All persons shall be equal before the courts and tribunals (and) everyone shall be entitled to a fair public hearing by a competent, independent and impartial tribunal established by law."*

The independence of the judiciary is also necessitated by the increasing power of the judiciary; to scrutinize the legality of government actions. Judicial review of the constitutionality and legality, of the actions, or decisions, taken by governments is, arguably, amongst the judiciary's most significant and sensitive roles in a democratic society; and this is only possible where the judiciary is independent. Judicial independence is essential to ensuring that individual rights and freedoms are respected, protected and fulfilled.

There is a general recognition that the protection of human rights is best achieved under a political system that is committed to the rule of law. The rule of law is fundamental to achieving communities in which every person has equal opportunity to succeed, in life, in accordance with his talents and application. The overall success of any community is enhanced by the perception, by the general populace, that the country's courts are independent and impartial; and that the rule of law prevails.

All international legal instruments, of significance, underscore the importance of a transparent appointment process. Transparency in making appointments depends, in large measure, on the mechanisms for appointment of judges. These play an important role in selecting persons who have the professional skills, and qualities, that are required for judges in an independent judiciary.

Mechanisms for Judicial Appointment

The mechanisms for appointing judges differ, from one jurisdiction to another. In some jurisdictions, there is an independent constitutional body that is assigned to recommend, to the president, judges for appointment. These bodies, in the main, go under the name 'Judicial Services Commission'. In the Seychelles, this body is called the

'Constitutional Appointment Authority'. There is nothing magical about the names of these constitutional bodies; which deal with judicial appointments. What is important is that the body, which is established to appoint, or recommend the appointment of judges, must be alive to the values, and processes, that underpin an independent judiciary.

Scrutiny of most judicial appointment mechanisms will reveal that there are no standardized systems of appointment. The selection processes range from executive appointments, popular elections, to selection by senior judges, and on occasion, in consultation with the legal profession. Once they are appointed, different terms of service exist for judges. These vary from life tenure appointments, to a specific number of years. The bottom line is that, whatever judicial appointment mechanism is used, in any particular country, it should be transparent; and open to public scrutiny.

Transparency and public scrutiny, in the mechanisms for judicial appointment, are of paramount importance. This is not only so as to ensure appointment of only the best available persons to judicial office, but also to enhance public confidence in the judiciary. The soul of justice is publicity and it is incorrect, in principle, to appoint judges under cover of darkness; without the public knowing what considerations were at play.

Broadly speaking, the mechanisms for judicial appointment, which are operational, in different countries, may be classified under two sub-headings, namely elective and appointive systems. Under the election model, judges are elected on the basis of either partisan election, or non-partisan election. The United States of America is well known for the election model of selecting judges. However, it is not all states that employ the election model. Some states employ a mixed system; that combines the features of both the appointment and election model. The model of election by the legislature is employed in a few states in the United States. The same model is employed in Switzerland, in the election of Federal judges, while, in Germany, it is used with respect to the election of Constitutional Court Judges. Notably, the practice of electing judges, in the United States of America, is slowly giving way to the non-elective methods of electing judges. Currently, a majority of states use non-partisan election, and a significant number of states use combined merit selection; and different election methods.

Proponents of the elective system often justify the election model; on the basis that judges make law and, therefore, they should be selected, or chosen, by the people who will be subject to, or affected by, their judgements. Opponents of the elective system argue that the elective system does not consider any formal qualifications, and competence, of the persons to be appointed as judges; and that the decisions which such judges deliver tend to be more political than legal.

In partisan election systems, political considerations are instrumental in the selection process; and judges are selected on the basis of their political credentials, rather than on merit. This may, almost certainly, compromise the quality of jurisprudence, and undermine public confidence in the judiciary. It may also render the law unstable in that another group of judges, with a different political agenda, may be more inclined to change the law, to the advantage of those to whom their loyalties lie; and not for the benefit of the communities in which they serve.

Appointive System

The most common system of appointing judges is, by far, the appointive system. In terms of this system, appointments to judicial office are made by the head of the executive, either a President or Prime-Minister; usually after a recommendation made by the Judicial Service Commission, or some other constitutional appointing authority. Although there is merit in the increased agitation that judges must be appointed by a body constituted mainly by judges and lawyers, and a minimal number of politicians, if any, the appointment of judges, by the executive, may be tolerated or acceptable; so long as the appointments are made in meaningful consultation with members of the judiciary and the legal profession; or by a body in which members of the judiciary and the legal profession participate.

The principle of judicial independence requires that the power of appointment, of judges, should not be vested exclusively in the executive government. This is because if the executive government enjoys an exclusive privilege, in selecting judges, a risk always exists, of misuse of the power of appointment. This may take the form of politicians paying lip service to merit considerations, and, instead, being swayed by political considerations; that would, ultimately, compromise the quality of the legal system. The result of this is that judges, who obtain their position as a result of executive discretion or favour, could be obligated to serve the interests of their appointing authority; in a manner which might undermine judicial independence. The appointment of judges, exclusively, by the executive government is, therefore, not well accepted by jurists and commentators.

A number of countries consider it appropriate to involve parliament in the appointment of judges. According to this system, candidates for judgeship have to go through a parliamentary vetting, or approval process, before they can be appointed by the executive. In terms of the parliamentary approval system, formal appointments, by the executive, are only permissible once parliament has approved the candidates; with this process often being preceded by interviews.

Parliamentary approval provides a check on the power of the executive; and there is scope for public scrutiny of the appointment process. Nevertheless, this system has some inherent defects. Firstly, parliament usually has nothing to do with the initial stages of selecting candidates. Since the initial selection of candidates is a vital issue in appointing judges, this system may not be effective in controlling pre-eminent political or other irrelevant considerations, in selecting candidates for judicial office.

In countries with strong party systems, parliamentary approval may just be a smokescreen; as it may merely be an extension of the executive. Consequently, parliament may not be effective in insulating the judiciary from being politicized.

As indicated earlier, most countries, at least in the commonwealth, use the independent mechanism of the judicial service commission, to appoint judges. The problem, however, is that not all Judicial Services Commissions are independent. Many are packed with executive appointees, whilst others are dominated by politicians. It is desirable that where the mechanism of a Judicial Service Commission is adopted, it should include representatives of the judiciary and the independent legal profession; as a means of ensuring that judicial competence, integrity and independence are maintained. Under no circumstances should politicians, or political appointees, outnumber the judges and members of the legal profession.

A properly functioning, and independent, Commission system, can provide a stronger form of scrutiny of prospective candidates; for judicial office. Such a Commission can ensure the selection of the best-qualified candidates, for judicial office, for as long as it uses a fair, and transparent, selection process. In addition, if the system used by an independent Commission is transparent, and open to public scrutiny, it can reduce the exclusive executive control over judicial appointments; and maintain public confidence in the appointment system. In reality, however, the mechanisms for appointing judges exhibit several weaknesses. For instance, the Judicial Service Commission in Botswana has been criticized for being dominated by executive appointees. It is, therefore, permissible to say that this model does not inspire confidence that it can increase transparency and accountability; or remove improper political control; or, indeed, other irrelevant considerations from the appointment system.

In Kenya, the executive is represented, in the Judicial Service Commission, by two commissioners; namely the Attorney General and the Chair of the Kenya Public Service Commission. The nominations of the Judicial Service Commission go to the National Assembly for vetting; first by a Parliamentary Committee, and then by the National Assembly. In contrast, the South African system, of appointment of judges, has a very high number of politicians; that potentially compromises its independence. The South African Judicial Service Commission, which was established under the Constitution of 1996, consists of the following members:

a) The Chief Justice; who presides at the meetings of the Commission;

b) The President of the Supreme Court of Appeal;

c) One Judge designated by the Judge President;

d) The Cabinet Member responsible for the administration of justice; or an alternate designated by that Cabinet Member;

e) Two practicing advocates; nominated from within the advocates' profession, to represent the profession as a whole, and appointed by the Republican President;

f) Two practicing attorneys, nominated from within the attorneys' profession to represent the profession as a whole, and appointed by the Republican President;

g) One teacher of law, designated by teachers of law at South African universities;

h) Six persons designated by the National Assembly;

i) Four permanent delegates to the National Council of Provinces, designated together by the Council; with the supporting vote of at least six provinces;

j) Four persons designated by the Republican President, as head of the National Executive, after consulting the leaders of all the parties in the National Assembly; and

k) When considering matters relating to a specific High Court, the Judge President, of that division; and the Premier, or an alternate designated by the Premier, of the province concerned.

It is evident that the South African Judicial Service Commission is dominated by politicians. It consists of judges, the Minister of Justice, practicing and academic lawyers, members of the National Assembly, including a substantial number of opposition political party members, members of the Provincial Parliaments and persons nominated by the President, of the Republic of South Africa, after consulting leaders of all political parties represented in the National Assembly; and, in some cases, the Premier of the Province, or the Premier's nominee. Thus, the composition of the South African Judicial Service Commission is representative, in nature, and, despite its potential to be compromised, on account of the large number of political representatives which the Commission has, it is not under the exclusive control of the executive government.

The system used by the South African Judicial Service Commission, in appointing judges, is credited with having 'a fair degree of openness'. In terms of the actual appointing process, the first step is that the Commission identifies a list of meritorious candidates; by advertising for judicial vacancies and then interviewing the short-listed candidates, in public, as if 'in open court'. After the interviews, the Commission must prepare a list of nominees, with three names in excess of the number of appointments to be made. The list is submitted to the Republican President; who may make appointments from the list. If any of the nominees are unacceptable, the President must advise the Judicial Service Commission of that fact; giving reasons.

The President must, similarly, advise the Commission, giving reasons, on any appointments to be made. Where the President advises that the candidates for judgeship are unacceptable, the Commission must supplement the initial list with further nominees; and the President must make the remaining appointments from the supplemented list.

It will be seen that this method of appointment, of judges, may be prone to executive interference, for the obvious reason that the final appointing authority is the Republican President who may, perhaps on account of the advantage of incumbency, somehow manage to get preferred candidates appointed. However, the fact that candidates are identified by an appropriate constitutional body, namely the Judicial Service Commission; whose membership is diverse, and are, thereafter, subjected to scrutiny through interviews, gives the judicial appointment process, in South Africa, some transparency.

It is very important to note that when the appointment of judges is based merely, or predominantly, on political considerations, then that could have an adverse effect on the distribution of a country's economic wealth. This would come about where a powerful economic block, having captured the executive arm of the government, dictates judicial appointments to the executive. The result of that would be that judicial decisions, which affect economic interests, would be controlled by the political economic elite, who would have the remote control to judicial decisions. They would achieve this because those decisions would be made by judges whose loyalty lay with the appointing authorities who, in turn, owed their loyalties to their 'captors', namely the political economic elite.

An Overview of problems posed by different selection methods

Now that the different selection processes of judges have been discussed, it is necessary to have a look at the challenges posed by that process. A close assessment of the different approaches, and/or mechanisms, of appointment of judges reveals the following problems:

- Lack of a truly independent body responsible for appointing judges;

- Lack of a clear selection procedure;

- Lack of objective criteria for the assessment of candidates;

- Lack of transparency in the selection procedure;

- Lack of meaningful Civil Society engagement.

Arising from the above observations, a transparent and merit-based selection procedure should comply with the following imperatives:

- The body responsible for appointing judges must be independent;

- The profiles of the candidates should be procured and considered;

- The requirements, or qualifications, for suitability of candidature, to judgeship, and the abilities of candidates should be published in advance of the competitions;

- The selection procedure should be clearly established;

- Transparency, at all stages of appointment, should be established;

- Public hearings must be held; to assess candidates' qualifications.

Criteria for appointment

The earlier chapters of this book have outlined the requisite qualities for judgeship. Flowing from this, it is important that the law prescribe a clear, and merit-based, system of appointment; in order to ensure that only the best lawyers ascend to the bench. The quality of its judges is a very important indicator of any judiciary's independence; and commitment to the rule of law.

I am aware, even as I make reference to the need for the law to prescribe a clear, and merit-based, system of appointment, that there are certain human qualities that cannot be legislated for; such as a good nature, kindness, love, empathy, integrity, goodwill and a host of other traits, emotions and characteristics, which are desirable in a judge. However, the point that I make is that the law should be very clear on the type of preferred characteristics, such as those that have been discussed in the earlier chapters of this book, which a good judge should possess.

One may ask how the law would achieve this. A simple answer would be that this could be done through a transparent judicial selection process; such as has been described above. If the profiles of candidates are procured and considered, by all the relevant stakeholders in the selection process, and the suitability and abilities of candidates to judgeship are published in advance of the competitions; then those who know the candidates, both professionally and personally, would be able to make submissions; for the consideration of the Judicial Service Commission and all concerned in the process. That way, a truly informed decision could be made as to the candidates to be shortlisted.

It is my hope that the above discussion has brought out the fact that it is not, necessarily, a good Curriculum Vitae (CV) that makes a person suitable for judgeship. In actual fact, there is so much more to being a judge than having obtained good results at university or, indeed, having a brilliant mind. Experience has shown that while a good brain is necessary, some judges who got excellent grades, for their law degrees, have not turned out to be the best of judges; and those that were, perhaps, given less intellectual respect have gone on to distinguish themselves as formidable adjudicators.

Stretching the discussion on the criteria and qualifications that are necessary for judgeship, it is suggested that in order to be appointed judge, a candidate should have the following qualifications and or competencies:

Judicial Independence and Impartiality

It is an essential requirement, of judgeship, that judges should not be influenced, in their decision making, by interests beyond the law. They are required not only to be independent and impartial, but must be seen to be so. Impartiality requires judicial temperament, the ability and willingness to engage in thoughtful analysis, and collegial deliberations; before reaching a final determination.

Integrity

A reputation of personal integrity is an essential qualification of a judge. The reputation of a judge must be impeccable. A judge whose reputation is questionable discredits the judiciary as an institution.

Knowledge of the law and legal analysis

A candidate for judgeship must demonstrate knowledge of the law; and legal analysis. This means that candidates with proven experience, in making independent and impartial judgements, must be given priority consideration for judgeship. To this extent, a judge's academic qualifications and scholarship are important; as they are indicative of his, or her, knowledge of the law.

Excellent oral and written communication skills

It is not enough that judges must be knowledgeable in the law. It is important that candidates for judgeship must demonstrate excellent oral and written communication skills. This is so because a judge must be able to express his, or her, opinions clearly; so as to be understood not only by lawyers, but also by the general citizenry of the nation; whom the judge is appointed to serve.

Sufficiently developed creative intelligence

A candidate for judgeship should demonstrate that they have the capacity to deal, creatively, with new situations and problems. To this extent, persons aspiring to be judges must demonstrate a capacity for problem solving, consensus building and the ability to listen, carefully, to the other side during any court hearing.

Demonstrated commitment to protection of human rights, democratic values and democracy

A candidate for judgeship must demonstrate commitment to the protection of individual human rights and democratic values; such as constitutionalism, the rule of law and accountability.

Ability to understand the social and legal consequences of one's decisions

Judiciaries have enormous powers; which they must exercise with extreme care. Candidates for judgeship must demonstrate the capacity to understand the social and legal impact of their decisions.

Diversity

It is important that a judiciary must reflect the diversity of its people. It is, therefore, imperative that, in the selection and approval process, consideration should always be given to the desire to see a fair representation of women and men.

Conclusion

All the mechanisms for judicial appointment may have some advantages and disadvantages and, as such, no particular system can be treated as the best one. Despite this, the Commission system is, perhaps, a very effective mechanism for judicial appointment. This is because it can ensure that judicial independence and public confidence, in the appointment system, are maintained; provided that politicians, or political appointees, do not outnumber judges and members of the legal profession; in terms of the composition.

It is worth noting that, for all its positive attributes, the Commission system of judicial appointment will only be effective if a Judicial Service Commission is representative in nature; comprising members of the executive, legislature, judiciary, legal profession and the general public. In addition to this, it should be ensured that a Judicial Service Commission uses a system of appointment, of judges, which is transparent and open to public scrutiny. In this regard, the composition and working system of the South African Judicial Service Commission model, subject to considerable reduction of the number of politicians, may be an acceptable model. If it is properly utilized, such a mechanism may be very effective in ensuring the appointment of only the best-qualified people; to judicial office.

Chapter Five

JUDICIAL INDEPENDENCE

The preceding chapter discussed the appointment of judges. This chapter discusses judicial independence; a topic which, inevitably, follows that of judicial appointments. This is because after appointment, to the bench, judges take on the task of adjudication; which requires them to be independent and impartial in the decisions that they take. The principle of an independent judiciary has its origins in the theory of separation of powers; in terms of which the executive, legislature and judiciary form three separate branches of government.

An independent judiciary is an essential pre-requisite to the rule of law; in any country with democratic aspirations. Its existence, in any legal system, depends on concrete constitutional arrangements; which must enable a judge to exemplify judicial independence. Some old constitutions do not expressly state that the judiciary is independent. The Constitution of Botswana is one such example. However, a progressive interpretation, of that country's constitution, has always made it clear that the independence of the judiciary is beyond question.

Reasons for judicial independence

There are several reasons why there is need for every judiciary, in the world, to have independence. These include the following:

- To insulate the judiciary from politics;

- To guard against abuse of executive power;

- To halt the erosion of fundamental human rights and;

- To provide an assurance, to the public, that judges are impartial and fair; in their decision making process.

It is important to emphasize that the two concepts, of independence of the judiciary and separation of powers, are mutually reinforcing; and that it is in the interests of the broader society that the three arms of the state must remain detached in their operations, and also in the personnel that run them. In this way, the judiciary is insulated from political pressures. This detachment from the pressures of the political process, and political debate, provides judges with the legitimacy that they require in order for them to adjudicate, effectively, over the legality of potentially divisive, and contested, political disputes.

Separation of powers

The doctrine of separation of powers refers to the distinct functions given to the three organs of the state, concerning the exercise of governing power; with the legislature making the law, the judiciary interpreting the law, and the executive implementing the law. It is widely accepted that a complete separation of powers, between the organs of state, is unattainable; because the legislature enacts legislation, in terms of which the courts must operate, and the executive, which formulates policy on the implementation priorities, is also tasked with enforcing court judgements.

Also embedded in the doctrine, of separation of powers, is the principle of checks and balances; which accommodates the 'unavoidable intrusion of one branch on the terrain of another'; in order to prevent the misuse of power. These three arms of the state constitute a system of mutual checks and balances, which are aimed at preventing abuses of power; to the detriment of a free society.

Many countries have beautiful constitutions; which make it clear that the judiciary must be independent and impartial in carrying out its functions. Sadly, some of these constitutions are empty shells, and the judges merely paper tigers; unwilling and unable to do the job that they are mandated to do by the constitution. This unwillingness or restraint, by the judges, may be for many reasons; including a democratic culture that is not conducive to a flourishing independent judiciary.

Judicial independence is not a privilege

I must, of necessity, emphasize that judicial independence is not a privilege, or prerogative of judicial office. It is a responsibility which is imposed on each judge; to enable him, or her, to adjudicate upon a dispute honestly and impartially, on the basis of the law and evidence; without external pressure, or influence, and without fear of interference from anyone.

Another point that needs emphasis is that at the heart of the principle of judicial independence is the complete liberty of a judge to hear, and decide, the cases that come before the court; without fear or favour. No authority, be it the executive, the legislature, pastor, friends, family members or other judges should interfere, or attempt to interfere, with the way in which a judge conducts a case; and makes his, or her, decision.

Another key aspect of judicial independence is that it refers to both the personal and the institutional independence that is required for decision making. Judicial independence is, therefore, both the state of mind of an individual judge, and a set of institutional and operational arrangements. The former is concerned with the judge's independence, in fact, while the latter's focus is on defining the relationship between the judiciary and others, particularly the other branches of government, so as to assure both the reality and the appearance of independence.

The personal independence of a judge is directly connected, and related, to the independence of the judiciary; as an institution. This is so because if the judge is independent, but the institution, itself, is not independent of the other branches of government, in what is essential to its functions, then the judge cannot be said to be independent. The need for judicial independence is critical to every democratic society; which is founded on good governance and the rule of law. This may be seen from the fact that the case law of many democratic countries has clarified the public value of the independence of the judiciary; and how the personal independence of a judge relates with the independence of the institution of the judiciary.

In the case of **Valente v The Queen**, the court defined judicial independence as follows:

> "…*judicial independence involves both individual and institutional relationship: the individual independence of a judge, as reflected in such matters as security of tenure and the institutional independence of the court or tribunal over which he or she presides, as reflected in its institutional or administrative relationship to the executive and legislative branches of government.*"

The court concluded that:

> "…*judicial independence is a status or relationship resting on objective conditions or guarantees as well as a state of mind or attitude in the actual exercise of judicial functions…*"

It is inherent in the concept of adjudication, that the judge must not be an ally, or supporter, of one of the contending parties. It follows, therefore, that judicial independence is as much about perception, as it is about reality. For this reason, a judge, who has an interest in a matter, must recuse himself/or herself from hearing and determining that case.

Personal independence

The concept of personal independence postulates that, in the decision making process, judges shall be independent from any influences, or pressure, from their friends, relatives and/ or colleagues at the bench. This means that any hierarchical organization of the judiciary and any difference in grade, or rank, shall in no way interfere with the right of a judge to pronounce his, or her, judgement freely. When I speak of the need for judicial independence, there is one experience that nearly always springs to mind. To wit, I once heard a judge, at a seminar on judicial independence, relate how when he was new on the bench, he used to submit his draft judgements to the Chief Justice, for approval, and only then, could he deliver the judgements.

The judge in question conceded, during discussion, that the Chief Justice would mark him wrong; and substitute his decision for a correct one. Being new to the bench, that judicial brother of mine reasoned that the intervention of the Chief Justice was part of legitimate orientation. To say that I was surprised to hear that story is to put it mildly because, in my mind, that was, plainly, wrong. No judge should ever subject himself, or herself, to the approval of another judge, not even a Chief Justice. To do that violates the personal independence of a judge; and makes a mockery of the concept of judicial independence.

It is a requirement of the rule of law that, in performing judicial duties, a judge shall be independent of judicial colleagues. He, or she, is no one's employee, or junior, in the performance of judicial functions. A judge is only answerable to the law and to his, or her, own conscience. In fact, apart from any system of appeal, a judge cannot, in deciding a case, act on an order or instruction from anybody. The hierarchical organization of the judiciary does not entitle senior judges, or even the Chief Justice, to instruct a junior judge on how to decide a case.

As has already been mentioned, the independence of a judge stretches far beyond that of just the individual. It extends to the judiciary; as an institution. In liberal democracies, courts founded on the rule of law depend on public confidence for their credibility. Citizens will not be willing to submit to the decisions of the judiciary; if they perceive that judges are subjected to influences, and/or pressures, by their friends, relatives and colleagues.

Public opinion and the fear factor

No discussion on judicial independence can escape the fact that, for all its positivity, there are some challenges associated with judicial independence. One such challenge is the tension that exists between the theory and practice of judicial independence all across the world. Threats to judicial independence come in many forms. Sometimes, they take the form of subtle attempts to influence how a judge should approach a certain case, or to carry favour with the judge in some way.

The solution to this type of threat to judicial independence is that any extraneous attempt, whether direct or indirect, to influence a judge on how to reach his, or her, decisions must be rejected completely. The role of a judge is to decide cases independently and impartially; at all times. A judge must never be swayed by public opinion; in any case of major national controversy. A judge must, similarly, never allow himself, or herself, to be caught up in what may be described as the eye of the storm.

Sometimes, the weight of the publicity, that a case attracts, may tend to promote a particular desired result. However, in the exercise of judicial functions, a judge must be immune from being influenced by public sentiments; and must only be instructed by the law and the evidence presented in a case. Under no circumstances should a judge be swayed by partisan interests, public clamour or fear of criticism. It should not matter, to a judge, whether the laws applied, in any particular case, are popular or not. A judge should act fearlessly, irrespective of popular acclaim or criticism.

I must say, however, that the matter of fear is problematic. Once I presided over a case that caused me fear on account of the history and antecedents of one of the applicants who had once committing the worst offence can commit against a presiding justice. I discussed my apprehension with a fellow judge; and it was agreed that security would have to be bolstered; when the matter served before me. I cite this personal experience in order to highlight the fact that, while it is natural for every person to be fearful, judges must not allow fear to sway them from the course of their duties; and neither must fear determine their verdict in any case that serves before them.

As an arm of government, the importance of the role of the judiciary, in ensuring the observance of the rule of law and good governance, by both the executive and the legislature, is without question. However, in carrying out its role, it is important that the judiciary should be perceived as independent. The test for independence should include that of perception. An aggrieved litigant, who wishes to challenge the independence of the court, needs to prove an actual lack of independence. The litmus test, for this purpose, is the same as that for determining whether a court is biased. Where the question of bias is raised, the test is whether a reasonable, and well informed observer, would perceive the court as independent.

Although judicial independence is a status or relationship resting on objective conditions, or guarantees, as well as a state of mind or attitude in the actual exercise of judicial functions, the test for independence is whether the court may be, reasonably, perceived as independent. In some countries, in Africa, the executive employs a wide array of strategies to intimidate, and undermine, the independence of judges. These strategies range from trumped up charges, to systematically harassing personnel and people around, or working with, judges. Examples of these strategies, and machinations, for the intimidation of judicial officers, and the people around them, abound. Some may have read stories of a judge whose driver died, mysteriously, on the eve of the judge hearing a high stakes political case; somewhere in East Africa in 2017.

A colleague narrated, to me, a case in which a judge was investigated for some offence; and the investigations revealed that no offence was committed. The judge was, accordingly, informed that the investigations were concluded, that he was cleared of any wrong doing and that the matter was closed. A few months later, the same judge was presiding over a high stake litigation, in which the President and other high ranking state officials were parties. Apparently, soon after submissions before him were concluded, and judgment was reserved, the police came visiting. They told him that it seemed that the matter which they had said was closed would have to be reopened, because of 'new evidence' that had emerged. The judge was advised that this should, however, not disturb him; because the police were aware he was handling an important case. The police left; with the parting shot that they would visit the judge, again, once he was done with the matter. After a few months, the judge delivered his decision. The President and the other high ranking state officials won the case. The police never paid the judge a return visit. I, obviously, have my own views on this story; but I shall leave it open to interpretation.

One of the most eminent jurists to serve as Chief of Justice of Botswana in the immediate post-independence era, Chief Justice Hayfron Benjamin, cut to the chase on the essence of judicial independence during an address to judicial officers. He sounded the caution that no judge, or magistrate, in Botswana should do that which his, or her, conscience told him, or her, was wrong and went against the constitution or laws and usages of Botswana; in order to gain the nod of approval from any official, or politician, or for the applause of thousands; or the daily praises of the press. These sentiments which, in my view, were very well founded, underlined judges' fidelity to the constitution; as the overriding consideration in the course of their judicial functions. During the same address, Chief Justice Benjamin emphasized that no judge should avoid doing that which his, or her, conscience told him, or her, was right and in conformity with the constitution; even if such a stand point should draw, upon the judge, a whole artillery of libels; and all that falsehood and malice could invent.

Returning to the main topic under discussion, in this chapter, the concept of independence of the judiciary is adequately reflected in several international legal instruments and/or declarations. The Universal Declaration of Human Rights of 1948 and the International Covenant on Civil and Political Rights of 1966 both declare that in the determination of their civil and political rights and obligations, or in any criminal charge(s) preferred against them, everyone is entitled to a fair hearing; conducted by an independent and impartial tribunal that is established by law.

In 1985, the United Nations General Assembly adopted a Statement on the 'Basic Principles of the Independence of the Judiciary'. In that Statement, it was acknowledged that governments and other institutions must respect, and observe, the independence of the judiciary. As a consequence of the adoption of those principles, the members of the General Assembly are each, expected to guarantee the independence of the judiciary; in their constitutions and laws.

In 2003, the Commonwealth developed the Commonwealth Latimer House Principles on separation of powers among the three branches of government, namely the executive, the legislature and the judiciary. The Latimer House Principles, state that 'An independent, impartial, honest and competent judiciary is integral to upholding the rule of law, engendering public confidence and dispensing justice'.

It becomes clear, having regard to the above cited international legal instruments, that an independent judiciary is the key to upholding the rule of law in a free-society. This independence may take different forms in different jurisdictions; but the principles that underpin it are the same in all democratic countries which subscribe to the rule of law.

Judicial immunity

Another important factor that helps to guarantee the independence, and impartiality, of the courts is the immunity that is afforded to judicial officers. Judicial officers are not liable to be sued for the legitimate exercise of their powers. It should be obvious that if judges were to be sued for delivering a judgement which was not in accordance with the law, but which the judge believed to be in accordance with the law, then judicial function would be impossible to exercise. However, and this immunity notwithstanding, a judge may be sued if it can be proven that his, or her, judgement was actuated by malice.

Judicial immunity may be traced back to the early 16th century. In an old English case, that of **Floyd v Barker**, Lord

Coke explained that the significance of judicial immunity lies in ensuring that judicial officers decide disputes before them freely; and without fear of adverse consequences that may arise. In the case of **Sirrors v Moore,** Lord Denning, likewise, expressed the significance of judicial immunity by stating the following:

> *"Each should be protected from liability to damages when he is acting judicially. Each should be able to do his work in complete independence and free from fear. He should not have to turn the pages of his books with trembling fingers, asking himself: 'if I do this, shall I be liable in damages?'"*

The reason underlying the principle of judicial immunity is clear. It is simply that it is better to excuse one judge, out of a thousand, that may have acted dishonestly, or one who gives a bad judgement to the detriment of a party before him, because it is less harmful, to the health of society, to leave that party without a remedy, than that nine hundred and ninety-nine honest judges should be harassed by vexatious litigation alleging malice; in the exercise of their proper jurisdiction.

In the South African case of **Penrice v Dickinson**, the court held that no liability attaches to a judicial officer who gives a bad judgement, as a result of lack of legal skill or knowledge; as long as the decision was arrived at in good faith. Even the failure to take reasonable care would not render the judicial officer liable for damages. The South African Appellate Division also considered a claim for costs, against a judicial officer, in the case of **Regional Magistrate**

Du Preez v Walker. The court held that a cost order, against a judicial officer, arising from the performance of judicial functions, solely because he had acted incorrectly, was incompetent. Judicial officers would be unduly hampered, in the exercise of their functions, if it were otherwise. The court also held that an exception to this rule would exist in circumstances where the judicial officer was shown to have been actuated by malice in his, or her, decision. It also appears to be settled that where the evidence does not support a finding of malice and/ or bad faith and there is, therefore, no question of awarding costs against the judicial officer personally; it would, also, not be appropriate to award costs against the State either.

Some years back, when I was a practicing lawyer, a judge ordered costs against our law firm; in the most unlikely of circumstances. One of our senior partners had commenced litigation against the Attorney General seeking, among others, an order that the Industrial Court was not a court of law; having regard to its composition and, more particularly, the fact that a judge of the Industrial Court sat with lay assessors. The matter was referred to the High Court because, at the time, the Industrial Court did not have jurisdiction over constitutional matters. In the interim, the senior partner, who had initiated the litigation, went on study leave; and duly handed the matter over to another lawyer, in the law firm, albeit one less experienced. When the matter was called up, the lawyer who had taken over conduct, of the matter, announced his appearance; to the great irritation of the presiding judge! He charged at the new lawyer; for the reason that he (the judge) would have preferred it if the senior partner had appeared for the matter; because 'he was the one who started it'.

The infuriated judge directed that the said senior lawyer was to appear, before the court, on a scheduled date; to explain why he should not be imprisoned for contempt of court. The judge then ordered our law firm to pay the costs for the adjournment. The law partners were, unsurprisingly, convinced that the costs order was inappropriate; in that the new lawyer, of the same law firm and whose name appeared in the power of attorney, was ready, and willing, to argue the matter. It was, thus, the view of the law partners that the judge had personalized the matter. For some months, the law partners deliberated on whether, or not, to sue the judge. However, the fact that the odds of proving malice, as compared to mere misdirection fuelled by ignorance, militated against suing.

Without proof of malice, no suit against a judge can be sustained. Take another example of a judge who sentences an accused person to what appears, to some, to be a harsh and disproportionate sentence. While many people may agree, or disagree, with the sentence, and the judge's reasons for imposing it, what must be remembered is that a judge has the authority, and the power, to be wrong; as well as to be right. The bottom-line is that disenchanted litigants, or other citizens, should not be able to influence a judge about a judicial decision, through the threat of suing him, or her.

In 1978, the Supreme Court of the United States of America held, in the case of **Stump v Sparkman**, that the doctrine of judicial immunity forbade a suit from being brought against a judge who had authorized the sterilization of a slightly retarded 15-year-old girl; under the guise of an appendectomy. Apparently, the judge had approved the operation, without a formal hearing, when her mother alleged that the girl was promiscuous. After her marriage, two years later, the girl discovered she was sterile. The girl's suit against the judge was adjudged incompetent because the judge was immune.

In another case, that of **Dykes v Hosemann,** the same Court held that a judge who had issued an 'emergency' order, granting custody of a child to its father, (a fellow judge), without either notice to the mother, or the holding of a proper hearing, was immune from a legal suit at the instance of the child's mother. Some may disagree with these decisions; but the courts did what they deemed best; in the circumstances of each case.

The principle that judges can be wrong, for as long as their decisions are arrived at in good faith, is meant to ensure that there should be no threat of personal liability for decisions which are later found to have been incorrect.

Turning the focus back to the independence of the judiciary, there are a number of concrete institutional arrangements which impact on the institutional independence of the judiciary. I discuss them, briefly, below.

Appointment

As earlier indicated, the manner in which judges are appointed impacts on their independence; in the performance of their duties. The method and safeguards in place, with regard to the appointment of judges, have deep implications on the independence of both the judiciary, as an institution, and individual judges.

Remuneration

Judicial independence requires that judges' salaries, and other terms of service, be secured by law. In Botswana, the salaries of judges, the Attorney General, and members of the Judicial Service Commission are charged to the Consolidated Fund; which permanently authorizes their compensation and prohibits the government from reducing salaries, arbitrarily, in order to pressurize, or influence, judges, in the performance of their functions.

In Kenya, the remuneration and benefits payable to, or in respect of, judges are charged on the Consolidated Fund. The Judiciary Fund is charged on the Consolidated Fund; and is used for administrative expenses of the judiciary, and such purposes as are necessary to discharge the functions of the judiciary. The establishment of the Judiciary Fund, charged on the Consolidated Fund, institutionalizes judicial independence. Furthermore, the Kenyan Constitution stipulates that the remuneration and benefits payable to, or in respect of, a judge shall not be varied to the disadvantage of that judge; and the retirement benefits of a judge shall not be varied to the disadvantage of the retired judge; during the lifetime of that judge.

Tenure

The security of tenure of judges is a key factor in determining whether, or not, a judiciary is independent. If judges can easily be removed from office, then there can be no independence of the judiciary. Security of tenure goes hand in hand with a lack of executive interference in proceedings for the removal of a judge; from office. This, in turn, reinforces the doctrine of separation of powers. Under the provisions of the Constitution of Kenya, the President has no independent power to remove judges. Removal can only be done by a tribunal composed of retired, or active, judges and senior legal practitioners, appointed by the President. Even then, the President can only appoint a tribunal if the Chief Justice represents, to the President, that the question of removing a judge from office, should be investigated.

In South Africa, a judge may be removed from office only if 'the Judicial Service Commission finds that the judge suffers from an incapacity, is grossly incompetent or is guilty of gross misconduct; and the National Assembly calls for that judge to be removed, by a resolution adopted with the supporting vote of at least two thirds of its members'.

Under article 144 of the Ugandan Constitution, the President shall remove a judicial officer if a tribunal consisting of judges and legal practitioners, appointed by the President to investigate the conduct of the judicial officer, recommends that he, or she, should be removed. Apart from the Judicial Service Commission, the Cabinet, which includes the President, may also recommend, to the

President, the establishment of a tribunal; to investigate a judicial officer.

The new constitution of Kenya establishes the Judicial Service Commission as the body mandated to petition the President to remove a judge from office. The petition may be initiated by the Commission, on its own motion, or by any person aggrieved by the conduct of a judge. This gives every consumer of justice an opportunity to petition for a judge to be removed; in the event that they are reasonably aggrieved by the conduct of the judge. Within fourteen days from the date of receipt of the petition, the President is obliged to suspend the judge, against whom the petition is made, and to appoint a tribunal to investigate the conduct of that judge. The tribunal is then required to expeditiously inquire into the petition; and make binding recommendations to the President.

During suspension, the remunerations and benefits paid to a judge are adjusted to one-half; until the judge is removed from, or reinstated, in office. A judge who is aggrieved by the recommendations of a tribunal may appeal to the Supreme Court; within ten days from the date on which the tribunal makes its recommendations. It is reasoned that the tribunal disciplinary mechanism instills a sense of accountability, in judicial officers, in exercising their mandate. However, critics have argued that not all breaches of regulations, by judges, should warrant their removal from office; and that there should be put in place some form of internal disciplinary mechanisms, by the head of the judiciary, for 'petty' breaches of regulations.

Adequate Resources

The institutional independence of the judiciary requires that the executive must commit sufficient resources, to the judiciary, which, once allocated, must be controlled by the judiciary. I recall one happy Chief Justice telling me that whilst the resources allocated to the judiciary were not adequate, the good thing was that once they were allocated, the resources were wholly controlled by the judiciary. He said this enabled the judiciary, which had initiated projects such as the construction of court buildings, to pay contractors in time.

Financial Autonomy

The matter of financial autonomy, of the judiciary, is extremely important; and it is discussed, in some detail; in the next chapter.

Still on the question of the independence of the judiciary, an assessment of case law and relevant constitutional prescriptions exposes the glaring need to reposition judiciaries to act as promoters, and defenders, of the constitution. However, this is a challenge in that the autonomy, or independence, of most judiciaries, in Africa, is largely compromised by the fact that institutionally, and individually, judges are exposed, and vulnerable, to pressure to administer the law in ways desired by the appointing authorities who, in most cases, are also vested with the power to decide on the judges' promotions, remuneration and removal from office. Some consolation, however, exists in the fact that the judiciary, itself, has the power of review of the exercise of these decisions and, hence, judges have the opportunity to pronounce the law in accordance with their independent understanding; and free from external and internal influence, to some degree, upon such review.

Another issue concerning their autonomy, or independence, is that judiciaries are still bedevilled by challenges in the form of judicial corruption, lack of adequate resources, judicial conservatism, huge backlog of cases leading to undue delays in the dispensation of justice and staff inefficiency. Other challenges include inaccessibility to the courts, by the poor, due to exorbitant costs associated with litigation; and the politicisation of the judiciary. In most African countries, judiciaries lack the capacity to execute their mandate freely; because of political interference. In light of these plagues, future endeavours on reform must focus on taking practical steps to enhance the independence of the judiciary.

Judicial independence is work in progress; especially in Africa. In 1832, the Cherokee Indians won a landmark case, upholding their rights to land, against white settlers. It is reported that President Andrew Jackson sent Federal troops to ensure that the decision was not enforced.

In 1955, in the famous **Brown v Board of Education** case, the Supreme Court in the United States of America ordered an end to segregated education. The decision was unpopular and was opposed by the public; but President Eisenhower sent in Federal troops to ensure that the judgment was enforced. In Botswana, judicial decisions are routinely enforced. In 2017 a President who had declined to appoint a judge, after a court order, ultimately relented and complied. In the same year, 2017, the Supreme Court in Kenya ordered a re-run of Presidential Elections, and the order was complied with; although not without protest and grumbling from some quarters.

The lesson from the above narrative is clear. It is that judicial independence is work in progress; and must be fought for every day. Judicial independence is grounded in public respect for the courts; and the judicial function. This independence cannot be legislated for, or be demanded by the courts. It must be earned.

In conclusion, it may be said, with some credibility, that both personal and institutional independence may appear more formalistic; and with a tendency to mask other equally relevant considerations. Some of these are that, to a large measure, the independence of the judiciary is also a function of the personal conviction of judges; to ensure that they, themselves, and the courts, as institutions, are independent; in reality.

Judges can achieve this by engaging in quality legal reasoning; and being willing to take a stand when the independence of the judiciary is threatened. One may pose the question as to what quality legal reasoning entails. Simply put, pursuing quality legal reasoning means showing complete fidelity to the rule of law, by applying autonomous legal values, while consciously avoiding overt political considerations. This position does not, naively, presume that the law is, necessarily, distinct from politics. It merely asserts that there are autonomous legal values which must guide judges; in their work. This commitment to the application of autonomous legal values permits judges to defend the weak and marginalized; even if such decisions are not politically popular.

It is also significant to mention that the independence of judges does not require them to believe that the law is a magic wand for any societal ills. That would be a total fallacy, as it cannot be so. Furthermore, judges cannot apply the law out of context and ignore the broader social, cultural and political context; under which they serve. As it is often said, judges cannot pretend that they live in caves devoid of any social, cultural and political context.

Chapter Six

FINANCIAL INDEPENDENCE OF THE JUDICIARY

In most discussions on judicial independence, there is a tendency to neglect, or down play, the subject of the importance of financial autonomy for judiciaries all over the world. The inescapable truth is that it is very important that a judiciary be sufficiently funded by the state. The reason for this is that it is most undesirable that an entity which is supposed to be independent, and impartial, should, at the same time, be a beggar who begs the government; which is a regular litigant before it. If this happened, then both the real and perceived independence, and impartiality, of judiciaries would be compromised. It is, in fact, for this reason that judicial self-governance is imperative.

A judiciary should be financially independent

At the barest minimum, judicial independence requires that the judiciary should be institutionally, financially and administratively independent. Institutional independence concerns the day to day operations of courts; and this type of independence is necessary in order to ensure that judiciaries are not, directly or indirectly, controlled, or seen to be controlled, by other arms of government. Institutional independence requires that the judiciary must have its own budget, sourced from the consolidated fund; and that it must have a separate accounting system. The judiciary should be able to have a budget that enables it to procure all that it needs to function efficiently, and independently, rather than it going down on its knees to beg for resources from the executive. In situations where the judiciary is at the mercy of the executive in terms of financial support, the people may, legitimately, take the view that the judiciary cannot be trusted; as it is too dependent on the executive.

In many jurisdictions, the executive and the legislature have their own financial vault. They are free to decide on administrative support, staff establishment, job descriptions and salaries. The executive and the legislature can even decide which projects to prioritize. Unfortunately, the same cannot be said of the judiciary; notwithstanding the fact that it is an independent organ of the state. Ideally, the judiciary should be co-equal to other arms of the state. But the reality is very different in many jurisdictions across the globe.

Vulnerability to manipulation

It is often, correctly, said that the moment a court accepts jurisdiction over a controversy between government and an individual, then government is demoted; in that it loses its claim to be the exclusive representative of the state. This much is true; as is the fact that a judiciary that perpetually begs the executive to fund its operations is vulnerable to manipulation and dictation. Such a judiciary cannot, independently, determine the controversy between the executive and the individual. The principle of equality before the law means that at the time of exercising jurisdiction, the individual is promoted to a public role and assumes an equal claim to represent the state. However, the principle of equality before the law is not possible in situations where the judiciary is not financially independent. It follows, therefore, that in order to properly, and effectively, adjudicate over controversies between the executive and the citizen, the courts need to be financially independent.

One of the accepted facets of 'institutional independence' is the one concerning the financial resources and financial freedom, or autonomy, which is to be given to the judiciary. Today, this concept has been developed, and accepted, in most of the democracies that are governed by the rule of law. The doctrine of separation of powers has, essentially, been suitably modified and adjusted in order to achieve the goal of financial freedom of the judiciary. Despite the development, and wide acceptance of the concept of financial freedom and autonomy, the reality is that in the scheme of power, and of the efficacy of institutions, the judiciary is not able to compete with an executive which has its roots in the legislature.

Financial dependency is a threat to judicial independence

While judicial independence may be guaranteed, under most constitutions, the financial and administrative aspects of the judiciary, in some jurisdictions, continue, in reality, to be controlled by the executive. There have been numerous views expressed on the judiciary's inability to compete with the executive and the legislature; in terms of financial autonomy. Alexander Hamilton correctly observed, in relation to the early constitution-making process in the United States of America, that:

> *"Whoever considers the different departments of power must perceive that...the judiciary, from the nature of its functions, will always be the least dangerous to the political rights of the constitution...the executive not only dispenses the honours, but holds the sword of the community. The legislature not only commands the purse, but prescribes the rules by which the duties and rights of every citizen are to be regulated. The judiciary, on the contrary, has no influence over the sword or the purse; no direction either of the strength or the wealth of the society, and can take no active resolution whatever. It may truly be said to have neither Force nor Will but mere judgment..."*

Also commenting on the issue of the financial autonomy of the judiciary, the former Chief Justice of Kenya, Mr. Justice Gicheru, said the following:

> *"The institutions that control the purse and the administrative support of the judiciary can also directly control the extent and efficiency in the execution of the role. It is simply a case of he who pays the piper calling the tune. The necessary judicial independence of the judiciary cannot be achieved if the court finances are determined and dictated by the political organs of the executive*

and the legislatures over whom the court should exercise judicial control".

According to Justice Browne-Wilkinson, the lack of financial support by a Government is a clear 'threat to the independence of the legal system'. He says:

"Control of the finance and administration of the legal system is capable of preventing the performance of those very functions which the independence of the judiciary is intended to preserve, that is to say, the right of the individual to a speedy and fair trial of his claim by an independent Judge...the enforcement of the rule of law by the Judges could be wholly frustrated by the refusal to appoint Judges, to provide court rooms for them to sit in or staff to service those courts... there is a failure of the provision of adequate courts and court staff to meet society's current demands for Justice...It is that aspect of the independence of the Judiciary which I wish to consider..."

Insufficient funds

In many jurisdictions, judiciaries complain of insufficient funds, citing that the funds availed to them, by the executives, are grossly inadequate; to meet the requirements of the judiciary. Undesirable as this may be, it is all too common for judiciaries to beg for resources for numerous purposes; such as to enable them to build courts, to hire adequate staff and to avail funds to accord judicial officers the opportunity to attend local and international conferences, in furtherance of their professional development.

Other reasons why judiciaries go to their executives, with begging bowl in hand, include seeking resources to provide accommodation, vehicles, security and all other matters that are incidental to secure the proper independence of the judiciary. Control of funds, by the executive, obviously breeds bureaucratic delays and red tape; and negatively affects the efficiency of the judiciary.

It will be noted, and as was indicated in the previous chapter, that the topic of financial autonomy, for judiciaries, has been discussed in some detail. This is because the performance of a judiciary, in its constitutional mandate, depends directly upon the financial autonomy of courts. It goes without saying that effective, and efficient, administration requires resources to support the remuneration of necessary, qualified, staff and the acquisition of equipment and facilities. In the interests of the independence of the judiciary, it is imperative that the administration of the judiciary be carried out either by the judiciary, itself, or by a professional agency under the superintendence of the judiciary. It may be useful to give a few examples of how judiciaries are funded in some jurisdictions, across the globe, and the law that regulates their funding.

South Africa, Kenya, Ghana, Tanzania and Uganda

South Africa adopted a democratic constitution in 1994 after decades of authoritarian rule. Its constitution is rated among the best in the world, in that it spells out the independence of the judiciary in the clearest of terms. However, the South African Constitution does not have adequate provisions to ensure the financial autonomy of the courts. As a result of this inadequacy, various Chief Justices have fought long, and hard, for a dispensation that allows the courts some financial autonomy. These battles resulted in the establishment of an enlarged office of Chief Justice; headed by a Secretary General. The Office of the Chief Justice (OCJ) is a national department. It was established in 2010.

In the year 2015, I had the honour, and privilege, to head a committee that was established by the Chief Justice, of Botswana, to undertake a comparative study on how various jurisdictions have tried to tackle the issue of financial autonomy for their judiciaries. That assignment led me to spend a number of days in South Africa; under the gracious hospitality of the Office of the Chief Justice. Our committee was informed that the judiciary, in South Africa was no longer controlled by the Ministry of Justice; but that everything to do with the judiciary was now coordinated from the OCJ. We learned that the mandate of the OCJ was to render support to the Chief Justice; as head of the judiciary. It was also brought to our attention that the OCJ was required to provide, and coordinate, legal and administrative support to the Chief Justice. It was also tasked with providing communication and management services, and to assist in the development of judicial policy, norms and standards. Suffice it to say that the South African study tour was valuable; as it gave me a broader picture of how various jurisdictions were dealing with the issue of judicial financial autonomy.

In Kenya, the position is that the constitution has established a Judiciary Fund; which is managed by the Chief Registrar. Each financial year, the Chief Registrar is required to prepare an estimate of the upcoming year's expenses, which estimate is submitted to the National Assembly for approval. This innovation came about in 2010. Prior to that, the Kenyan judiciary was seriously underfunded; which limited its autonomy from the executive and legislative branches.

The Judiciary Fund, of Kenya, is paid from the Consolidated Fund. In addition to the Fund, the judiciary is permitted to accept grants, gifts, donations, or bequests towards the achievement of its objectives. In another departure from the pre 2010 position, the Kenyan judiciary is required to open, and maintain, a bank account. A number of Kenyan judges, whom I have spoken to, suggest that the fact that the judiciary can receive grants, gifts and donations from other bodies opens the door to minimizing the ability of the executive to starve the judiciary of funds. I daresay that there are others who may hold a contrary view; but that may be for another discussion.

The Judicial Service Commission, which was established by the 2010 constitution, of Kenya, was meant to facilitate, and promote, the independence and accountability of that county's judiciary. As part of achieving that independence, the judiciary as been granted the power to purchase, or otherwise acquire, hold, charge and dispose of movable or immovable property; and also to enter into contracts.

While the Kenyan innovation, with regard to fostering judicial financial autonomy, is an interesting one, it is important to point out that care must be taken when accepting gifts, and donations, from potential litigants in court. If that happens, the perception of independence and impartiality may be compromised; because of the adage that 'he who pays the piper dictates the tune'; which simply means that he who pays the money, for something, decides what will be done.

In the Republic of Ghana, the independence of the judiciary is provided for in its constitution. Article 127 deals with the independence of the judiciary; and it reads as follows:

1. *In the exercise of the judicial power of Ghana, the judiciary, in both its judicial and administrative functions, including financial administration, is subject only to this Constitution and shall not be subject to the control or direction of any person or authority......*

2. *Funds voted by Parliament, or charged on the Consolidated Fund by this Constitution for the Judiciary shall be released to the Judiciary, in quarterly instalments.*

3. *For the purposes of clause (1) of this article, financial administration includes the operation of banking facilities by the Judiciary without the interference of any person or authority, other than for the purposes of audit by the Auditor General, of the funds voted by*

Parliament or charged on the Consolidated Fund by this Constitution or any other law, for the purposes of defraying the expenses of the Judiciary in respect of which the funds were voted or charged".

From the above provision, it is very clear that the Ghanaian judiciary is independent in both its judicial and administrative functions; including financial administration. It may even operate banking facilities; with respect to the funds voted to it by Parliament or charged on the Consolidated Fund.

In terms of Ghana's constitution, neither the President nor Parliament shall interfere with judges or judicial officers; or other persons exercising judicial power. Furthermore, all organs and agencies of the state shall accord, to the courts, such assistance as the courts may reasonably require; in order to protect the independence, dignity and effectiveness of the courts; subject to the constitution.

Tanzania promulgated a law called 'The Judiciary Administration Act, 2011'. Section 52 of that Act establishes a special fund called the Judiciary Fund. Sums of money, required for purposes of the judiciary, are paid by the Treasury into the Judiciary Fund. The overall administration and control of the Judiciary Fund is vested in the Chief Administrator; who is the accounting officer, and is responsible for the day to day administration, and operation, of the Judiciary Fund. The Tanzanian Judiciary may also receive grants, made for the purpose of the judiciary, by a foreign government, national and international organizations, or associations, or by an individual person.

The Chief Court Administrator is mandated to cause to be kept, proper books of accounts and to, within and not later than three calendar months after the end of each financial year, cause to be prepared a statement of income and expense during the financial year. The accounts relating to the operations of the Judiciary Fund shall be submitted for audit by the Controller, and Auditor General, on the last day of the financial year, in accordance with the Public Audit Act, the Public Procurement Act and the Public Finance Act.

In terms of Section 55 (1) of Tanzania's Judiciary Administration Act, the Judicial Service Commission, in consultation with the Minister of Finance, is mandated to make financial regulations for the proper management and financial control of the operations of the Judiciary Fund. In terms of Section 56, the Chief Court Administrator is mandated to submit, to the Minister, copies of a statement of income and expenditure and a copy of the Auditor's report, together with a report on the activities of the Judicial service Commission during the financial year. This is for submission, by the Minister, to the National Assembly; and is done in each year.

The Judiciary Administration Act provides for the process of submitting and presenting budget estimates. Section 57 provides as follows;

1. *"Prior to the beginning of each fiscal year, the Judicial Service Commission shall direct the Chief Court Administrator to prepare estimates of the sums of money which the Judiciary may require for payment of various costs and expenses to be incurred by the*

Judiciary during the next fiscal year for the following purposes.

i. *administrative and support provided to the Judiciary;*

ii. *salaries and remuneration of judicial and non-judicial officers;*

iii. *funding requirements for Judiciary purposes".*

The Chief Court Administrator makes a presentation, to the Judicial Service Commission, of the estimates of the sums of money required to be appropriated by Parliament; for the purposes of the Judiciary. The Judicial Service Commission shall review the estimates and make any alteration considered, and found to be, appropriate and shall, then, concur and adopt those estimates. The Chief Court Administrator is then mandated to present the budget estimates as adopted by the Judicial Service Commission, to the Treasury, and, thereafter, to submit a copy of the budget estimates to the Minister; for the purposes of appropriation by Parliament.

The independence of the judiciary, in Uganda, is provided for in its constitution. Section 128 of the Ugandan Constitution provides for the independence of the judiciary; in its judicial functions. It says that the judiciary shall not be under the control, or direction, of any person or authority; when exercising its judicial functions. It also provides that all organs, and agencies, of the State shall accord, to the courts, such assistance as may be required to ensure the effectiveness of the courts. The Constitution of Uganda, additionally, provides that the judiciary shall be self- accounting; and may deal directly with the Ministry responsible for finance, in relation to its finances.

Australia, Canada and the United States of America

In Australia, the administration of Courts is governed by the Courts Administration Act, 1993. The objects of this Act are:

a) to establish the State Court Administration Council as an administrative authority, independent of control by executive government;

b) to confer, on the Council, power to provide courts with the administrative facilities and services necessary for the proper administration of justice.

Section 6 establishes The State Courts Administration Council as a corporate body. The Council is an instrumentality of the Crown. It consists, among others, of:

a) The Chief Justice of the Supreme Court;

b) The Chief Judge of the District Court and;

c) The Chief Magistrate of the Magistrates Court

The Council's responsibilities include the provision, or arrangement for the provision, of the administrative facilities and services for the courts; which are necessary to enable the courts to carry out their judicial functions properly. The Council may establish administrative policies and guidelines; to be observed by Courts in the exercise of their administrative responsibilities.

In terms of Section 11, the Council has the powers of a natural person and may, for example, enter into any form of contract or arrangement. It may acquire, hold, deal with and dispose of real and personal property. It may also provide services on terms and conditions determined by the Council. It is also the Council's mandate to prepare and submit, to the Attorney General, a budget showing estimates of its receipts and expenditures for the next financial year; or for some other period determined by the Attorney General. The Attorney General may approve the budget with or without any modification. The Council must keep proper accounting records of its receipts and expenditures. It must ensure:

a) That expenditures are not made out of money under the Council's control without proper administrative authorization;

b) That proper control is maintained over the Council's property.

The Auditor General must, at least once a year, audit the accounts of the Council. Commenting on the funding of Australian Courts, the Chief Justice of the High Court of Australia, the Hon. Robert French, once noted:

> "*The funding of the courts is important and difficult. It is important because it is necessary to the rule of law which lies at the heart of our representative democracy. It is difficult because it must respect the independence of the judicial branch and because it requires judgments about needs where criteria to*

guide such judgments are difficult to define with precision".

The Chief Justice of Victoria, the Hon. Marilyn Warren AC, also commenting on the funding of the Australian Courts, noted that it was important for judges and magistrates to have spacious courtrooms and offices to work in; and for the public to view proceedings. He, additionally, noted that such courtrooms should be fitted with modern technology, to enable judicial officers to work better. The Chief Justice argued that judicial officers needed proper accommodation to enable them to work at home. More importantly, he noted that courts needed people to run them; such as registry staff, judicial staff and administrative staff. All these facilities would help the courts to dispense justice effectively and expeditiously and, therefore, the judiciary needed to be sufficiently funded, argued the Hon. Chief Justice. He, further, noted that:

> *"Of course the judiciary, as the third arm of government, does not simply ask the executive for a cheque and expect it to be written. The judiciary must explain, to the executive, what its needs are. This places the judiciary in the position of having to compete with various parts of the executive; to persuade treasury as to why the needs of the courts should take priority over the other needy parts of the executive. For courts this is very challenging. We are not necessarily our best advocates".*

In Canada, the administration of courts is regulated by the Courts Administration Service Act of 2002. The purposes of this Act are to:

a) facilitate coordination and cooperation among the Federal Court of Appeal, the Federal Court, the Court Martial Appeal Court and the Tax Court of Canada, for the purpose of ensuring the effective and efficient provision of administrative services to those courts;

b) enhance judicial independence by placing administrative services at arm's length from the Government of Canada and by affirming the roles of Chief Justices and Judges in the management of the courts; and;

c) enhance accountability for the use of public money in support of court administrations while safeguarding the independence of the judiciary.

In terms of Section 7, the Chief Administrator is the Chief Executive Officer of the Service, and has supervision over and direction of its work and staff. He or she, in consultation with the Chief Justices of the Federal Court of Appeal, the Federal Court, the Court Martial Appeal Court and the Tax Court of Canada, shall establish and maintain the registry, or registries, for those courts; and prepare budgetary submissions for the requirements of those courts and for the related needs of the Service.

The case of **R v Valente** is the leading authority on the content of judicial independence. In that case, the court held that there were three essential conditions for judicial independence, namely security of tenure, financial security and institutional independence. The court, further, held that institutional independence would necessarily include judicial control over the administrative decisions that bear directly, and immediately, on the exercise of the judicial function.

In the USA, the Chief Judge has a leadership role in court management and stewardship. While most day to day administration should be handled by court unit executives, ultimately the responsibility for the integrity of the court's management practices rests with the court and the Chief Judge.

The Chief Judge, the unit executive(s), and the court, as a whole, share the responsibility of ensuring that the court is properly managed. Together, they ensure that organizational structures and planning processes are established to guide the expenditure of funds, and that systems are in place to prevent waste or abuse; and that important decisions are elevated to an appropriate level in court.

The judiciary obtains its funding, each year, through appropriations from Congress. The process is governed by statute, congressional directives and preferences, and Judicial Conference procedures. The process requires massive, coordinated effort by the Budget Committee and other conference committees, the Administrative Office and many other offices and employees. The budget cycle requires eighteen (18) months to complete. By statute, the Director of the Administrative Office prepares the judiciary's budget requests. After consideration by the Budget Committee, a recommended budget is then sent for approval by the Judicial

Conference, and submitted to the Office of Management and Budget and Congress.

The judiciary's appropriations are divided into twelve (12) separate accounts, in accordance with their court structure. The appropriations are made out of salaries and expenses, maintenance of buildings and grounds, and payment to Judicial Retirement Funds. Each account is treated separately, in the judiciary's submission to congress, and is supported by detailed statistics and narrative justifications. Funds are appropriated by Congress, for each segregated account, and may not be transferred from one account to another without specific congressional approval.

It is important to note that while for most government agencies, funds appropriated by Congress generally lapse each year, the judiciary is able to avoid this problem, to some degree, because it has specific authority to carry over, to following years, the unused monies collected in filing and other fees; and the multi-year funding for planned automation expenses in the Judiciary Information Technology Fund.

In the USA, the construction of courts is different from other judiciary programs; because it is funded through the executive. The judiciary, however, still has an input into the construction budget process.

The situation in Botswana

In Botswana, the judiciary finds itself in the rather unfortunate situation where it has to explain itself to the executive; in terms of what its needs are. The Ministry of Justice, under which the courts fall, treats the judiciary, for all practical intents and purposes, as its department. Perhaps the name under which the courts falls, that is to say 'The Administration of Justice' (AOJ) gives it away; and reinforces the perception of the judiciary as a department under the Ministry of Justice.

The budgeting system of Botswana is such that the Ministry of Finance sets ceilings for ministries; including the judiciary. It is taken that the Ministry of Justice, as a whole, is supposed to represent the interests of the judiciary and, because of that, the judiciary is hardly, ever, consulted in a meaningful way. It has to be said that this type of budgeting, where the judiciary, as an arm of government, does not have any meaningful say in its financial needs, presents a problem for the judiciary.

At one stage, in the past, the judiciary of Botswana resolved, after a thorough analysis of its needs, that every judge, or magistrate, should have at least two court reporters at any given time. This was because there was a public outcry that records, of proceedings, were taking too long to be transcribed; for purposes of appeals. At the time, all the judges and magistrates had one reporter each; meaning that the court reporter who was expected to transcribe court proceedings, was the same one who was expected to be in court; almost on a daily basis. This meant that the court reporter had no time to transcribe court records which were required for appeal purposes. One may ask why this example has been cited.

The judiciary of Botswana has no power to employ support staff. Such power is vested in a government agency, namely the Directorate of Public Service Management (DPSM), which determines the vacancies in all government ministries, including those in the judiciary. However, even if the judiciary had the powers to employ support staff, it would still face a challenge in that it does not have the budget for that kind of activity. For that reason, and despite identifying it as an important need which would improve its efficiency, the judiciary of Botswana was not able to employ more court reporters. That was a move which would have ensured that every judicial officer operated with two court reporters and which, in turn, would have alleviated the problem of delayed transcription of records.

To add to the above woes, if the management of the judiciary decides to cause court reporters to work overtime, that is to say after hours or during weekends, there are no funds to pay overtime for those officers. The result is that the court reporters are not in the position to work outside of working hours; as they will not be remunerated.

It is almost certain that if the judiciary of Botswana had a firm say in its budgeting process, including the choice of ceiling, then some of the challenges it faces, due to budget limitations, would not exist.

At the end of the day it is plain that the judiciary in Botswana is constrained to cater, adequately, for all its budgetary needs; because of being at the mercy of the Ministry of Justice for its budget. At this point, I mention, with a measure of confidence that this is not a problem that is unique to the judiciary of Botswana. Discussions with judicial colleagues, especially across the continent of Africa, have revealed that most judiciaries face operational challenges due to the lack of financial autonomy. This, and as has been discussed earlier in this chapter, affects judicial independence.

The approach in Lesotho

Taking another example, the Lesotho Constitution casts an obligation upon the Government to 'accord such assistance as the courts may require, enabling them to protect their independence, dignity and effectiveness and to discharge their functions under the constitution and law'. In practice, however, the judiciary of Lesotho lacks financial autonomy; and its finances and administration have been directly controlled by the Ministry of Justice.

England and India

Moving further afield, from my native and neighbouring jurisdictions, in England, judges are not involved in any policies or planning. The court officers are integrated into the civil service; with the officers in the Lord Chancellor's office being part of the executive. Judges are not consulted in the budget formulations. That is a matter which is under the exclusive control of the Lord Chancellor's office; which prepares the budget and, thereafter, causes it to be submitted to Parliament; through the executive. There is no place for judges in any of these matters and processes. The Lord

Chancellor has, however, expressed grave doubts, as to whether such a system is conducive to judicial independence. In sum, the position in the area of court finances, in England, is that the judges have no say. However, in the matter of salaries and emoluments, the United Kingdom is far ahead of many countries.

In India, there is the advantage of court officers, and staff, being under the complete control of the judiciary; from the highest court to the lowest courts. In that way, the Indian system is better than that of the United Kingdom and France. The main problems, for the judiciary in India, are in regard to policy-making and finances. Judges there are not involved, directly, in any policy making; and neither are they involved in the preparation of the judiciary's budget. The Chief Justice, of India, and the heads of the courts prepare a budget, with the help of their Registrars. However, these are routine budgets; which are based upon an increase of the figures of previous years. They are not based on any long, or short range, plans for the judiciary. After preparation, the budgets are sent to the executive; and suffer serious cuts. The budget is so even at State level, in terms of cuts.

India has no independent judicial council, or a conference with statutory status, or even an independent bureaucracy, of court administration, through which budgets can be prepared and the lump sum allocation, to the judiciary, can be spent, independently, under various heads; subject to supervision by the Judges' Council. The judiciary's budget is part of the executive budget.

Having outlined the practice in a number of jurisdictions, with regard to the finances of the judiciary, it clearly emerges that the judiciary should not be treated as if it were another administrative department under the Ministry of Justice; for it is not. It is a co-equal of the other two branches of the state. The judiciary is an institution under the constitution, which qualifies as an independent institution; and whose accountability and responsibility should go hand in hand. When all is said and done, judicial independence without administrative and financial autonomy may turn out to be meaningless. Autonomy implies control of both human and material resources and, without this autonomy, there can be no accountability to speak about. The needs of the judiciary can only be addressed if, and only if, the judiciary, itself, can assess and determine these needs and concerns.

As a person who, because of being a judge, is acutely aware of the challenges that the lack of financial autonomy, for the judiciary, brings about, I am of the firm view that sufficient, and sustainable, funding should be provided to enable judiciaries to perform their functions to the highest standards. Such funds, once voted for the judiciary by the legislature, should be protected from alienation or misuse. The executive should not be allowed to use funding as a means of exercising improper control over the judiciary.

Appropriate salaries and benefits, supporting staff, resources and equipment are essential to the proper functioning of the judiciary. Furthermore, and as a matter of principle, judicial salaries and benefits should be set by an independent body; and their value should be maintained, as part of guaranteeing the institutional, and personal, independence of the judiciaries. It makes sense to peg the salaries at the highest segment in the industry if the judiciary is to attract lawyers of requisite experience and knowledge. I am aware that, in some jurisdictions, brilliant legal luminaries, who would have made excellent judges, have declined offers for appointment, to the bench, on account of remuneration issues. It suffices to say that such situations would be averted; if judiciaries were adequately funded and given a wide berth to use their funds as per their needs.

Chapter Seven

JUDICIAL IMPARTIALITY

Impartiality, just like independence, is a supreme judicial virtue. A judge should have no interest in any matter before him, or her, whether directly or indirectly. Traditionally, the requirement for impartiality, by judges, is depicted by the image of a blindfolded 'Lady Justice'; holding the scales of justice in one hand, and the sword in the other. The scales reflect even handedness, while the sword is a symbol of power; that executes decisions without favour, fear or ill-will. Being blindfolded indicates that justice does not depend on who is a party in court. It is also said to indicate that justice cannot see any signal that the ruler may want to send; as to which way a case must be decided.

In short, the blindfold represents neutrality and impartiality. A blindfolded justice should administer objective justice between the president, of a country, and a pauper; between a judge and a lowly paid servant, between the Director of Public Prosecutions and a hardened criminal; and between a widow and a wealthy insurance company.

A judge should conduct himself, or herself, in such a way as to vindicate their independence and impartiality. Some judges are known to hold certain lawyers in low esteem; or even to hate them. This suggests that judges are only human. However, it is not desirable for a judge to harbour ill-will or hatred against a lawyer; who is representing a litigant in that judge's court. Such conduct should, as far as is humanly possible, be avoided altogether and if that is not attainable, it should, at the very least, be managed. This is because there is always a danger of arbitrariness; where this is the case.

While it is expected of a judge, or any other adjudicator, impartiality is not, necessarily, a natural trait. But it is one which can be learnt, and practiced. When they are appointed to the bench, professional lawyers know that it is part of their profession to be impartial. As has been stated, in the earlier part of this book, the appointment process, for judges, has implications for their independence in deciding cases. A transparent, and merit based, system of appointment is more promotional of the independence of the judiciary; than a system which lacks openness, and bases judicial appointments on certain considerations which do not, necessarily, include merit.

Legal knowledge

The ancient Philosopher Maimonides, (1135-1204) indicated that it would be wrong to appoint, to judgeship, a person who did not have adequate legal knowledge. He said that even though such a candidate may have some other admirable qualities, if he doesn't have legal knowledge, it would be a travesty to appoint him or her. I am sure that there are many who agree with this view; even in the present day.

A judge must be impartial at all times

A judge is required, and expected, to be impartial at all times. A judge will be disqualified from hearing a case if a fair-minded lay observer might, reasonably, apprehend that the judge might not bring an impartial mind to bear, when deciding the issues before the court. It is a basic requirement that justice must both be done; and be seen to be done. So, even the appearance of departure, from impartiality, is prohibited in the dispensation of justice. The reason for this is that even if there is no bias, but there is the appearance of bias, then the integrity of the judicial system can be undermined. It cannot be over-emphasized that public confidence depends upon the impartial administration of justice. Equally important, to remember, is the fact that public confidence also depends, significantly, on appearance and reality. If, during pending litigation, the question arises as to whether the judge might not be impartial, no attempt will be made to work out how the judge may actually decide the case. The only thing that matters is whether there is a possibility of real, and not remote, bias.

The doctrine of necessity

The doctrine of necessity accepts that in exceptional circumstances, a judge who, otherwise, should not sit in a matter, on account of apparent bias, may be forced to preside; notwithstanding the apparent bias. The doctrine of necessity enables a judge, who is otherwise disqualified, to preside over a case where failure to do so may result in an injustice. This may arise where an adjournment, or mistral, will work undue hardship on a litigant. The doctrine of necessity may, also, be invoked where there is no other judge, reasonably available, who is not similarly disqualified; with the result that if the judge, in question, does not sit, then another court cannot be constituted to hear and determine the matter in issue. Such cases will, of course, be rare and special.

Recusal

If it is, absolutely, necessary for a judge not to hear and determine a matter for personal, or other legitimate, reasons, then the procedure to be followed is for the judge to recuse himself, or herself, from the matter. Recusal may be on a judge's own motion; or on application by a litigant. An application for recusal may be brought when there are grounds of appearance of bias on the part of the presiding officers. It must be noted, and stressed, that actual bias need not be proven. All that is needed is for there to be reasonable apprehension of bias. Once it is established that there are grounds for reasonable apprehension of bias, then an application for a judge to recuse himself, or herself, from hearing a case may be made. The rationale for this is that in order for a judiciary to maintain society's trust, and confidence, 'justice must not only be done, but be seen to be done'. Typically, bias or prejudice means that the judge has acted, or spoken, in a way that prevents him, or her, from treating the party, or attorney, in a fair and impartial manner.

The applicable test, for recusal, was stated in the South African case of **President of the Republic of South Africa and others v South African Rugby Football Union and**

others. In that case, which is commonly known as the SARFU case, the Constitutional Court, of South Africa, formulated the test as follows:

> 'The question is whether a reasonable, objective and informed person would, on the correct facts, reasonably apprehend that the Judge has no or will not bring an impartial mind to bear on the adjudication of the case, that is a mind open to persuasion by the evidence and the submissions of counsel. The reasonableness of the apprehension must be assessed in the light of the oath of office taken by the Judges to administer justice without fear or favour; and their ability to carry out that oath by reason of their training and experience. It must be assumed that they can disabuse their minds of any irrelevant personal beliefs or predispositions. They must take into account the fact that they have a duty to sit in any case in which they are not obliged to recuse themselves. At the same time, it must never be forgotten that an impartial Judge is a fundamental prerequisite for a fair trial and a judicial officer should not hesitate to recuse herself, or himself, if there are reasonable grounds on the part of the litigant for apprehending that the judicial officer, for whatever reasons, was not or will not be impartial.'

The test in SARFU requires that judges should decide cases which come before them without fear or favour, according to facts and law; and not according to subjective personal views. In considering an application for recusal, the court, as a starting point, presumes that judicial officers are impartial in adjudicating disputes. The applicant, for recusal, bears the responsibility of rebutting, or countering, the presumption of judicial impartiality.

It must be stated that the presumption is not easy to dislodge. It requires 'cogent' or 'convincing' evidence to be rebutted. Having served as a judge for over 15, years I must say that the notion of 'absolute neutrality' is something of a myth in the judicial context. This is because judges are human; and they are, unavoidably, the product of their own life experiences. Their perspective, on certain issues, is derived, inevitably, from their individual experiences and that, distinctively, informs each judge's performance of his, or her, judicial duties.

Impartiality is that quality of open-minded readiness to persuasion; without a rigid adherence to the position of one of the litigants, or to the judge's own predilections, preconceptions or, indeed, personal views. Total detachment, from the position of the litigants, is the keystone of a civilized system of adjudication. In short, impartiality requires 'a mind open to persuasion by the evidence presented and the submissions of counsel'. In contrast to neutrality, impartiality is an absolute requirement in every judicial proceeding.

The reason for the law insisting on an open mind is because the absence of an open-minded and impartial adjudication of disputes, which come before the courts, is more likely to impair confidence in the proceedings; rather than in the actual bias, or the appearance of bias, in the official, or officials, who have the power to adjudicate on disputes. Those whose confidence, in court proceedings, may be impaired, if there is a lack of open-mindedness and impartiality, on the part of an adjudicator, could either be the litigants; or the general public.

In the SARFU case, the court also alluded to the, apparently, 'double requirement' of reasonableness; that the application of the test, for recusal, imports. This is that not only must the person apprehending bias be a reasonable person, but the apprehension, itself, must, in the circumstances, be reasonable. This two-fold aspect also finds reflection in another South African case, that of **S v Roberts,** which was decided shortly after SARFU, and where the Supreme Court of Appeal required that the apprehension of bias be that of the reasonable person, in the position of the litigant, and that it be based on reasonable grounds.

What has been called the 'double' unreasonableness requirement also highlights the fact that mere apprehensiveness, on the part of a litigant, that a judge will be biased, or even a strongly and honestly felt anxiety is not enough. The court must, carefully, scrutinize the apprehension; to determine whether it is to be regarded as reasonable. In adjudging this, the court super-imposes a normative assessment on the litigant's anxieties. It attributes a legal value to the litigant's apprehension and, thereby, decides whether it is such that it should be countenanced in law.

Where the claimed disqualification is based on a reasonable apprehension, the court has to make a normative evaluation of the facts; to settle the question of whether a reasonable person, faced with the same facts, would entertain the apprehension. The enquiry involves a value judgement of the court; applying prevailing morality and common sense. It should be common knowledge that the cornerstone of any functional legal system is the impartial adjudication of disputes; which come before courts and tribunals. What the law requires is not only that a judicial officer must conduct a trial open-mindedly, impartially and fairly; but that such conduct must be manifest to all those who are concerned in the trial and its outcome; especially the accused.

It is settled law that not only actual bias, but also reasonable perception of bias, disqualifies a judicial officer from presiding, or continuing to preside, over judicial proceedings. Once bias is established, the disqualification is so complete that continuing to preside, after recusal should have occurred, renders the further proceedings a nullity. This dual aspect is captured in the oft repeated words that 'justice must not only be done, but must manifestly be seen to be done.'

In **BTR Industries South Africa (Pty) Ltd and Others v Metal and Allied Workers' Union and Another,** the Appellate Court, in considering the grounds for recusal, held that an applicant, for recusal, is required to show the existence of reasonable suspicion of bias, on the part of decision maker. The court also held that a real likelihood of bias was a pre-requisite for disqualifying bias; provided that the suspicion, of partiality, was one which might reasonably be entertained by a lay litigant.

It must be noted that the reviewing court is not required to measure the precise extent of apparent risk. The hypothetical reasonable man is to be envisaged in the circumstances of the litigant who raises objection to the court. However, and very importantly, the notion of 'a reasonable man' cannot vary according to individual idiosyncrasies or superstitions; or the intelligence of particular litigants.

In the case of **S v Roberts,** which has been referred to above, the court mentioned four requirements to test 'the appearance of judicial bias'. These were that, firstly, there must be suspicion that a judicial officer 'might' and not 'would' be biased. The second test was that the suspicion must be that of a reasonable person; in the position of an accused person, or a litigant. The third was that the suspicion must be based on reasonable grounds; while the fourth test, for the appearance of judicial bias, was that the suspicion must be one which the 'reasonable person', referred to, 'would' and not 'might' have. Where an application for recusal is found to be 'a transparent and dishonest strategy to obtain postponement', a presiding officer will be correct to refuse the application; and to proceed with the matter.

The Court of Appeal, of Botswana, also had occasion to deal with the test for recusal; in the case of **Mafeelela v The State.** In that case, the court held that the right of a litigant, to ask a judicial officer to recuse himself, or herself, was a very important one; which had to be fully protected. However, that right had to be honestly exercised, in appropriate cases and upon well-established grounds. The Court also held that a magistrate, or judge, cannot sit in a case where he, or she, might not be able to administer justice impartially; and where there is a possibility of bias either on the ground of hostility, or the ground of interest in the case.

The concept of judicial impartiality and neutrality is embodied by an icon, the goddess of justice. The image of the goddess has been known to western culture for more than two thousand years. In Ancient Greece, thousands of years ago, the goddess of justice was called 'Themis'. To the ancient Romans, she was known as 'Justitia'.

The duty of impartiality manifests itself in a number of principles in the common law tradition; with the overriding one being that a judge with a direct interest in a matter should not preside over it. The most obvious example of a judge with a direct interest, in a case, is one who accepts a bribe; in order to decide in favour of one of the parties. Suffice it to say that there can be nothing more inimical, to the idea of justice, than a judge being bribed. Another common example, of direct interest in proceedings, is where a judge has a direct financial interest in the litigation. Such an interest will be sufficient to disqualify the judge from presiding over a case. The principle behind this is that, in such cases, a reasonable observer would always hold the reasonable apprehension that the judge might not bring an impartial mind to the question that is to be determined.

Direct financial interest, as a disqualifying factor, is illustrated by an old English case; which involved the then Lord Chancellor of England, Lord Cottenham, who owned a substantial shareholding in a company; which was a party in an appeal on which he sat. It was held that he should have disqualified himself. In arriving at that decision, the House of Lords said: "No one can suppose that Lord Cottenham could be, in the remotest degree, influenced by the interest that he had in this concern; but, my Lords, it is of the last importance that the maxim that no man is to be a judge in his own cause should be held sacred. And that is not to be confined to a cause in which he is a party, but applies to a cause in which he has an interest."

It is necessary to make it known that financial interest need not always be direct, for it to disqualify a judge. There is also indirect financial interest; which occurs where a judge has a remote, and very small, financial interest in the dispute. There is, however, a challenge with indirect and remote, and even inconsequential, financial interest; in that it may occasion difficulties as to whether, or not, it should lead to disqualification. But, at the end of the day, the question as to whether a judge, in those circumstances, should recuse himself, or herself, depends on the answer to another question; that of whether a reasonable person, knowing all the relevant facts, could not entertain a reasonable apprehension that the judge, concerned, would not decide the case impartially, or without prejudice.

The case of General Augusto Pinochet, the former Head of State of Chile, is another famous authority for the preposition that financial interest may disqualify a judge, from sitting. On 25th November 1998, the House of Lords, in England, ruled that General Pinochet was not immune from arrest, and extradition, in relation to crimes against humanity which he, allegedly, committed whilst in office.

At the start of the hearing, the Court gave permission for Amnesty International, which is an international premier human rights organization, to intervene in the case. After the Court had delivered its judgement, information emerged; to the effect that one of the five judges, Lord Hoffmann, was an unpaid director and chairman of Amnesty International Charity Limited; an organization set up, and controlled, by Amnesty International. It also became known that Lord Hoffmann's wife was employed by Amnesty International.

Unhappy with the decision of the Court, and believing that Lord Hoffmann was disqualified to sit, on account of his interest in Amnesty International, an intervening party, General Pinochet applied to the House of Lords to set aside its earlier decision. The ground he advanced was that the relationship between Lord Hoffmann and the intervening party would give rise to the appearance of possible bias.

In December 1998, a newly constituted panel of five judges, in the House of Lords, held, unanimously, that the relationship between Amnesty International and Lord Hoffmann did, indeed, disqualify him from hearing the case. The judgement of the House of Lords, which had previously been given, had to be set aside. In the new judgement, it was held that Lord Hoffmann had an interest in the outcome of the proceedings; simply because he had some involvement with Amnesty International Charity Limited which, in turn, had a close relationship with Amnesty International Limited.

At this point, I am compelled to state that it is both difficult and unwise to seek to enumerate, exhaustively, all the possible interests that could lead to the disqualification of a judge; from presiding over a case. For instance, the interest of a family member, or an intimate knowledge of the judge in a dispute, which may qualify the judge to be a witness, may legitimately lead to disqualification. This is so because one cannot, at the same time, be judge on the bench, controlling the proceedings, and witness in the same case. In the case of the interest of family members, the question whether a judge ought to have disqualified himself, or herself, would depend on whether a reasonable person, aware of the facts, might, reasonably, have apprehended that, because of a family member's interest, in the case, then a judge might not bring an impartial mind to the resolution of the dispute. In reality, it is elementary that where cases involve close relations, or friends, then the judge cannot sit.

In some jurisdictions, the courts have even held that there is a real danger of actual bias, and the appearance of bias, if the child of a judge appears before him, or her, as a lawyer for one of the parties. Similarly, it seems to me that where a judge has a personal friendship with one of the parties, to the proceedings, or has a serious, intimate and ongoing relationship with a lawyer for one of the parties, an appearance of bias is generated.

Still on the issue of bias, whether actual or perceived, it is a salutary rule that judges should not accept gifts from litigants, potential litigants or witnesses. This makes it uncertain from what sources a judge may, properly, receive money; in addition to his, or her, judicial salary. It must be said that there can be no objection to a judge receiving the proceeds of ordinary investments, or the rental monies from any property that the judge may own. Indeed, in many jurisdictions in the commonwealth, judges do engage in some business; including sitting as members of business entities. The cardinal rule to observe, in all of this, is transparency and integrity. A judge must never be involved in any business, or money making venture, which would call his, or her, integrity into question; and bring the office of judgeship into disrepute.

The duty of impartiality may be breached by a judge exhibiting animosity to one of the parties or his legal representatives. The primary principle, in this respect, is that each party must be given a fair opportunity to convince the judge of the merits of their case. This cannot be so if a judge exhibits personal animosity to one of the parties. If the animosity is expressed by questions, or remarks, that show that the judge is biased, then he, or she, may not preside. This being said, difficulties may arise, in terms of proof, where the animosity is in the body language, or the tone, of the judge.

Judges are required to be patient; and listen to both sides of a case that serves before them. Not allowing a party, or a party's lawyer, a proper opportunity to present his, or her, case is contrary to one of the fundamental principles of fairness. History is replete with examples of judges whose behaviour exhibited a lack of impartiality. A few examples will suffice, in this regard. It was said of Lord Campbell, a 19th century English Lord Chief Justice, that during submissions, by counsel, the judge would not keep to his seat. Instead, he would get up and march up and down, while casting, at intervals, the most furious glances at the imperturbable counsel, and throwing his arms into the air. This, of course, spoke volumes about the judge's lack of impartiality. Unfortunately, Lord Campbell has not been alone in this kind of behaviour. Another Lord Chief Justice of England, Lord Hewart (1870-1943), has been described as follows:

> *"He lacked only the one quality which should distinguish a judge: that of being judicial. He remained the perpetual advocate. The opening of a case had only to last for five minutes before one could feel, and sometimes actually see, which side he had taken; thereafter the other side had no chance".*

Judges should always allow parties to submit freely and without undue interference; save where it is necessary to seek clarification. Persistent, unwarranted and prejudicial interference, with counsel's submission, may be a basis for recusal; especially where a judge's conduct, through unwarranted interruptions, makes it, virtually, impossible for counsel to put his case properly before the court.

While judges are only human, they must tame the inclination for humour during court proceedings; as that may, often, be misconstrued as indicative of lack of impartiality or, indeed, indifference to the seriousness that should attach to court proceedings. Sometimes, judges fall into the temptation to make jokes in the court room. If such a risk is taken, then care must be taken to ensure that it does not appear that the judge is taking the occasion lightly, or is making fun of someone involved in the case.

Improper, or ill-timed jokes may be a threat to the appearance of impartiality. They may also dent confidence in the judicial system. If people who are seeking justice, from the courts think, or believe, that their cases are taken lightly, by adjudicators, they will not be wrong to think that they will not get any justice.

Another important aspect of impartiality is that it demands that judges avoid giving the impression that they have pre-judged an issue. It is a travesty, of justice, for parties to walk out of court with a credible sense that the judge has already prejudged the issues before him, or her. Quite clearly, a party who believes, on reasonable grounds, that the judge has decided, in advance, to disbelieve his, or her, evidence cannot have confidence in the result of the proceedings. A judge must, at all costs, avoid making statements, during the hearing of a case, which indicate, or even suggest, that he, or she, has made up their mind, about which way the case should be decided, even before the case is concluded.

In the era of case management, modern judges, responding to the need for more active case management, may intervene, actively, to ensure that issues are clearly defined, as early as possible, and that cases are expeditiously disposed of. However, and whilst judges who manage cases are permitted to take charge and effectively manage cases, by ensuring that they are disposed of expeditiously, and efficiently, a judge is still not permitted to prejudge a case; under the guise of expeditious management of the case in question. This being said, the prohibition against judges prejudging cases does not mean that they cannot form a superficial view on the case; at the earliest stages or, indeed, that they cannot express a tentative view of the matter. On the contrary, judges often form tentative opinions on matters in issue, and lawyers are, usually, assisted by hearing those opinions; and being given an opportunity to deal with them.

It is important to point out that although judges may express a tentative view on a matter, at any time before delivery of judgement, it may be good judicial policy to do so sparingly. This is so because a judge may think that any view that he, or she, may express before the conclusion of a case is merely provisional and that evidence, or argument, presented later may cause the judge to change his, or her, mind. However, litigants often do not understand this; and may mistake a provisional view for a concluded pre-judgement.

Judges have many duties to carry out; in the course of performing their judicial functions. One such duty is to control proceedings; and ensure that there is always decorum, and professionalism, in their courts. To this extent, a judge may, legitimately, place time limitations on submissions and/or ask counsel to wind up. This is so because a judge's duty, in the interests of justice, is to secure a fair, efficient and expeditious trial. For this reason, judges are permitted to intervene, when parties before them are speaking, so as to avoid irrelevance, to curb prolixity and to protect witnesses. As is often said, tolerance and patience are the ultimate judicial virtues; but to allow parties the freedom to place before the judge evidence that is irrelevant, and to argue for the sake of arguing, is inimical to the efficient management of cases. I think I can, confidently, say that it is not many adjudicators who have a quarrel with this notion.

It is all too common, in a number of jurisdictions, for judges to decide cases on points not pleaded or raised. This should be avoided, at all costs. It is an undesirable practice which is, inherently, unfair; as it does not give litigants the opportunity to address the court; per the tradition with judicial adjudication. Where a judge comes across a point, or case, which is not raised in court and which may sway the case, either way, it is good practice to reconvene the court, let the lawyers know of the lapse and, thereafter, invite them to address the court on the point, or case, in issue.

The duty to remain impartial also means that while a case is pending, a judge must not communicate with one party, or that party's lawyer, without the other parties being present. Having brought out this critical aspect of impartiality, I must mention that whilst communicating with the other party, to a law suit may not, on its own, be evidence of bias, in certain circumstances, it may lead to perceptions of bias and should, thus, be avoided.

As a general rule, a judge cannot be asked to disqualify or recuse himself, or herself, from presiding over a case, because the judge has, in the past, decided a case presenting similar facts and the law. That fact is not a basis to seek a judge's recusal. However, if a judge has made credibility findings against a particular party, in one case, it would be wrong for that judge to hear another case involving the same party; where that party's credibility would, again, be an issue. The reason for this is that the judge would have a preconceived idea of whether, or not, the witness will tell the truth; when the rule is that a judge must decide a case only on evidence before him, or her.

In my experience on the bench, it has come to my notice that a judge's academic writings or other extra judicial opinions are, occasionally, cited by lawyers; as evidence of bias. It suffices to say that this may not, necessarily, be so. But where such writings, or extra judicial opinions, become the basis for recusal, the test remains the same; namely that if a reasonable person, aware of the facts, may reasonably conclude that the judge would not bring an impartial mind to bear, on the matter, then the judge ought not to preside in the case.

The approach of judges, as to what should be done where a reasonable apprehension of bias may appear, differs from one jurisdiction to another. The practice, in most jurisdictions, is that judges would generally disclose to the parties, at the outset of a case, the existence of some facts or circumstances that may be misconstrued as evidence of bias. The disclosure is designed to advise the parties of the facts upon which they can make an informed decision, as to whether the judge's interest could possibly lead him, or her, to prejudge the issues in a case. Once disclosure has been made, the parties are then able to direct argument as to whether the outcome of the case might, possibly, be affected by the interest disclosed. Quite often, the parties may advise the judge that, notwithstanding the disclosure, they do not think that he, or she, must disqualify themselves from sitting; and the judge may then proceed to sit. However, there may be instances where a judge may disqualify himself, or herself, from sitting; even though the lawyers did not think that the judge should do so.

It is good practice, if cost, delay and inconvenience are to be avoided, that a judge must disqualify himself, or herself, at the earliest opportunity; if circumstances so warrant. The parties should not be confronted with a last minute choice between adjournment, of a case, and waiver of an otherwise valid objection. In fact, it is generally desirable that disclosure should be made, to the parties, in advance of a hearing. It is also a good judicial policy for judges to disclose matters; rather than for parties to 'investigate' the judge.

While litigants have every right to demand the recusal of judges, from hearing matters, judges must always keep it in mind that they are under an obligation to preside over cases. For that reason, they should not readily accede to requests for recusal; especially when such applications are mischievous, tactical, or otherwise intended to put pressure on the judge. Recusal must only be based on reasonable grounds of perception of bias.

Justice must be seen to be done

It needs to be remembered that although it is important that justice must be seen to be done, it is equally important that judicial officers discharge their duty to sit in cases. The objectivity that surrounds the concept of the fair-minded person means that a judge should not, automatically, disqualify himself, or herself, when requested to do so, by one of the parties, on the basis of an allegation of prejudgment or bias. By acceding too readily to suggestions of appearance of bias, judges may encourage parties to believe that, by seeking the disqualification of a judge, they will have their case tried by someone who will be inclined to decide the case in their favour.

Judges, as fountains of justice, must avoid a myriad of partiality, based on political and religious grounds. It is all too common for judges, often unconsciously, to show bias based on gender. Judges are human beings; and they have strengths and weaknesses, just like every other person. They may, intensely, dislike counsel appearing for a party. Perceived favouritism for opposing counsel, by a judge, is a common ground of complaint by litigants appearing in person. The converse occurs when a judge goes to extreme lengths to demonstrate that he, or she, does not favour a lawyer with whom the judge is known to be friendly.

In carrying out their duty to adjudicate, judges should know that the more aware they are of their subconscious feelings, the better judicial officers they will be; as that awareness will enable them to, better, control their internal bias. Judges are not angels; and it would be unrealistic to expect complete impartiality from them. It is, therefore, inevitable that they should harbour likes and dislikes, prejudices and emotions for, and against, different people. It is also not unexpected that judges should support, or oppose, social and political causes; or that they should have personal views about many issues that arise, in the general course of human life. However, and even in the face of all these factors, what is required of a judge is to curb these feelings and to try and prevent any of them from having a bearing on the decision to be made in a court case. In short, judges must refrain, at all costs, from doing anything that would give any indication of bias.

In my many years at the service of the law, I can readily testify that unconscious bias is a major problem. Bias is such an insidious thing that even though a person may, in good faith, believe that he, or she, was acting impartially, that person's mind may, unconsciously, be affected by bias. As is often said, judges may try to be as objective as they, possibly, can be; but the bottom line is that much as they can try to do that, they still see things with their own eyes and process legal disputes with their own brain; and this takes place in the context of their individual backgrounds, upbringing and habits.

Still on the subject of impartiality, the right to be tried by an impartial court and, or, tribunal is one of the universally recognized aspects of the right to a fair trial. It is a given that justice is contaminated when a judge enters the temple of justice already pre-disposed to determine a matter, in a particular way, on account of prejudice, bias or ill-will which he, or she, may harbour against one of the parties to the dispute. Impartiality is one of the core values that guide judges' work; and it is incumbent upon judges to, as far as is possible, act as dispassionate arbiters; being persuaded only by the evidence before them.

It must be emphasized, in closing but by no means exhausting the discussion on impartiality, that much as they are required to be impartial, society should never make the mistake of assuming that judges are angels. As has been repeatedly stated, in the pages of this book, judges are human beings; with human passions and emotions. But these human weaknesses, notwithstanding, they must always strive to be impartial, because the lack of impartiality erodes the confidence, of people, in the courts; and also undermines judges' moral authority to preside, over disputes, impartially and fairly.

Chapter Eight

JUDICIAL ACCOUNTABILITY
· ·

The preceding chapters of this book have discussed a range of topics; that are all closely associated with, and form the core of, judgeship. It will be noted that theoretical reflections on judgeship, qualities and attributes of a judge and the appointment of judges, have been discussed; in some detail. Other topics, of equal importance, which have been given attention, in the earlier chapters of this book, include judicial independence, financial independence of the judiciary and judicial impartiality. This chapter continues with the insights into judgeship; and looks at the topic of judicial accountability. The starting point, of this discussion, is that judicial power is, by definition, a delegated one. It is the people who delegate this power that ordinarily belongs to them; in a democratic dispensation. In other words, judges are trustees, and it stands to reason that they must account for the power that they exercise on behalf of the people.

Growth of judicial review

There is another reason why judges must be accountable. The increase in the power of the judiciary, as manifested by the power of judicial review, has resulted in a corresponding increase in the need for judicial accountability. Invariably, politicians, ever apprehensive of the growth of judicial power, and in an effort to free themselves from what they perceive as the 'undue power' of the judiciary, are keen to ensure that the judiciary is accountable. The question of accountability requires that judges, as holders of public office, be held accountable; in the same way as the other branches of the state must be held to account. However, and while it is not in dispute that the institution must be accountable, the accountability of the judiciary must be such that it does not undermine its independence.

Politicians sometime miss the point

I recall that some years back, in Botswana, politicians were concerned that judges were handing down lenient sentences for stock theft. This worry stemmed from the fact that pastoral farming, in Botswana, is one of the mainstays of the economy; and the rural areas are a potent source of political power which, I dare to add, the politicians did not want to risk losing grip on. The Politicians were, similarly, concerned that judges were letting criminals on the loose, by granting them bail. So, they approached the Chief Justice and informed him that since the people were concerned, about those matters, he should assign a judge to accompany the Minister of Justice to a series of community meetings; so that the judge could answer the concerns of the people. The Chief Justice, politely, declined the invitation; pointing out, with regard to the issue of criminals being let loose, through the granting of bail, that it was incumbent upon the politicians to understand the prescriptions and stipulations of the constitution; such as the meaning, and import, of concepts such as the 'presumption of innocence'.

With regard to the concern on the perceived lenient sentences, the Chief Justice made it known that sentencing was in the discretion of the judge. He additionally pointed out to the Minister, and correctly so in my view, that a judge appearing alongside him at meetings, as a form of accounting, was not permissible, as it had the effect of compromising the independence of the judiciary; by putting undue pressure on the judges to be accountable to politicians.

Accountability should not undermine judicial independence

The accountability mechanisms required must protect judicial independence by keeping the political branches of government at arm's length. Furthermore, accountability mechanisms of the judiciary should reside within the judiciary, broader civil society and the nation at large; but not within the executive. This is because placing the responsibility for judicial oversight outside of the judiciary, and within the executive, introduces the risk that judges will be investigated, and removed from office, for political reasons; unless mechanisms are in place to prevent the oversight body being hijacked by politicians.

It is a reality that judges wield a lot of power and, imbued with so much power and independence, there is a temptation to develop 'arrogance of office'; which is a feeling of being untouchable. Suffice it to say that 'arrogance of office' should not be allowed to take root in any jurisdiction.

In a number of jurisdictions judges have been criticized and attacked, sometimes savagely and severely, by Heads of Governments and States, Members of Parliament, government officials, the press and even the public, for decisions they have made in particular cases. This has often been used as a misguided stratagem to have judges account for their decisions. I say misguided because to attack judges is not the appropriate way to engender accountability. Accountability by the head of state of a government is particularly reprehensible; given the duty that resides in that authority to protect, promote, fulfill and defend the constitution.

In the United Kingdom, back in 2005, a former leader of the Conservative Party launched a vicious attack on the law Lords, for what he called their "aggressive judicial activism". What had triggered this unwarranted attack was their decision that the indefinite detention, without trial, of foreign terror suspects contravened the Human Rights Act. The attack, by the politician, suggested that the decision of the court was political, and dangerous, as it opened the country to attacks by terrorists.

In the modern environment, the concept of accountability permeates public life. In a democracy, based on the rule of law, it is now the expectation of every citizen, that all aspects of government ought to be highly accountable. As it is often said, the exercise of public power, and the performance of public functions, necessarily demand some form of justification. This requirement, for justification, need not be spelt out, in express terms, in any legislation; although to do so would be preferable. To my mind, justification flows from the very concept of democracy, the rule of law and constitutionalism.

Levels of Accountability

There are, arguably, three levels on which one has to consider judicial accountability; these are the personal conduct, personal decision and the conduct of the judiciary, as an institution. At the personal conduct level, judges are expected to behave in a manner befitting the office of a judge. If they misbehave, they must be some machinery by which they can be disciplined. However, care must be taken to ensure that the executive does not harass judges under the guise of enforcing the law, and that no one is above the law -a principle which no judge can, legitimately, question.

In view of the, sometimes misguided, expectations as to accountability, it may be good to insulate judges from undue harassment, under the guise of enforcing the law; by providing that where judges are suspected of the commission of an offence, or any improper conduct, then the matter must be brought to the attention of the Chief Justice, or the next most senior judge, who may institute an enquiry into the allegation against the judge. Where there is some evidence, at the peripheral level, that an offence has been committed, the Chief Justice or Senior Judge should be obliged to refer the matter to prosecutorial authorities.

It may also make sense to provide that the police may not arrest a judge; without the prior consent of the Chief

Justice, or the most senior judge. If it is the Chief Justice, without the consent of the most senior judge.

With respect to decisional accountability, judges cannot be forced to resign because of making a decision that is considered to be wrong. This is a very important aspect of judicial independence. It is, generally, accepted that judges must make their decisions without fear or favour; and this explains why they cannot be disciplined, for making a decision that is perceived to be wrong.

There is an inbuilt system that ensures that judges are held accountable for decisions that they make. The starting point is, perhaps, the oath of office which they take. That oath is significant, and judges must live up to its prescriptions. It is necessary to mention that an oath of office is not a fanciful, or rhetorical, citation. It is a weighty pronouncement; meant to guide the judge throughout his, or her, career. The second aspect of the inbuilt mechanism for judicial accountability is the requirement for judges to sit in open court and deliver their decisions publicly. They are also required to give reasons as to why they have decided a dispute in the manner in which they have done. These decisions are open to public discussion and, indeed, criticism. A decision that is unsupported, by reasons, is untenable and constitutes a strong ground of appeal.

The system of appeal is meant to correct wrong decisions; that may have been given by the lower courts. It must be said decisional independence does not mean that a judge is at liberty to decide arbitrarily. Even in cases where the law gives him, or her, the discretion, a judge cannot decide whimsically. Any decision, that a judge makes, must be based on sound legal principles and reasons. Judges must always remember that the bottom line, in the adjudicatory process, is that judicial decisions must always be based on the evidence and the law; and nothing more.

Where a matter is taken on appeal, the appellate court may criticize the lower court for getting the facts, or law, wrong. Once a judgment is delivered, armies of highly paid lawyers take all the time in the world to find errors in the judgment. As it often happens, with the advantage of time and resources which the judge may not have, these armies of lawyers scrutinize every word, sentence, paragraph and authority to expose any error they can find. Some of the things that can happen, when a judgement goes on appeal, are that the criticisms, of the appeal courts, may be published, without limitation, and academic lawyers are free to criticize judicial reasoning. Additionally, books may be written about the errors that judges have committed. Academics often spend years studying these judgements; and writing to expose any weaknesses found.

It is should be noted that the media usually attend court hearings; and report accordingly. They, too, may be critical of judgements, as is their prerogative. The only condition is that if the media must criticize judgements, they must do so respectfully, and based on facts. Judges should not stand above legitimate criticism; because they are not sacred cows. However, any criticism that is ill informed, malicious or done in bad faith; and whose intention is, simply, to damage the reputation of a judge, or bring the court into ridicule, or disrepute, must not be allowed. In fact, that kind of criticism may be legitimately censured.

The judgements of the appeal courts, overturning the decision of the lower courts, are a matter of public record. They stand forever, with judges' errors recorded for posterity; and for succeeding generations of lawyers to examine and discuss. This should, however, not deter judges, of the lower courts, from delivering judgements as they see fit; from the evidence, presented to them, and the applicable laws. It is part of the judicial process, for a higher court to disagree with the decision given by a lower court, and for the higher court to upset the lower court's judgement; if it is necessary to do so.

Despite these structural guarantees of exposure of the business of the courts to the scrutiny of legal examination, and the glare of public scrutiny, it is still considered that the judicial branch needs to become more accountable. Thus, it is contended that the absence of 'a constitutional referee', to review the wrongs of judges imposes, on them, an awesome responsibility to exercise self-accountability. On a positive note, a commentator once said, "If you have judges with high character, knowledge and commitment to the rule of law, that, in itself is a measure of accountability."

With respect to the accountability of the judiciary, as whole, the point that needs to be emphasized is that judicial accountability must be sufficiently balanced; so as to strengthen judicial integrity. One of the ways through which judicial integrity can be achieved is by ensuring that the appointment process is beyond reproach. As indicated earlier, in most jurisdictions, judges are appointed through a system over which the public has no control.

The power to appoint is, usually, vested in Judicial Service Commissions which, in some countries, tend to be dominated by representatives of the executive. Where this is the case, it is common for doubt to exist, over the integrity of judges who are appointed through those Commissions. As was emphasized during the discussion on appointment of judges, a transparent and merit based system, overseen by an independent constitutional appointing authority, accounts better for institutional independence of the judiciary.

The Judiciary needs to be held in high regard, by the public, if it is to function properly. However, that respect is not an entitlement; it must be earned. In a situation where a large segment of the population takes the view that judges do not decide cases in accordance with the law, much is at stake. Former Chief Justice Marshall, of the United States of America, once cautioned that "The people have made the Constitution, and they can unmake it".

Elements of institutional Accountability

In my mind, institutional accountability, when reduced to its barest minimum, requires that:

- The judiciary, as a whole, to explain to the public how the judicial system works; and how it is essential for the interests of every person;

- That the system works efficiently and fairly;

- The public is assured that there is a dignified process, in place, to deal with errant judges.

From the discussion on the concept, one may assert, without fear of contradiction, that even in the absence of specific provisions in a constitution, judicial accountability is now accepted as the reverse side of judicial independence; and is not seen as being an interference, or a limitation, to the functions of judgeship. As long as judges are charged with the responsibility of protecting the human rights and freedoms of the citizenry, they are stewards who should, therefore, account to the public; for their judicial performance. This, in turn, means that the public should be allowed the freedom to make adverse comment on judicial performance; which they perceive as errant from the norm.

In a functional democracy, the legislature is accountable to the people through regular and periodic elections. The executive is accountable to the legislature and, ultimately, to the electorate. In both cases, the courts, in the exercise of their powers of constitutional and judicial review, may invalidate any law that is passed by the legislature. The courts also have the mandate to overturn decisions, made by the executive, which are not in accord with the constitution or with the law.

Judges, on the other hand, are neither subject to periodic elections, nor to censure. They serve until they reach retiring age; or the expiry of their contractual term. Judges may be removed, form office, only for a cause; and no other authority hovers over their shoulders, to see whether, or not, they are performing their functions properly. Consequently, this has led to a perception that judges, particularly those who serve in the superior courts, may be unaccountable and undemocratic; especially when they invalidate laws passed by representative legislatures; and overturn decisions of popularly elected governments.

It could also be said that the seeming 'freedom from accountability' to the executive and legislature, by judges, is another factor that may contribute to the apprehension, by politicians, that judges wield too much unchecked power. Stretching this observation, it could also be the reason why politicians will seize every opportunity, that they can, to try and get rid of judges who are deemed to pose a threat to political power.

The question may be asked, if the judges are accountable to the people who, then, should judge the judges? Thomas Jefferson once said: *"Man is not to be trusted for life, if secured against all liability to account"* In a democracy, judges are not liable to be sued in the good faith performance of their duties. However, if they are actuated by malice, the protection falls away. The question who judges the judges is a difficult one. The answer must, of necessity, be the people, themselves, as they are the ones who delegated judicial power, to the judges, in the first place.

The Bangalore Principles of Judicial Conduct

The need for judicial accountability without eroding judicial independence has now been recognized in most democracies. It is found in both international instruments and national statutes. At the international level, I find the **2002 Bangalore Principles of Judicial Conduct** to be instructive. The first principle is that 'impartiality is essential to the proper discharge of judicial office, and it applies not only to the decision, itself, but also to the process by which the decision is made'. The second principle is that 'integrity is essential to the discharge of the judicial office'. The fourth principle is that 'ensuring equality of treatment to all, before the courts, is essential to the due performance of judicial office'. The fifth principle is that 'competence and diligence are prerequisites to the due performance of judicial office'.

Most jurisdictions have adopted codes of conduct, which establish standards for the ethical conduct of judges. This is in a bid to regulate the conduct of judges and to provide a mechanism, and a forum, for those who may have complaints against judges. The rationale, for such codes, was best described by Laurance M. Hyde, Jr. (1892-1978), Chief Justice of the Missouri Supreme Court, when he said:

> *'This vital independence must be balanced by concepts and duties which will assure our citizens that Judges will impartially interpret and apply the law of the land. Judges must be, and just as important, must appear to be above reproach. Much of this will always be up to the consciences of those individuals who are called to the bench, and no code of ethics can substitute for the personal qualities which are the makings of good judges. However, just as there must be laws, not merely the sense of justice of good and wise people serving as*

*Judges, so there must be not only Judges of good
conscience, but rules of ethical judicial conduct
which are mandatory, and sanctions for the
violation of those rules.'*

Mr. Hyde quotes an interesting utterance by John
Marshall at the Virginia Constitutional Conference in
1829-30, when he said:

*'I have always thought, form my earliest youth till
now, that the greatest scourge an angry Heaven
ever inflicted upon an ungrateful and sinning
people, was an ignorant, a corrupt or a dependent
judiciary.'*

On the need for Codes of Conduct, the Latimer House
Guidelines, which have already been alluded to, provide that:

*'A Code of Ethics and Conduct should be developed
and adopted by each judiciary as a means of
ensuring accountability of Judges.'*

The guidelines also state that legitimate public
criticism, of judicial performance, is a means of ensuring
accountability. They add that criminal law and contempt
proceedings are not appropriate mechanisms for restricting
legitimate criticism of the courts.

Codes of conduct

Codes of Conduct, and constitutions, contain various do's
and don'ts; relating to judicial officers. The purpose is to
regulate the conduct, and performance, of judicial officers.
In other words, these constitute sufficient mechanisms

for making the judiciary accountable, notwithstanding its independence. One may add that most constitutions of the commonwealth countries, especially those crafted in the 1960's, use the term 'misbehaviour' as founding a basis to trigger disciplinary measures against a judge; which may be, suspension or impeachment. This term appears, to me, to be ambiguous or providing inadequate protection to a judge. The ordinary meaning of 'misbehaviour' is 'inappropriate behaviour, bad behaviour, disobedience, mischievousness' and similar appellations. Other countries have interpreted 'misbehaviour' in their constitutions, for purposes of triggering disciplinary measures to mean, 'gross misconduct'. Personally, I suggest that, as a matter of principle, the law should prescribe a higher threshold, of what constitutes 'misbehaviour', in order to forestall possible abuse, especially by politicians.

Latimer Principles

The Commonwealth (Latimer House) Principles on the Accountability of and the Relationship between the Three Branches of Government encapsulates judicial accountability in these words:

> *"Judges are accountable to the Constitution and to the law which they must apply honestly, independently and with integrity. The principles of judicial accountability and independence underpin public confidence in the judicial system and the importance of the judiciary as one of the three pillars upon which a responsible government relies".*

Justice Sandra Day O'Connor, a retired Associate Justice of the Supreme Court of the Unites State of America, once stated that, *"judicial accountability, however, is a concept that is frequently misunderstood, at best, and abused at worst"*.

Experience shows that 'judicial accountability' sometimes becomes a rallying cry for those who want to dictate substantive judicial outcomes. It has also been argued that such a warped representation, of what is meant by accountability, ignores the role of the judiciary and, indeed, the very structure of a democratic government; based on the separation of powers, the rule of law and constitutionalism.

Judicial accountability also serves to promote judicial integrity. It is indisputable that an independent, and accountable, judiciary is indispensable to the rule of law. Equally indisputable is that fact that judicial accountability advances judicial competence. A fundamental value of the rule of law is that judicial decisions are not made arbitrarily; but through a process of reasoned decision making. The rule of law requires that decisions must be justified in law and, therefore, should be reasoned, analytical, rational and non-arbitrary; with respect to legal standards. At the end of the day, independence, integrity and competence are the hallmarks of a judiciary that is committed to upholding the rule of law. These are the cardinal principles by which a judiciary should be held accountable.

In addition to the mechanisms which have been outlined, in this chapter, lawyers also play an important role in ensuring that judges are held accountable. It helps, immensely, if the organized legal profession is independent, adheres to a strong code of professional ethics and keeps regular watch over the conduct of the legal profession; by making its views known if judges are discourteous in court, or take too long to deliver judgments. An organized, and effective, law society may also litigate, in court, in cases where the Judicial Service Commission does not take action against an offending judge.

As part of accountability, individuals may petition the Judicial Service Commission to inquire into the behaviour of judges; where there is reason to believe that judges have breached their code of conduct. For instance, in 2015 the Chief Executive Officer of the Law Society of Kenya, Apollo Mboya, brought a complaint, against judges, to the Judicial Service Commission. This followed a 'go slow' that was staged by judges; over the retirement age question. After his complaint, the judges were reprimanded for their conduct. Mr. Mboya was not happy with the reprimand. He protested that the Judicial Service Commission had 'reprimanded' the Supreme Court Judges, rather than recommend a tribunal to consider their dismissal. Although no removal ensued, Mr. Mboya was, at least, able to make a complaint that put judges on notice; that if they did anything untoward, people would come forth and complain.

Judicial Service Commissions, which are established in terms of the Constitution in most countries, are important vehicles for ensuring accountability. For instance, in South Africa, the Judicial Service Commission is established in terms of section 178 of the Constitution; and is responsible for holding judges accountable for various issues; including misconduct and incapacity. However, the Judicial Service Commission has met a lot of criticism; with regard to cases involving judges. In the past, cases involving misconduct by judges have been in the litigation pipe-line for close to ten years or more; and during all this time the judges, in question, would be on the pay roll. Clearly, this process was protracted; and the negative side to such drawn out proceedings is that they can serve to bring the judiciary into disrepute.

There is merit to ensuring that cases which involve allegations of misconduct, by judges, are expeditiously disposed of; to avoid a situation where an errant judge is on the pay roll for years on end; when he, or she, is not presiding over matters and is, effectively, drawing a free salary. In South Africa, the case that comes to mind, in this regard, is that involving one Judge Motata. That case dragged on for years and in the year 2016, or thereabout, it was reported, in the media, that during the period of his suspension, the judge had been paid almost fourteen million Rand (R14, 000,000.00); since being placed on special leave in 2007.

Yet again in South Africa, in 2008, a complaint was lodged, against one Judge Hlophe, the Judge President Constitutional Court, by 11 judges of the same court. The complaint held that Judge Hlophe had approached two members of the Constitutional Court; and tried to, unduly, influence them over the pending trial of Jacob Zuma, who was the President of the Republic of South Africa. After reporting the allegedly improper approach, to them, by Judge Hlophe, the two complainants, Judges Jafta and

Nkabinde then lodged a statement, with the Judicial Service Commission, placing it on record, among other things, that they were not willing to make any statement to the Commission. This case has also been stalled, for years, as Judges Jafta and Nkabinde brought their refusal to deliver a statement all the way to the Constitutional Court.

In May 2016, the Constitutional Court dismissed an appeal, by the two judges, and ordered that the investigation of Judge Hlope proceed. In a highly unusual move, Judges Jafta and Nkabinde then asked for that order to be rescinded. The lesson from these two cases is that it is desirable for disciplinary cases, or complaints, against judges to be concluded speedily; both in order to maintain the integrity of the judiciary and to do justice.

The adage 'justice delayed is justice denied' applies to judges, just like everybody else. The judges under scrutiny need to know their fate, whether it be favourable or otherwise, in a timely manner. In any case, while protracted proceedings may offer those who are truly errant a free meal ticket for as long as their cases drag on, such proceedings offer no solace for those judges who are innocent of the charges, or complaints; as their reputation remains on the line for as long as the case against them is continuing. Justice should be for all people; including adjudicators.

The discussion on judicial accountability has, so far, focused on individual and institutional accountability in the performance of judicial functions. Apart from this, there is also the issue of financial accountability of the individual judges; and the judiciary as an institution.

Financial Accountability of individual judges

In many judiciaries, judges are required to account for their personal wealth. This is seen as essential for maintaining the integrity of judicial office. In those jurisdictions where judges are expected to account for their wealth, there is a general prohibition on judges holding any other office, of profit, or receiving payment for any service; other than that rendered by virtue of being a judge. As part of this regime, for rendering judges financially accountable, judges are also required to disclose their own registerable interests; as well as those of their immediate family members.

An earlier chapter discussed the issue of financial autonomy for the judiciary. This part of the book, briefly, discusses the need for the judiciary, as an institution, to properly account for the state funds appropriated to it, to enable it to run its affairs. As a starting point, it is very important to take note of the fact that the independence of the judiciary should not be misconstrued to mean that the judiciary should not account for monies entrusted to it. As indicated, earlier, it is all too common for the executive and the judiciary to fight over the control of the budget. The judiciary often complains that monies allocated to it are insufficient; while government counters this by always pointing out that there are many other competing interests, apart from those of the judiciary.

It must be accepted that any government would, of necessity, have to put a ceiling on the expenditure of any state institution. However, what is not acceptable is the deliberate, and arbitrary, financial suffocation of the judiciary as a control measure. It is inevitable that there should be a degree of give and take between judicial independence and judicial financial accountability. Once funds are allocated to the judiciary, by government, they it must be accounted for. In this regard, the judiciary cannot claim any entitlement to be treated differently from any other government institution; in terms of the responsibility to account for allocated funds and expenditure. The funds are, after all, public funds for which government must, in turn, account to the people.

Performance

One other important issue, concerning accountability, is that the judiciary must account for its performance; as an institution. It will be noted that the individual attributes, such as integrity and impartiality, which judges need in the performance of their judicial duties, have already been visited. In terms of institutional performance, the judiciary must be able to account to parliament, through annual reports, how it is carrying out its duties and, generally, whether cases, both criminal and civil, are being disposed of expeditiously.

Annual reports

The judiciary's annual reports should include statistics on the number of cases filed into its civil and criminal registries; and should also account for any revenue acquired from the filing of court cases. Challenges faced in the performance of judicial functions, such as insufficient numbers of adjudicators, insufficient court buildings, etcetera, should also be made known, to government, so as to explain why the performance of the judiciary, as an institution, may be affected on account of those challenges. Personally, I think that there is nothing wrong with this form of accounting. Many countries do it; including Papua New Guinea.

In other jurisdictions, there are internal mechanisms, in place, for evaluating judicial performance and holding judges accountable. In Kenya, for instance, the judiciary conducts biennial reviews on the integrity and performance of the judges, through the Ethics and Governance Sub-committee of the Judiciary. There is also the continuous complaints system, under the Office of the Chief Justice, through which litigants are able to seek corrective redress on the workings of the process of the courts.

The judiciary, as an arm of the state, must always be accountable for the exercise of its power, both to the public and to other arms of government. In my mind, there can be no other profession where the work of an individual is subjected to such a wide array of intense scrutiny. The argument that judges are not accountable is, therefore, largely fueled by ignorance. In my experience, judges are held accountable in the most intense and merciless fashion; and heaps of books are written about the supposed errors that judges have committed. I think many will agree that members of the executive and legislature are subject to less intense individual and institutional scrutiny.

My last thoughts, for the purposes of this chapter, are that in as much as accountability is important, it should never be of the kind that subordinates judges to the control of another authority, other than the law. Whatever model of enforcing accountability, it must not undermine the independence of the judges to apply their minds and enforce the law without fear, favour or any prejudice. It must always be borne in mind that judges have a very different role to perform, from the members of the other organs of state; and they should be allowed to carry out their judicial duties unfettered by extraneous considerations, or impediments, under the guise of accountability.

Chapter Nine

JUDICIAL ETHICS
· ·

The position of judge is one that carries significant responsibility and weight; and so a judge must accept restrictions that would, otherwise, be considered burdensome. Appointment as a judge, inevitably, brings with it certain duties and responsibilities. It is because of the onerous responsibilities of judges that they cannot complain if their conduct, on and off the bench, elicits criticism; or even censure. As a matter of course, judges' integrity, honesty, impartiality and independence from external influences, be they corruptive or intimidating, should be above question. Their private lives should also be exemplary.

Ethical judiciary

The community, at large, accepts that judges are only human; and that they should not be made to feel too restricted. However, the stature that they enjoy, in the community, requires them to be extra vigilant in ensuring that they, themselves, comply with the demands of the law; and with the ethical and moral rules of conduct, consistent with their elevated office. I have known of judges who, soon after joining the bench, resigned because they found the restrictions on their lives to be unbearable. These restrictions include a relatively isolated, and lonely, life. Judges always have to be on the alert that the company they keep is appropriate; and have to be cautious, at all times, about what they say in public.

Taking an example of my own experience, when I arrived in Papua New Guinea, a colleague took me around and introduced me to some coffee shops and restaurants. He then warned me to avoid two other restaurants; because they were frequented, or owned, by politicians. When I asked what was wrong with that, he answered that politicians were better avoided, because they could compromise a judge. The caution showed me that this was but one example of a judge who worried about where he went, whom he may meet and the potential for being compromised. After explaining why, I was well advised to avoid the named restaurants, my colleague opened up, a bit, and informed me that most of the politicians in the country were litigants, in court, and in an innocent discussion with a judge, they could try to obtain the judge's view about a matter that was serving before the court. The obvious effect of this was that it could give rise to the perception of favouritism and lack of impartiality, and that, in turn, had the potential to undermine confidence in the administration of justice.

International codes

Most of the international codes that have been written to govern judges' conduct, such as the Bangalore Principles of Judicial Conduct, espouse the viewpoint that those in public positions have the responsibility to behave in an ethical fashion. The codes also outline that there has to be a basic code, or guidelines for ethical conduct, which can be acknowledged and accepted as a fundamental standard to be followed. In this context, judiciaries are encouraged to adopt Codes of Ethics and Conduct, for judicial officers, and to embark on judicial outreach programmes to communicate, to the general public, the role and functions of the Judiciary.

There has been a recent upsurge in the popularity of Judicial Codes in Africa. In 1984, Tanzania adopted a Code of Conduct for judges; which inspired many other countries to follow suit. Kenya is one of the countries that, possibly inspired by the Tanzanian example, came up with a Judicial Code of Conduct. The adoption followed an earlier meeting of judges and magistrates; in which the idea of a Code was debated and supported. The Kenyan Code has been reviewed for its compliance with international standards; specifically the Bangalore Principles of Judicial Conduct and it has been found to be compliant. Botswana has a Judicial Code of Conduct that was conceptualized, debated and adopted by judges.

It is critical to the effectiveness of codes, that they have the respect and the support of the judiciary. Taking part in the development of a code also allows judicial officers the opportunity to address concerns and establish guidelines. The support and interest in establishing and adopting of codes by judicial officers, in Africa, is indicative of the importance of, and the desire to uphold, the highest standards of ethical conduct. It is also a demonstration that, contrary to some misguided beliefs, that may be held by certain sections of society, judicial officers, on the whole, are neither averse to being held accountable for their conduct; nor do they fear to come under scrutiny for the performance of their judicial functions.

The power of life and death, which judges exercise over their fellow humans, is so extensive, and pervasive, that it demands, of necessity, that judges' conduct must be beyond reproach. Ronald Dworkin discussed having faith in the ability of a judge to distinguish between law and politics, and to find the correct legal answer. He admits that objectivity is more of an ideal, than a reality. It is often said that the judge who realizes, before listening to a case, that people have a natural bias of mind and that thought is apt to be coloured by predilection, is more likely to make a conscious effort at impartiality, and being detached, than the judge who believes that his, or her, elevation to the bench makes him, or her, the dehumanized instrument, of infallible logical truth, at once.

While there may be some general principles that have a universal appeal, at least within Commonwealth trained judges, judicial ethics, like most concepts, is context specific. One of the most important contexts is the historical, geographical and political setting in which judges operate. At the international level there are many Covenants, Declarations and Codes that all judges must endeavour to read; so as to discern some ethical obligations expected of them. These include the following:

- *The Universal Declaration of Human Rights, 1948.*

    '19. Everyone is entitled in full equality to a fair and public hearing by an independent and impartial

tribunal, in the determination of his rights and obligations and any criminal charge against him.'

- *The International Covenant on Civil and Political Rights, 1976.*

  '14(1). All persons shall be equal before the courts and tribunals. In the determination of any criminal charge against him, or of his rights and obligations in a suit at law, everyone shall be entitled to a fair and public hearing by a competent, independent and impartial tribunal established by law.'

- *The United Nations Basic Principles on the Independence of the Judiciary.*

- *2005: The United Nations Convention Against Corruption identifies the judiciary as a key institution to prevent, and counter, corruption.*

- *2006: The Bangalore Principles of Judicial Conduct, define six main principles: independence, impartiality, integrity, propriety, equality and competence and diligence.*

- *The African Charter on Human and Peoples' Rights 1986.*

- *The Principles and Guidelines on the Right to a Fair Trial and Legal Assistance in Africa proclaimed by the African Commission on Human and Peoples' Rights and endorsed by the Heads of State of the African Union 2003.*

- *Commonwealth Principle on the Accountability of and the Relationship between the Three Branches of Government 2003.*

Public acceptance of, and support for, court decisions, depends upon public confidence in the integrity and independence of judges. This, in turn, depends upon judges upholding a high standard of conduct in court. It follows, therefore, that if public confidence in the courts is to be maintained, judges should demonstrate, and promote, a high standard of judicial conduct; as one element of ensuring the independence of the judiciary.

Public confidence requires that a judge be impartial at all times. The absence of bias is both a legal and ethical imperative. As has already been mentioned, bias is, quite often, unconscious; and it can manifest either verbally or physically. Bias comes in many shapes and sizes. It may take the form of negative stereotyping and ill-considered jokes, based on stereotypes perhaps related to gender, culture or race. Other examples of bias include threatening, intimidating or hostile acts; suggesting a connection between race, or nationality, and crime, and irrelevant references to personal characteristics.

Many of those who have been on the bench for long know, fully well, that bias, or prejudice, may also manifest in body language. Body language can convey an appearance of bias to parties, in the proceedings, or to lawyers and also to the media and others. The bias, or prejudice, may be directed against a party, a witness or an attorney. A judge must, at all times, avoid unjustified reprimands of counsel; just as a judge must also avoid displaying any conduct that may destroy the appearance of impartially.

It is unethical for judges to communicate information, on matters serving before them, in the absence of the others; unless the consent of those that are absent has been obtained. The principle of impartiality, generally, prohibits private communications between the judge and any of the parties or their legal representatives. It is also unethical for a judge to communicate, to the Registrar of a court, anything adverse against a party; either about the pleadings, of any case, or some accusation of improper conduct, in a manner that may be construed, by a reasonable bystander, as indicative of bias.

Outside court, judges must take care not to talk recklessly about public controversies, in the public domain; as these issues may end up in court. A judge who expresses a hostile position against a party, in private, may not be well suited to preside in a matter in which he, or she, has already expressed a hostile position. Everything from a judge's associations or business interests, to remarks which the judge may consider to be 'harmless banter', may be perceived, by a reasonable bystander, as evidence that the judge is biased.

An example of very high ethical standards was shown by a friend, and a colleague, in Botswana. In 2018, soon after the new president, of the Republic of Botswana, was inaugurated, a political party challenged the propriety of the president's ascension to office; alleging that his inauguration was unlawful. When the case was registered, it was allocated to my colleague, and friend of many years, Motswagole J; who was, in fact, my former law partner. The judge decided to recuse himself; and the matter was allocated to another judge. My friend made known the reason for his recusal: he indicated that, prior to the matter being filed into court, he had had an informal discussion with the Attorney General, as friends, about the matter; and had expressed a view, during that discussion, which he thought disqualified him from sitting. For that reason, the judge declined to preside over the matter.

I think that, in recusing himself, the judge exhibited very high ethical standards. This is because if he did not care about judicial ethics, he could simply have kept mute about his conversation, with the Attorney General, and gone on to preside over the matter; knowing very well that he held a view that could well have, ultimately, clouded his judgement. I give this example not because Judge Motsagole is my friend; but because his conduct, with regard to that case, epitomized the observance of judicial ethics; which every judge should strive to attain, in carrying out their judicial functions.

Upon appointment a judges relinquishes partisan politics

Another dimension of judicial ethics is that upon appointment, a judge who may have been a politician, prior to appointment, must absolutely and unequivocally cease all political activity, and association, with the assumption of judicial office. A judge who uses the privileged platform of judicial office to engage in partisan political debate risks his, or her, impartiality being doubted; when he, or she, has to preside over a matter in which he has already expressed a view. Speculation of bias often arises with respect to those judges who have formerly held political office. In my experience, some of the speculation is simply paranoia but, in a few instances, there may be substance to perceptions of bias.

I recall that some years back, a judge in Botswana, who used to be an opposition politician, presided over a very partisan dispute. The judge ruled against the ruling party. A prominent lawyer, who was, at the time, a minister of the governing party, remarked to me, half in jest and half seriously, that in truth, they should have known that they stood no chance. Those remarks suggested that the loss of the case, by the ruling party, was on account that they had appeared before a judge who was opposed to them.

Still on the issue of speculation of bias sometimes being without basis, in the year 2018, I spoke to a friend of mine, who is a judge in a country where the opposition had just won a bitterly, and closely contested, election; and there were fears that the Chief Justice, a former politician of the defeated ruling party, would not swear in the new president; as required by law. As it turned out, such fears were unfounded; and the new leader was, seamlessly, sworn into office.

A judge must, as far as is practicably possible, avoid placing himself, or herself, in conflict of interest situations. Such a conflict arises when the personal interests of a judge, or of those close to him, or her, conflict with the judge's duty to adjudicate impartially. Political allegiances, whether actual or perceived, must be avoided. For instance, although members of a judge's family have every right to be politically active, a judge should not be seen to share, or be too close, to the political activities of the family members; in such a manner as to credibly, and objectively, raise issues of potential bias. To this extent, a judge must avoid making donations to a political party.

A judge must also not allow his, or her, financial activities to interfere with the duty to preside over a case that comes before the court. Although some disqualifications will be unavoidable, a judge must reduce unnecessary conflicts of interest that arise when the judge retains financial interest in some business organizations.

A monkey cannot be a judge over the affairs of the forest

It is also unethical, and improper, for a judge to be a judge in his own cause. This is akin to a monkey being a judge over the affairs of the forest. This sacred principle, as developed by the courts, has two similar, but not identical, implications. It may be applied literally; that is to say if a judge is, in fact, a party to the litigation or has an economic interest in its outcome, then he, or she, is indeed sitting as a judge in his, or her, own cause. A judge who is conflicted in this manner is disqualified from sitting; because justice should not only be done but must be seen to be done.

It has been, repeatedly, stated that integrity is central to the function of judgeship; and that a judge's conduct must be beyond reproach. This cannot be over-emphasized. A judge should embody the qualities of a morally upright person.

Essentially, the qualities, conduct and image, that a judge projects, affect those of the judicial system, as a whole, and are critical to engendering public confidence. The public demands, from judges, conduct which is far above what is demanded of their fellow citizens. The standards of conduct, to which judges must adhere, are much higher than those of society as a whole. In fact judges are expected to have, virtually, irreproachable conduct.

A judge must maintain high standards in public life and, in that regard, should not engage in activities that clearly bring disrepute to the courts, or the legal system. Whenever a judge is confronted with a moral dilemma, on any given matter, he, or she, must not do that which he doubts is proper. It has been suggested that the proper inquiry, when faced with an ethical dilemma, is not whether an act is moral, or immoral, or, indeed, whether it is acceptable or unacceptable by community standards. Rather, proper inquiry, in the face of ethical dilemma, should be how the act reflects upon a judge's ability to dispense justice independently and impartially.

A judge cannot alter a judgement after delivering it

In court, a judge is prohibited from altering the decision which he, or she, has given orally; even if the judge may, subsequently, realize that the decision was wrong. This is so because once a decision has been given, it should stand; unless reversed by an appellate court, or properly rescinded by the same court, where the rules permit such a cause of action. It is, however, permissible for a judge to correct poor expression and grammar.

Public scrutiny

By virtue of the sensitivity of judgeship, a judge must expect to be the subject of constant public scrutiny and comment and must, therefore, accept restrictions on his, or her, activities. This might be viewed as unduly burdensome; by the ordinary people. In public spaces, the judge must behave in a manner that engenders confidence in the judicial office that he, or she, holds. A judge must, also, behave with the sensitivity and self-control that is demanded by the judicial office; because a display of injudicious temperament is inconsistent with the dignity of judicial office.

It is inevitable that judges would know, and be friends, with many lawyers. Some of these lawyers may be former class mates at law school. What is required of a judge is to maintain a respectful distance in the manner he, or she, relates to such lawyers. Since judges do not live in ivory towers, but in the real world, they cannot be expected to cut all their ties with the bar. It would be unrealistic for judges to isolate themselves from the rest of society, including from school friends and colleagues in the legal profession. To this end, a judge is not prohibited from attending a function organized by the bar; or to exchange light banter with lawyers. But being seen, regularly, in the company of an attorney may reasonably raise concerns of possible bias; when that lawyer appears before the judge. It is a good practice, and principle, for a judge not to discuss, with any lawyer, the merits or demerits of any case serving before the judge.

Intimacy with a member of the bar

A judge should, generally, refrain from having a personal, or intimate, relationship with a member of the bar; in circumstances in which such relationship may give rise to legitimate concerns. If that cannot be avoided, the judge must, at the very least, exercise extreme caution, and avoid any perception of bias; by a reasonable and well informed bystander. This, however, is easier said than done; because judges are human beings who are entitled to fall in love with whomsoever they choose.

The obvious problem of the appearance of bias, and favouritism, exists when a judge's partner appears before the judge. In such circumstances, the judge is the ultimate arbiter of whether, or not, the relationship is such as to disqualify him, or her, from sitting. The test is whether the romantic relationship interferes with the discharge of the judge's judicial responsibilities; and whether a reasonable and well informed bystander, who is aware of the nature of the social relationship, is likely to entertain significant doubt about justice being done.

When I was doing my last year at Law School, our legal ethics professor used to have a laugh at his time, when he would use his previous life experiences as an example to drum home the importance of ethics. Amidst laughter, he would say "During my time as a legal practitioner, I had a judge as my girl-friend and I would appear, routinely, before her. Do you think it was proper for me to do so; do you think any person who knew of our relationship would believe that justice would be done under those circumstances"? The class would roar, in unison, "No way!" Many of my former class mates would remember this particular professor, with some nostalgia, because even though his lesson, on ethics, was infused with humour, he brought forward a very valid point whose importance, I am certain, remains appreciated to date.

A judge should not preside in cases where he, or she, has close relationships with litigants; as that is a situation which would lead a reasonable bystander to believe that if the judge were to preside, justice would not be done. The rationale for this rule is the promotion of impartiality. It does not need to be over-emphasized that the obvious reason, for discouraging judges from presiding over cases where they have close relationships with litigants, is because litigants with whom a judge is close are in a position to improperly influence the judge in the performance of his, or her, judicial functions. It is, of course, not every familiarity, with a litigant, that should disqualify a judge from sitting.

A judge is only disqualified from presiding in a case in which a close family member is a party to the litigation. It seems plain to me that a judge is, similarly, disqualified, to sit in a case in which a member of the judge's family, or other person in respect of whom the judge is in a fiduciary relationship, is likely to benefit, financially, from a positive outcome of litigation. In such a situation, a judge has no alternative but to disqualify himself, or herself, from presiding.

Abuse of judicial office

Moving on from the topic of impartiality, there is one vice that judges must guard against at all times; and that is the abuse of their judicial office, in any form or manner. A judge should distinguish between proper and improper use of the prestige of judicial office. It is improper for a judge to use, or attempt to use, his or her position to gain personal advantage; or preferential treatment of any kind. A judge should not use his, or her, office to disregard the dictates of the law. For instance, it would be inappropriate for a judge to seek to avoid a traffic fine by pointing out, to the law enforcement officers, that he, or she, is a judge.

Judicial officers should never, in any way, give the impression that they are above the law; and neither should they ever seek directly, or indirectly, to defeat the ends of justice. For a judge to use his, or her, exalted office in an attempt to influence other public officials, in the performance of their lawful duties, is to misuse the prestige of the judicial office. Such conduct is both unethical and unacceptable; for the disrepute that it brings to judicial office.

Judges are not above the law

It is very important to point out that judges are not above the law. They have to obey the law; just like everyone else. Sometimes, judges may be called upon to testify as witnesses. When that happens, a lawyer who regularly appears before that judge may be placed in an awkward position, in terms of cross-examining the judge. The caution to offer judges, who perform witness duty, is that when they find themselves aggressively cross-examined by a lawyer; and, in the process, the lawyer makes uncomfortable insinuations, judges must, in the larger scheme of things, understand that lawyers are expected to represent their clients; to the best of their ability. Judges who have been cross-examined in a manner that they may not appreciate should not, when they next preside in a matter in which the same lawyer, who cross-examined them, appears, seek to humiliate or, otherwise, treat the lawyer unfairly. By the same token, lawyers are well advised not to throw courtesy to the winds when they cross-examine judges. They should not use cross-examination as an opportunity to humiliate, or unduly harass, and embarrass judges; or to settle scores with them. While judges are not above the law, they hold an office that entitles them to some respect.

Academically inclined judges

Some judges are academically inclined; and write books. When a judge writes or contributes to a publication, whether related or unrelated to the law, such a judge should not permit anyone associated with the publication to exploit his or her office. On occasion, lawyers may seek to use the views expressed by a judge, in a book, as a ground to disqualify the judge from presiding over a case. Others may use the views that the judge expresses, in a book, to good effect; by attempting to persuade the judge to act consistently with those views. I experienced the latter, once, in Kenya, when I had gone there on a Trial Observation Mission; by the Africa Judges and Jurists Forum. A lawyer made reference to a published article, by the Chief Justice, in which he critiqued a previous decision of the same court; before he became its member and later the head of that court.

In the course of performing judicial duties, a judge may acquire information of commercial, or other, value that is unavailable to the public. In such instances, the judge must not reveal, or use, such information for personal gain; or for any purpose unrelated to judicial duties.

Increasingly, there is growing acceptance that judges must keep abreast with developments in the law. A judge is in the unique position to contribute to the improvement of the law, the legal system and the administration of justice; both within and outside of the judge's jurisdiction. Such contributions may take the form of speaking, writing, teaching or participating in other extra-judicial activities. To the extent that time permits, a judge is encouraged to undertake such activities. A judge may, also, contribute to legal and professional education; by delivering lectures, participating in conferences and seminars, judging moots and acting as an examiner.

Judges are intellectual leaders

It is my view that judges, as intellectual leaders of their communities, must be encouraged to write books; and share their experiences with the public. A judge may also contribute to legal literature as an author or editor. Such professional activities, by judges, are in the public interest; and are to be encouraged. However, a judge should make it clear that comments made in an educational forum are not intended as advisory opinions; or commitments to a particular legal position in a court proceeding. Until evidence is presented, arguments heard and when necessary, research is completed, a judge cannot weigh the competing evidence and arguments impartially; nor can he, or she, form a definitive judicial opinion.

Judges chairing independent bodies

Judges are often called upon to chair independent bodies; such as Electoral Management Bodies and Commissions of Enquiry. In some countries, it has been suggested that judges should not be deployed to bodies such as Electoral Management Bodies; as that may compromise their independence. There is, however, no consensus on this concern. Some countries in Southern Africa still deploy judges to chair the Electoral Management Bodies; or to head Constituency Delimitation Commissions or Commissions of Enquiry. In considering an assignment to be a member, or chair, of any of the above bodies, a judge should think very carefully about the implications, on judicial independence, of accepting the assignment. There are examples of judges becoming embroiled in public controversy and being criticized and embarrassed; following the publication of reports of Commissions of Enquiry on which they have served.

The terms of reference and other conditions, such as time and resources, should be examined, carefully, so as to assess their compatibility with the judicial function; bearing in mind that the function of a Commission of Enquiry belongs not to the judicial, but to the executive sphere. The function of enquiry, is one of investigating and ascertaining, for the information of the executive, facts on which appropriate action may be taken. Such action may, well, involve proceedings either of a civil or criminal nature, in the courts, against individuals whose conduct has been investigated by a commission. Like all executive action, the proceedings and findings of a Commission of Enquiry may properly be, and frequently are, the subject of public controversy.

Community activities

Despite the demands of their office, judges are at liberty to participate in community activities. Examples include charitable organizations, university and school councils, religious bodies, social clubs, sporting organizations and organizations that promote cultural, or artistic, interests. However, in relation to such participation, the following matters should be borne in mind:

- A judge should ensure that membership to those bodies does not make excessive demands on his, or her, time.

- A judge should refrain from being legal adviser; as this may bring a judge into a conflict of interest situations; if a matter, in which the judge had given a legal opinion, should come to court; and be allocated to the particular judge.

- A judge should not personally become involved in, or lend his, or her, name to any fund raising activities.

- A judge should not hold membership in any organization that practices discrimination on the basis of race, sex, religion or national origin; because such membership gives rise to perceptions that the judge's impartiality is impaired.

While there may not be too much of a challenge in judges' participation in the events alluded to, above, the matter of their involvement in business is a little more problematic. Many countries require judges to register their business interests. Quite obviously, a judge cannot be active in a business enterprise; without risking compromising his, or her, independence. A judge's participation in a family business, while generally permissible, should be avoided if it takes too much time, or involves the misuse of judicial prestige, or if any issue to do with the business is likely to come before the judge's court. It is not advisable for a judge to serve on the board of directors of a commercial enterprise, that is to say, a company whose objects are profit related. This applies to both public and private companies; whether the directorship is executive or non- executive, and whether it is remunerated or not.

Conflict of interest

A judge should not act as arbitrator, or mediator, or otherwise perform judicial functions in a private capacity; unless authorized by law. The integrity of the judiciary is undermined when a judge takes financial advantage of judicial office; by rendering private dispute resolution services for pecuniary gain, as an extra-judicial activity.

Even when performed without charge, such services may interfere with the proper performance of judicial functions.

A judge should neither ask for, nor accept, any gift; in relation to anything done, or to be done or omitted to be done, by the judge, in connection with the performance of judicial duties. The prohibition does not include:

- Ordinary social hospitality that is common in the judge's community, extended for a non-business purpose, by an individual not a corporation, and limited to the provision of modest items such as food and refreshment;

- Items with little intrinsic value intended solely for presentation, such as plaques, certificates, trophies and greeting cards;

- Loans from banks and other financial institutions, on terms that are available based on factors other than judicial status;

- Opportunities and benefits, including favourable rates and commercial discounts, that are available based on factors other than judicial status;

A judge is not prohibited from accepting honoraria, or speaking fees, provided that the compensation is reasonable and commensurate with the task performed. These days, judges travel the globe to attend conferences and they are often given subsistence allowances, by conference organizers, and no one ever suggests that that may compromise their independence. However, receiving honoraria in a domestic setting may not be advisable; as it may compromise the independence of a judge. It is also advisable that a judge should not spend significant time away from court duties, in order to meet speaking or writing commitments; for compensation. In addition to this, the source of the payment must not arise any question of undue influence; or the judge's ability, or willingness, to be impartial.

It cannot be over-emphasized that judges should maintain the dignity of judicial office, at all times, and that they must avoid both impropriety and the appearance of impropriety, in their professional and personal lives. Judges should aspire, at all times, to maintain conduct that ensures the greatest possible public confidence in their independence, impartiality, integrity, and competence. In this digital age, the power of public confidence is swiftly, and mercilessly, wielded using social media. Perceived infractions, that would tarnish the image of a judicial officer, are a simple WhatsApp share away; thereby making it that much trickier to live up to the yardstick of the appearance of ethics; and not just the actual maintaining of ethics.

In conclusion, it is safe to say it is difficult to prescribe a uniform code of conduct, as the circumstances of each country may differ. However, the fundamental principles that inform the judicial codes of conduct remain the same. The ideal judicial conduct, in any setting, is based on a set of values which should govern judicial conduct; in the performance of judicial function. The content and extent of the said values are, hopefully, determined by, and amongst, the judges themselves. Ideally, the values should respond to and reflect public confidence and, therefore, implicate the social context of every country. This should be so because the judiciary does not exist in isolation. It is an institution of particular societies.

Chapter Ten

STATUTORY AND CONSTITUTIONAL INTERPRETATION

. . . .

Most disputes are resolved through interpretation. It is difficult to define in precise terms what, exactly, interpretation means; but many would agree with the suggestion that interpretation involves the process of giving meaning to a legal text. This may pertain to rules of court, an employment contract, a will, a statute or constitution. In other words, interpretation is about giving meaning to words employed in a legal text.

Transformation of words

The judge, in the process of interpreting legal texts, transforms static texts into dynamic words that have consequences. This often happens when the law is vague, inconsistent or if there is a gap in the law. Interpretation can be a very complex exercise that is pregnant with the possibility of diverse, or multiple, conclusions. The conclusions arrived at may depend on which approach to interpretation the judge is persuaded to adopt. Some of the approaches, to statutory interpretation, are discussed in this chapter.

Interpretation is a contested terrain

Some scholars contend that there is a fundamental difference between interpreting and filling a gap. They argue that whilst interpretation gives meaning to a text, gap filling subtracts from or adds to the text; by way of analogy or by applying the system's fundamental values. According to this school of thought, a gap in a text exists when its interpretation leads to the conclusion that the absence of a solution, to the identified problem, conflicts with the purpose of text.

The difficult question that often confronts judges is whether or not there is a reliable, and coherent, system of interpretation; which does not occasion undue violence to the text. Legal history, as scholars would readily testify, is replete with many systems of interpretation. The challenge that faces all systems of interpretation is the limitation of language; and what happens when the plain language seems to be unsupported by the context. Context in law is important; with some saying it is everything. What I am prepared to say is that all interpretative systems must tow a fine line between the real, and hypothetical, intention of the author.

A coherent theory of interpretation is extremely important; in that it yields predictable results and brings integrity to the law. As a judge serving in a common law jurisdiction, I cannot say that there is a coherent theory of interpretation; that may be applied to diverse interpretative situations. This is troubling, in the extreme, because interpretation is a judge's primary tool for pronouncing what the law says, in differing circumstances. Over the years, judges have articulated their understanding about what interpretation involves, and its purpose. Quite often, the question that presents itself, when dealing with interpretation of legal texts, is what the purpose of interpretation is.

Lord Denning is famous for having once said that in a case involving statutory interpretation, judges try their best to find out the intention of parliament and of ministers, and carry it out. He observed that this is better done by filling in the gaps, and making sense of the enactment, rather than by opening it up to destructive analysis. This much is partly true but, certainly, not the whole truth. There may be many other factors to be considered; other than finding the intention of parliament.

Lord Simonds, of the House of Lords, in the United Kingdom, then considered as the ideological rival of Lord Denning, had a radically different opinion to that of Lord Denning. Lord Simonds took the view that the general preposition, namely that it was the duty of the court to find out the intention of parliament could not, by any means, be supported. He maintained that the duty of the court was to interpret the words that the legislature has used. He was, also, opposed to the view, championed by Lord Denning, that the court, having discovered the intentions of parliament, must proceed to fill in the gaps; and argued that this amounted, in effect, to saying that 'what the legislature has not written, the court must write'. Lord Simonds rejected this preposition on the basis that it amounted to a naked usurpation of the legislative function, under the thin disguise of interpretation.

On the whole, courts all over the world either take the view of Lord Denning, or Lord Simonds, or a combination of both; to varying degrees. For instance, the Canadian courts have also been torn between the two schools of thoughts. In my personal view, the answer to the question posed, earlier, on the purpose of interpretation, would depend on the circumstances of each case. In a contract between two individuals, the purpose may be to discern the true intention of the parties; and when dealing with a statute it may be to realize the purpose of the law. If it is a statute that falls for determination, issues such as the purpose, for which the law was designed or intended to achieve, or what mischief it was intended to address, may loom large.

Those who have been servants of the law for a long time would, readily, testify that the journey of the law is a never ending struggle to strike a proper balance between social goals, intended to be achieved by legislation, and the context. This is so because a statute can never be considered in isolation. It exits in the context of society, and as part of general social activity. It is also known, to seasoned judges, that there is no single meaning, to a single word, in a statute. It is possible that the term 'may', in one statute, may be permissive, and while in another, it may be mandatory.

In my experience, the concept of 'purpose' is normative legal construct. The purpose of a particular text may contain both subjective and objective elements. While the real intent of the author is important, to discern, it may not be decisive; because the objective elements may force a conclusion that departs from the subjective intention of the author.

On occasion, the intention of the legislative body receives imperfect expression, from the author, and it then becomes necessary for judges, having regard to relevant objective factors, to make sure that the logically defective letter of the enacted law should be made logically perfect. This is so as to give effect to the legislative intention which may be gathered from the context, and other compelling objective circumstances.

In considering the meaning of a text in a statute, the function of a court of law is to construe the language of the legislature and to ponder, to the extent necessary, the social goal that the legislation was intended to achieve. Another function of a court is to consider whether any other interpretation, of the legal text, would lead to an absurdity. The court must, thereafter, pronounce what the meaning of the law is. It is notorious that the cannons of statutory interpretation are, more often than not, a body of rules that overlap, and even contradict, one another. In the final analysis, the cannon of interpretation, that should be applied, depend on the exigencies of each other.

The legal fraternity is all too familiar with what is called the 'literal' rule. In its pure form, this approach enjoins the courts, when interpreting statues, to concentrate, primarily, on the literal meaning of the provision to be interpreted. The literal rule is, by far, the most important rule to guide the courts in arriving at the intention of parliament. This is done by scrutinizing the language of the instrument, as a whole, and, when the words are clear and unambiguous, to place their grammatical construction upon them; and give them their ordinary effect. The literal rule, basically, enjoins the courts to give effect to clear, and unambiguous, words that are used in a statute. In terms of this rule, which is often called the 'golden rule', if the words that are used in a statute are vague, or if strict literal interpretation would result in absurd results, then the court may deviate from the literal meaning of the word, in order to avoid absurdity.

The literal rule regards the ordinary, grammatical, meaning of the text to be analogous to the intention of the legislature; which is a decisive factor in construing statutes. It has been held, in a number of cases, that if the legislature had a specific intention, it would be reflected in the clear and unambiguous words of text. The literal rule of interpretation of statutes, attempts to minimize, as far as possible, the discretion of the courts. This is because it is said that the function of the courts is interpret the law; and not to make it. Essentially, if the words of the statute are, in themselves, precise and unambiguous, then effect must be given to them. There are, however, situations where clear and unambiguous words may appear to be at variance with the legislative intention.

According to another canon of interpretation, called contextual or purposive approach, an attempt must be made; to ascertain the intention of parliament. In terms of this approach, the purpose of legislation is the prevailing factor in interpretation. The text, context and objectives of the Act, or statute, are taken into account, so as to establish the purpose of legislation. This approach usually involves a rule of interpretation called the 'mischief rule'. The mischief rule includes the application of external aids i.e. the law prior to the problem in question, defects in the law and the mischief that was intended to be addressed by the legislation. It also includes new remedies, proposed, and the reasons for such remedies. The contextual approach obliges the court to examine all the contextual factors in ascertaining the intention of the legislature. This is irrespective of whether, or not, the words of the legislation are clear and unambiguous.

According to the contextual approach, if the literal interpretation, of a statute, leads to a result which the legislature could not have intended, the courts must reject that interpretation; and seek another that can give effect to the intention of parliament. In this regard, it appears, to me, to be fair to indicate that the concept of 'the intention of parliament' is problematic because, popularly understood, it may signify anything from an intention embodied in positive enactment, to speculative opinion as to what the legislature probably would have meant. In my respectful view, to depart from the literal interpretation, on account that to follow it may lead to absurdity, requires that the absurdity must be glaring, and the intention of the legislature must be clear; and not a mere matter of surmise or probability.

The purposive approach accepts that the courts can make modifications to an Act; if that would best achieve the intentions of the legislature. However, such modification is only possible if, and when, the scope and purpose of legislation is absolutely clear; and it also supports such modification. In such circumstances, modification would not be an infringement of the legislature's function to legislate. It would only be a logical extension of the powers of the court.

The purposive approach does, however, have several limitations. Firstly, it must be possible to determine, from a consideration of the provision of the Act, and read as a whole, the mischief that the Act was supposed to remedy. Secondly, it must be apparent that the draftsman, and parliament, had by inadvertence overlooked, and so omitted, to deal with a particular matter that required to be dealt with; if the purpose of the Act was to be achieved. Thirdly, it must be possible to state, with certainty, what the additional words were that would have been inserted, by the draftsman, and approved by parliament, had their attention been drawn to the omission before the Bill passed into law.

It is the position of the law that, unless this third condition is fulfilled, any attempt, by a court, to repair the omission, in the Act, cannot be justified as an exercise of its jurisdiction to determine the meaning of a written law; which parliament has passed. Such an attempt crosses the boundary between construction and legislation. It becomes a usurpation of the function of the legislature.

I alluded, earlier, to how central the mischief rule is, to the purposive approach. The mischief rule attempts to answer the following questions:

1. What was the law before the measure was passed?

2. What was the mischief, or defect, for which the law had provided?

3. What remedy did the legislator appoint?

4. What was the reason for the remedy?

The mischief rule is now of almost universal application. It is useful for avoiding manifest absurdity, or repugnance, arising out of rigid adherence to the literal rule of interpretation. The mischief rule appears, to me, to be particularly relevant; as it enables the courts to apply the principles of justice, equity and good conscience; in realizing the objectives of the Act, or statute, that is being interpreted. Alongside the rules of interpretation, that have been discussed, there are some useful guidelines, for interpretation, called presumptions. These guidelines form the material foundation of statutory interpretation; and are useful in helping to determine the scope and object, or purpose, of the particular provision. In the premises, a brief over-view of these presumptions is in order.

There are three important presumptions worthy of discussion. Firstly, there is the presumption that legislation does not contain futile, or meaningless, provisions. This presumption forms the crux, and basis, of the most important principle of interpretation. It is imperative upon a court of law to determine the purpose of the legislation, and give it effect. As a matter of general judicial approach, the courts often take the view that futile legislation has to be avoided; and that an attempt should be made to promote the 'business efficacy' of a provision. This presumption relates to the reasonable and logical thought processes of the legislature. It is a presumption that the courts endeavour to uphold consistently.

The second presumption is that a statute should not be construed so as to oust, or restrict, the jurisdiction of the courts. This is an important presumption; because it is the function of the courts of law, whenever their jurisdiction is invoked, to adjudicate disputes; whether of fact or law, arising between citizens, amongst themselves, or between citizens and officers of the state, or other administrative authorities. Thus, there is a presumption against interpretation of statutes that would have the effect of excluding the jurisdiction of the courts.

The third presumption is that the legislature does not intend that which is harsh, unjust or unreasonable. This presumption is applied to the interpretation of statutes on the basis that every legal system strives to achieve standards of reasonableness, justice and fairness; and that the law-making organ of the system must, thus, be presumed to enact laws with this aim in mind. As a general rule, where two meanings may be given to a section, and one meaning leads to harshness and injustice, whilst the other does not, the court will hold that the legislature, rather, intended for the milder meaning; than the harsher meaning to prevail.

Having shed light on the interpretation of statutes, in general, it is important to bring out the fact that interpreting a constitution is different from interpreting an ordinary statute; because of the nature, and character, of a constitution. There are many things to be said about a constitution. To begin with, a constitution is, unquestionably, a unique document; as it lays down the architecture of the state, its political and social views and, its values.

A constitution determines the commitments of the state and its orientations. It is a promissory note; of a unique and superior character. The superiority of this document is such that it is difficult to amend; for the reason that a constitution is meant to direct society for years to come. A constitution usually places the judiciary at the helm of its existence; both as its custodian and guardian. As guardians of the constitution, judges should be mindful of the fact that they are partners to the constitutional enterprise. They are duty bound to interpret the constitution so as to ensure its continued relevance to society. The purpose of the constitution, as an organic instrument, is to provide an enduring framework for the legitimate exercise of governmental power, both for the present and in the future.

The task of interpreting a constitution requires an understanding of its nature and character. In interpreting a constitution, a judge, just like for a statute, assigns a meaning to a legal text. The judges who interpret the constitution must always be mindful of the fact that its language changes with time; because a constitution is a living document. It is, precisely, because of the constitution being a living document, that it would be incorrect to read it with the mindset of the past. Judges interpreting the constitution must look to history; but at the same time, must not be enslaved by the meaning that was appropriate at that time. In their interpretation of the constitution, judges must ask the all-important and decisive question: 'what is the meaning of the legal text in our time?' It is, fundamentally, because a constitution is a living document that it must be able to provide relevant solutions to all stages of society; as it matures. For its part, the role of the judiciary is that it must breathe life into it, ensuring that the constitution remains relevant to the lives of the people whom it is meant to serve.

The genius of the constitution lies in its elasticity and organic nature. It is, precisely, because of its being organic, in nature that a constitution should not be allowed to 'talk' in the language of the past. A constitution must be able to adapt to the changing circumstances of contemporary times. What this means is that generations, yet to be born, must find a constitution, which was crafted long before they were born, fundamentally relevant to their challenges and reality.

A constitution is sacred document; which should never be turned into a playing field, by anyone. The judges who interpret it must be learned and independent. They must be part of an independent, and impartial, judiciary which is not just insulated from the passions of the moment, and the pressures occasioned by the ebb, and flow of politics, but is best placed to render decisions without fear or favour.

Alexander Hamilton said, independent courts serve as an "excellent barrier to the encroachments and oppressions of the representative body," and they play a "peculiarly essential" role in safeguarding individual rights and liberties. On the other hand, "the judiciary has no influence over either the sword or the purse"; it has neither force, nor will, but merely judgment.

There are, in theory, many models of constitutional interpretation; namely, doctrinal, which based on judicial precedents, textual, which is based on the provisions of the constitution, judicial restraint, positing that judges must be restrained when interpreting the law and prudential interpretation, which is based on cost and benefit analysis. It is generally accepted that in interpreting the constitutional guarantees of human rights and freedoms, the court must adopt a generous approach to constitutional construction, on the basis that a constitution must be regarded as a living document; and the meaning of its provisions may change, with time, as society evolves.

It is an accepted truism, in constitutional construction, that the bill of rights, in a constitution, is a declaration of values and that the constitution, as the supreme law, is the compass that guides society, in times of peace and societal stress and tension. It is equally true that a bill of rights is a statement of the nation's concept of the society it hopes to achieve, and that it is the duty of the court to make it identifiable as such. In most cases, the words used in a constitution are, necessarily, general. The exact meaning of those words can, often, be understood in the context of the dynamic of time, and as society evolves. Time, invariably, illuminates the meaning of words and, when this happens, it does not mean that the words used change; but only that the dynamic of time assigns new meaning to the words used.

It would be retrogressive thinking to consider that a document as general as the constitution, crafted with an eye for the future, and meant to be enduring, should not be interpreted progressively.

The question of whether, or not, a particular piece of legislation, policy or act violates the terms of a constitution requires an objective assessment; for the precise reason that the constitution is a dynamic document. The assessment must be informed by the text, the scheme of the constitution, the contemporary norms, aspirations and the emerging consensus of values in the civilized community of nations. Additionally, the assessment must be informed by the expectations and sensitivities of the society that the constitution is meant to govern; with the result that on some occasions, a cost benefit analysis easily commends itself.

A constitution cannot be interpreted in a vacuum

A very significant point, of note, is that a constitution cannot be interpreted in a vacuum. The process of constitutional interpretation must be context- sensitive. It may well be that, depending on the issue to be resolved, one method, or a combination of methods in varying degree, commends itself. In interpreting a constitution, it is not advisable to treat a particular provision in isolation; or divorced from the broader scheme of the constitution. As has already been indicated, it is the pre-eminent function of the judiciary to keep a constitution alive and relevant. For that reason, the judiciary has the heavy responsibility not to interpret the constitution in a manner which may cause it to cease serving the interests of society. The beauty of the constitution rests not in any static meaning, that the founders may have found appropriate at the time, nor does it depend on the meaning it might have had in a world that is dead and gone. Rather, it rests in the adaptability of its principles and values to cope with current problems and needs.

The concept of values is hardly unpacked. It is important to say that when we speak of values, in the context of interpreting a constitution, we do not mean the personal values of a judge. We mean the values of a society; as a whole. The values of a constitutional democratic society include, among others, liberty, defined as our right to think, act, or behave without undue or unjustified interference from our government and the right to pursue happiness, subject to respect of other people's rights. Other societal values are unity of purpose, to achieve the common good, self-determination, sovereignty and being fair to each other; as citizens and as persons. Yet other values are treating each other equally, where such does not occasion any injustice to anyone and respecting difference, truth, order and peace.

The listed values constitute the national consensus that underlies, and underwrites, the legal system to which the courts, as the guardians of the constitution, must give effect; as they interpret the constitution. Judges who interpret the constitution derive these values both from the constitutional text, and the history of a nation. Thus, no one should read the constitution with an expectation that he, or she, will find the values listed in some chronological order; in some section, or page, of the constitution. Some of the values are expressed, but others are implied; or are to be deduced from the structure of the constitution and the history of a people.

The voice of the judiciary on constitutional questions must, ultimately, draw its authority from the public's acceptance of its institutional role; even when its specific decisions are controversial. A court's judgements must reflect the nation's best understanding of its fundamental values. It is often said that the power of great constitutional decisions rests upon the accuracy of the court's perception of this kind of common will; and upon the court's ability, by expressing its perception to, ultimately, command a consensus.

In interpreting and applying the constitution, the judiciary must be independent from politics and must reflect the values of the constitution, in order to secure the democratic legitimacy of its decision. In interpreting the constitution, a judge must pay heed, not only to the text, but to the values of the constitution. He, or she, must also be consistent; and not render an interpretation that renders the constitution unpredictable. Inconsistency, in constitutional interpretation, is a form of infidelity.

The metaphor, of a 'living constitution', misleadingly, suggests that the constitution, itself, is the primary site of legal evolution, in response to societal change; and that the constitution can come to mean whatever a sufficient number of people think it ought to mean. It must be clear, though, that to say a constitution is a living organism does not, in any way, suggest that a constitution has no enduring character; because it, most certainly does. The meaning, and interpretation, assigned to particular provisions of the constitution may change, but the constitution, itself, does not change; until it is properly amended.

There has never been, and can never be, one, and only one, legitimate mechanical and timeless way to derive constitutional meaning. Notably, the constitution, itself, does not prescribe a specific method of interpretation of its provisions. Interpreting the constitutional text and principles, in light of changing norms and social consequences, is not radical. If there is anything radical, at all, it is the insistence, by some scholars and judges, that the meaning of a constitution must remain static; and divorced from contemporary context.

As a matter of general rule, in giving appropriate meaning to the constitution, the courts usually adopt a multi-pronged approach; which considers diverse considerations such as the constitution's history, text, values, purpose and structure. To this extent, at least two approaches are discernible, from the case law and constitutional literature. There are authorities of respectable lineage that suggest that constitutional meaning is a function of both text and context. In many instances, a court cannot be faithful to the principle embodied in the text; unless it takes into account the social context in which the text is interpreted.

Most judges, in constitutional democracies, take an oath, upon appointment, to be loyal to the constitution. A question may be posed as to why there is need for loyalty to the constitution. The simple answer is that fidelity to the constitution serves, not only to preserve its meaning over time, but also to maintain the constitution's authority and legitimacy. The words and principles of the constitution endure, as our fundamental law, because they have been made relevant to the conditions and challenges of each generation; through an ongoing process of interpretation.

Some judges, and lawyers, believe that a judge should interpret the law based on the original meaning of a constitutional text. This method of interpretation is called textualism, or originalism. Textualism, as the name suggests, looks for meaning, of the law, in the text, itself. A key part of this process is to ascribe, to the constitutional text, the meaning it has borne since the time that it was adopted. In other words, originalism gives the original meaning of the text; rather than a new meaning that may shift unpredictably. The textualists, or originalists, argue that the original meaning should be the preferred method of constitutional interpretation; because in a democracy, the law passed by the legislature should be binding; and should not be the preference of a judge.

Originalism is the approach to constitutional interpretation that gives weight to the intentions of the original authors of the constitution. Originalism requires a judge, who is confronted with a constitutional dispute, to ask how informed individuals, living at the time that the constitution was ratified, would have applied it to a similar dispute. Originalism ignores the evolving nature of society, and the significance of the dynamism of time to constitutional interpretation. As a society evolves, its understanding, and application, of constitutional principles deepens; and the notion of expansive interpretation of rights gains traction.

Judicial restraint is a constitutional interpretation approach that urges judges to be restrained, in interpreting the constitution. It is the opposite of judicial activism; which is considered to be an unacceptable way of using judicial power to achieve personal and even partisan objectives; by conservative jurists. Interestingly, the proponents of strict construction hardly provide a clear definition of the term. It is often said that judges should not 'legislate from the bench' and should not 'make law' but should, instead, apply it. Beyond these agreeable platitudes, strict constructionists seem to suggest a method of interpretation that takes the words of the constitution literally. Proponents of strict construction argue that judges must read the constitution to simply mean what is says; nothing more and nothing less. They contend that strict construction limits judicial discretion. With the greatest of respect to its proponents, strict construction is unattractive; to the extent that it suggests that judges should be enslaved by the text; and that they should not pay heed to other considerations such as purpose, or values of the constitution. If it is to be of any benefit to society, a text should be construed reasonably, and not strictly, for the purposes of realizing the core values of the constitution.

A constitution is a living organism

By its nature, a constitution is intended to stand the test of time and endure for ages and, as such, judges should not, unduly, water down its potency and dynamism. It is safe to make the observation that, generally and save for societies that are in transition, each generation lives under a constitution that it inherited. But inevitably, and with time, notions of original meaning gradually sink into the annals of history. I think it is just as safe to observe that as society evolves, the people and its judges may find the constitutional text meanings of yesteryear ill-suited for the problems, and challenges, of the present day. When this happens, the intention of the originators of the constitution becomes less relevant as time goes on.

Chapter Eleven

JUDICIAL CASE MANAGEMENT

Having walked the reader through a number of critical issues surrounding judgeship, it is time to address another important issue, namely judicial case management, which judges have to deal with on an increasing scale, especially in today's contemporary society. It cannot be denied that the rate, at which people are litigating, in many countries, is increasing. In some jurisdictions, this is happening at an alarming rate; and the courts are, literally, struggling to dispense justice as quickly as possible.

As a result of this development, many countries have a backlog, of unfinished cases, which runs into years. This state of affairs does not sit well with the notion of access to justice as a human right. In the words of Lord Macaulay; if justice is a human right, and it is, then easy and inexpensive access to judicial justice is a fundamental pre-condition.

Case management is an imperative of our time

In order to dispense justice speedily, and cheaply, many countries have introduced some techniques on judicial case management; in terms of which judges try to manage cases efficiently, resulting in the timely delivery of judgements. The aim of this chapter is to describe case management;

and how to take control of a docket. It is aimed, primarily, at judges and not the general readership. But the general readership may, also, benefit from reading the chapter; as it will give them an idea of how judges should manage cases that are serving before them. I also highlight the principles that underpin judicial case management.

Essentially, case management is better demonstrated than defined. To that extent, it is like driving; in that it is better taught by demonstration. The term 'case management' is described as a 'managed process of managing cases'; from registration to disposal. It is a process in terms of which cases progress from one phase to another in a timely, and organized, fashion; which ascribes timelines to each key stage. At all these stages, which are often characterized by pre-trial conferences, is the expectation of an open approach to litigation; by which parties disclose all relevant material, that is important, in order to ensure that cases are dealt with expeditiously, by the courts.

In all jurisdictions where judicial case management is in place, the common expectation is high efficiency. It is expected that cases would be processed expeditiously, based on the principle of first come first served, and that cases are not delayed by technical procedural objections; when they are supposed to be heard. This means that there is a designated phase to deal with technical objections; so that they do not delay the matter, once a date of trial is fixed, and the matter is due to be heard on the merits. Efficiency and fairness ensure that the costs of litigation are kept to the very minimum.

It has been shown that, in order for judicial case management to work efficiently, and as it should, the directions, and timelines, that the judges give must be obeyed; and there should be effective sanctions in cases of unwarranted non-compliance that occasions unnecessary postponements. To this extent, and in order to avoid sanctions, the parties need to be encouraged to cooperate, and talk to each other. They should not just meet in court, sometimes with no idea as to what has brought them there; and yet others not even knowing who they represent. This is no exaggeration. It happens, quite frequently, and I, personally, have seen it happen; and have reprimanded lawyers for such conduct.

One abiding lesson, that is highly instructive when dealing with managing cases, is that speedy, and cheap, disposal of cases does not happen where the courts, routinely, grant adjournments; without the party requesting the adjournments giving good, and valid, reasons for seeking to postpone the matter. Some jurisdictions have admirably developed adjournments policy that help promote consistency in the manner in which the courts deal with adjournments.

I am aware that not all jurisdictions practice judicial case management; and that those who do, do not necessarily have similar rules or approaches. The emphasis of the discussion will, therefore, be on the principles and philosophy of case management. It may be proper to give some examples from the jurisdictions I am familiar with; these being Botswana and Papua New Guinea. Judicial Officers have a duty to exercise judicial authority, with commitment to service. They must be accountable for their decisions and must, also, promote public interest in judicial work. Servants of the law must act impartially and objectively.

The essence of case management, and/or individual docket management, is so as to render each judge responsible for the management of their own cases; from commencement to finalisation. The system aims to promote more proactive, and effective, judicial case management; in order to streamline processing. It is also designed to encourage early settlement, of cases, and overall, to dispose of cases more efficiently and speedily.

Before setting out its principles, it may be helpful to briefly discuss the genesis of judicial case management. In doing this, and for ease of reference, I shall draw, in part, on my own experiences. I was called to the bar in 1989, and was inducted into a system in which lawyers were in charge of the pace of litigation. I understand that this has been so for centuries; at least in the Commonwealth. It suffices to say that this system of litigating, in which lawyers controlled the pace of litigation, proved inefficient in most parts of the world where it was practiced.

The old system in which lawyers drove the pace of litigation was highly inefficient. Delays became all too frequent, and litigation also became very tedious and expensive. Pleadings were exchanged over a protracted period, with no sense of purpose, or urgency, at all. Cases would often stall for years; in the worst cases. After pleadings closed, some more delays would ensue. A pre-trial conference was a mere formality; and trial dates were allocated a long way off; only to end up being abandoned continuously. In fact, postponements were the chief enemy of progress.

As a result of inefficiencies, in the system, the confidence of the public, in the efficient and speedy resolution of disputes, waned. People were no longer keen to use the courts; and that prompted many countries to start reforming their systems. Progress was recorded but, still, the overall situation was unsatisfactory.

The breakthrough

The breakthrough came in the USA, in the 1970's, with the emergence of case-flow management. The techniques, that were introduced, put the individual judge in charge of the management of his, or her, cases. The role of lawyers was minimized, if not eliminated. New rules were formulated, that included pre-trial meetings intended to eliminate delays, and get rid of the back log of cases; especially old cases that were just clogging the system. Most countries also amended their rules, of practice, to allow for mediation in appropriate cases.

Essentially, the driving idea of the reforms was to remove the control of the pace of litigation from litigants, and their lawyers, and to place it in the hands of the courts. This was to be either in the hands of a court administrator, in the early phases, and then a managing judge, thereafter, or in the hands of a judge from an early stage. The reforms to enhance the efficiency of court process, by giving the central power, to progress matters, to the judge, accompanied by alternative dispute resolution mechanisms (ADR) gained ground in many countries; such as the United State of America, the United Kingdom, Australia and other Commonwealth jurisdictions.

Although different countries practice different versions of judicial case management system, the core fundamental principles are the same. These are:

- Judges drive the litigation process.

- Use of trial scheduling practices, and adopting postponement policies to create an expectation for all.

- Ensuring that firm and credible dates for trials are fixed and trials proceed as scheduled.

- Emphasis on readiness to try cases rather than settle cases as an inducement to settle.

- Creating a conducive environment promotional of settlement of issues by litigants

- Increase in judicial accountability and productivity.

- Speedy resolution of cases

- Reduce legal costs by increasing efficiency and reducing delay and, thereby, improving access to the courts; and to justice for more people.

Case management in Botswana

It is tempting to illustrate how judicial case management works; by giving examples of Botswana, which I have some knowledge of. In Botswana, the previous system left litigation in the hands of lawyers and litigants; who dictated the pace. Cases were taking long to be processed; and no one was holding the lawyers accountable. In a number of cases it suited lawyers to delay matters. Judges were only allocated cases on the eve of a trial. One of the consequences of this laxity was that lawyers hardly prepared for trials in advance. Many would come to court late, which triggered postponements. Some lawyers would not take full instructions; and judges were helpless to do anything. They couldn't sanction the lawyers because the rules of court did not make provision for that. So, invariably, preparation was left to the last moment.

On the eve of the trial, witnesses would only be consulted and discovery then made. In a number of cases, it often dawned, on lawyers, on the eve of a trial, that they would need expert evidence. In my experience, this usually happened in cases allocated a week, or more, for trial; mostly because the issues involved would be complex. Invariably, counsel was briefed close to the trial date. Inadequate discovery, or pleadings only then identified, required belated discovery and/or amendments; with the inevitable result being postponements, if the case was not settled.

A further cause of delay was occasioned by interlocutory applications, which would often be sprung upon the adversary without much thought; let alone following the rules. On a few occasions, the substance of some would make sense; but the required forms prescribed by the rules, would be wanting.

An accumulation of all these problems, communicated the clear message to the leadership of the judiciary, that the time for reform, had clearly, arisen. The Chief Justice embarked on formal consultations with the judges, the magistracy and the law society; and an agreement was eventually reached, despite initial resistance, that change was required. The rules were first amended in 2008, and on a few occasions, thereafter, to build into the rules, lessons learnt. When judicial case management was implemented, in Botswana, in the year 2008, it was envisaged that, at some point, there would be court controlled mediation. However, that issue is still pending; and is the remaining phase of the judicial case management project in Botswana.

Judicial case management is founded upon the compelling public interest to ensure that scarce judicial resources are better employed. Increasingly, many jurisdictions are realizing that judicial time is a prime national resource; which must be used, and managed, prudently. The rule of law depends as much on judges' time, as it does on progressive legal prescriptions. Judicial time can be unlocked with judges properly managing cases, and ensuring that every litigant is heard within the allocated time. Most judges, in Botswana, would readily testify that, generally, judicial case management has been a huge success. At times, and inevitably so, the wheels of justice may be slowed down by lawyers who do not want to litigate by the rules.

My experience, over the years, has been that cases are being finalised far quicker, and more efficiently, because of the intervention, and control, by managing judges. Judicial case management, markedly, reduced delays in litigation; but did not entirely eliminate them.

An example that I always cite is the reduction in the load of a judge; in terms of backlog. When I joined the High Court in 2005, it was not uncommon for judges to have a backlog of cases running into thousands. Some of these would have been registered in the preceding five years, or so, but would still be awaiting assignment to a judge. After the introduction of judicial case management, judges' backlog of cases reduced, dramatically, to a few hundred; with the oldest of the cases, in backlog, being about two or three years. It became clear, to everyone, that judicial management of cases works; and happy users of judicial services reported a reduction in costs of litigation; because cases were being determined much faster than before. This, of course, was a huge achievement for the judiciary of Botswana.

The role of a managing judge should not be that of a passive administrator; if results are to be achieved in judicial case management. Sitting back and being passive may be perilous. Judicial case management entails that, instead of sitting back, and waiting for the parties to proceed in the fullness of time, a judge is required to play a far more active role in controlling and managing the process. Returning to the example of Botswana, the rules of practice empower judges to be proactive; and to sanction, as appropriate, any attempt to defeat the objectives of judicial case management.

The trigger for the allocation of a case to a judge, to start managing, is the filing of an appearance to defend and/or the notice of opposition. There are, fundamentally, three distinct phases before trial. They are as follows:

- A case planning conference occurs, before the managing judge. It sets out the timelines for exchanging pleadings, and discovery, and also for summary judgment, if it is sought.

- A date is also set for the case management conference; preceded by a case management report, in which dates for pre-trial steps are set and dates for other, envisaged, procedural steps are indicated, with compliance dates, such as joinder, amendments, etc;

- A date is set for the pre-trial conference, after the exchange discovery and witness statements, in order to narrow down the issues that are in dispute, to specify issues that are no longer in dispute and to supply lists of witnesses and intended exhibits.

The rules in Botswana prescribe about three pre-trial conferences, namely the first, the additional and the final pre-trial conference. The second is optional and is held only when it is warranted. The final pre-trial must define the issues for trial; in a concise fashion.

It is necessary to mention that pre-trial conferences should never be seen as a mere formality. They are very useful in eliminating unnecessary delays and in delineating the issues. Lawyers are required to use them as an opportunity to understand each other's case; even if they may not agree. Once the parties have delineated the real issues, in controversy, they are required to agree on the way forward. The significance of a pre-trial conference is that its primary purpose is to discern what the case is really about; and to map out the steps to take, until the matter is fully disposed of.

It is equally necessary to let it be known that the attendance, at a pre-trial conference, of the lawyers responsible for running a case, is very important. By doing so, they will familiarize themselves with the issues in the case, and will, thus, be able to obtain proper instructions from their clients; as they will have a background knowledge of the case. This is useful because it is only those lawyers who know the history of a matter, who can attend at court and be in a position to argue matters competently. The lawyers' attendance at pre-trial conferences also helps the judge to remain in charge of the case; as it will enable the judge to allocate a hearing date, for a matter, only after ensuring that the scheduled dates are convenient to both the parties. Once lawyers have committed to a date, it is expected that they should turn up, in court, on the scheduled date; to progress the matter and reduce or avoid any delay.

In Botswana, Order 42, of the High Court Rules, which states the agenda of the initial case management, is very pivotal. Lawyers must prepare for it and must make sure that they, seriously, deliberate on all the items listed, therein. After the initial case management conference, the parties are required to place, before the court, the initial case management draft order; which is to be confirmed by the court. Before confirming the proposed draft order, after the initial, additional and/or final pre-trial judicial case management conferences, it is expected that the court should identify the pivotal issue (s) in the case. This may entail the following:

- Questioning of the parties, often beyond the pleadings, in a fair and even handed manner; in order to clarify issues, in dispute, and the steps to be undertaken.

- Careful identification of issues. This can reduce the issues that are in dispute, and is time well spent.

- In an appropriate case, the court may wish to find out whether the parties are considering settlement. This should be done in neutral terms and without indicating any direction for a settlement; so as to avoid any question of being accused, or creating the perception, of pre-judging the issues.

- A judge should try to control discovery, and avoid unnecessary motions and delays. Discovery is, arguably, the greatest cause of delay in most jurisdictions.

- Reduce duplication of documentation, or exclude those documents that are no longer in dispute.

- Identification of expert witnesses, the exchange of summaries and a meeting of experts should also be addressed; and timetables agreed upon.

  ○ Possible amendments to be addressed, and disposed of, within a timetable.

  ○ Exchange of witness statements, if appropriate.

  ○ Identification of witnesses and consideration of the length of the trial.

  ○ Establishing ground rules for the trial, and further final pre-trial steps to be undertaken.

At the end of it all, especially after the final pre-trial conference, in the case of Botswana, it is important to fix firm and credible dates; that may not be vacated without a valid reason. Before dates are set, a managing judge should be satisfied that the time periods are reasonable. The best way of doing so is for the judge to obtain confirmation, from the parties, for the dates; either by adopting their proposals, or the judge setting his, or her own, dates; after enquiring, as to their suitability, from the parties and, thus, having their buy-in. If there are any issues remaining, after the last conference, then there is no point in setting a date, for trial, when the matter is not ripe for trial. Under those circumstances, the proper way to proceed is to postpone the pre-trial conference, to ensure compliance and trial readiness.

In my experience, the principles of judicial case management, intended to achieve speedy and efficient disposal of matters may be applied during the course of the trial. For instance, the judge must:

- Guard against being too interventionist.

- Set time limits, and ground rules, but remain reasonably accommodating; by ensuring even-handedness.

- Consider evidence in chief by way of an affidavit, or written statement.

In order to achieve efficiency, and the speedy disposal of matters, a judge may, in opposed applications, set ground rules for the hearing of the application. Some of these ground rules include setting dates for exchanging of written arguments and setting time limits for oral arguments.

Competencies of a managing judge

Judicial case management presupposes that a managing judge has certain competencies or attributes such as:

- A working knowledge, and experience, of civil procedure; that is to say, an understanding of the role, and importance, of pleadings, discovery and the principles governing interlocutory procedures; such as summary judgment proceedings, amendments, interim interdicts and the like. Without a sound working knowledge of the rules, and principles, governing civil procedure, proper judicial case management can be a difficult, and even a messy affair.

- A thorough preparation for each phase of case management. In order to properly control the process, and manage it in the best way possible, a managing judge would need to prepare for each phase; so that appropriate directions are given, which will reduce issues or provide direction to the parties; as to the how to conduct the litigation.

- Pleadings need to be scrutinised, closely, and issues such as discovery and amendments, that often hold back progress, are dealt with speedily and adequately.

- Setting realistic, yet very firm, dates to take and finalise the necessary pre-trial steps.

- Ensuring that witness statements are exchanged.

- Ensuring the setting of firm, and credible, trial dates that are not easily vacated.

In addition to the above competencies, or attributes, it is also important that a judge must have an appreciation, and understanding, of the impact of judicial case management, on legal practitioners, and the tasks that they are supposed to undertake; in pursuance, thereof. When all is considered, it seems, to me, that much as it requires managerial skills, from judges, judicial case management also requires the same skills from lawyers; in terms of time management and how litigation is, generally, conducted. In addition to this, my observation is that if a case is, haphazardly, managed; in such a manner that there are too many postponements or too many status conferences, then, costs of litigation in such a case will, invariably, go up.

It follows, from the discussion, so far, that if case management is properly navigated, the overall litigation costs will be reduced, the prospects for delay diminished and clients, and the justice system, are better served. Furthermore, the identification of documentation and of witnesses, and the taking down of statements are exercises which are better undertaken at an earlier stage, rather than at a very late stage such as on the eve of trial, when peoples' recollections are, obviously, not what they were when events were fresh; and potential shortcomings, only identified at that late stage, instead of earlier on.

The judge and court staff must work together

In any discussion on judicial case management, it is important to mention that if such an initiative is to be efficient, then judges and court staff must work together, as one. Judges, in particular, must ensure that lawyers comply with the time-lines that are issued by the court and do not complicate simple matters, in order to, possibly, justify a higher fee. The benefits of judicial case management, in the form of low litigation costs, would increase access to the courts and, by extension, confidence in the court system. An efficient judicial case management system should translate the slogan 'justice delayed is justice denied' into reality.

Time management is an important feature of a well-functioning judicial case management system. For instance, a case management session which lasts for several hours, where lawyers are required to sit around for hours when their contribution just takes a few minutes, is not efficient. Some courts take a whole morning to postpone cases that could have been postponed by phone or video. An efficient judicial case management system must be able harness technology; in order to achieve speedy disposal of matters.

Reiterating that judicial case management is as much about judges as it is about lawyers, the success of the system also depends on lawyers being well prepared, at all times. The lawyers must ensure that all the issues that they need to address, in the various stages of pre-trial conferences, are attended to. Once in court, they only need to confirm their agreement; that progresses the matter forward. If all other issues are properly addressed, in a proposed case plan or in a case management report, then they don't need to be canvassed in any detail in court.

In conclusion, I must emphasize that, in managing cases, judges must be strict but reasonable. They must be careful of allowing postponements routinely; for the obvious reason that postponements are inimical to effective judicial case management. This being said, it is important to add that whilst postponements must be strongly discouraged; they must not be routinely refused either. An example, of postponements that may be problematic, are those where an attorney says his colleague telephoned to say he, or she, was unwell; but provides no proof of such a claim. Some judges adopt a strict approach and would proceed, with a hearing, if there is no medical proof; whilst some judges would give the lawyer the benefit of doubt.

I must, also, emphasize the importance of excellent knowledge of procedural and substantive law. In particular, knowledge of the rules governing civil procedure is imperative. Time-lines which are imposed by the court must be credible, and breach must be sanctioned. If lawyers know that the judge's time-lines mean nothing, they will breach same with impunity and, in the long term, the judge's management of cases may lose credibility. There may be few cases were slavish adherence to rules may yield injustice. Fortunately, those cases are few in number. In the majority of cases, disregard of rules should not be tolerated or encouraged. Justice must be done in accordance with law.

Chapter Twelve

FACT FINDING

This chapter seeks to provide an introduction on how judges make findings of fact, and draw inference from primary facts. In law, facts matter because law has to be married to facts; if disputes are to be properly resolved. It follows, therefore, that facts are foundational and fundamental to judicial decision making. I tend to believe that once the facts have been determined, the application of relevant law is relatively easy.

It not all facts that matter

It is not all facts that matter; only those that are relevant do. Relevance can only be gleaned by reference to the issues implicated in a trial, or application. Evidence that is relevant, in a proceeding, is evidence that, if it were accepted, could rationally affect, whether directly, or indirectly, the assessment of the probability of the existence of a fact in issue; in the proceedings. The range of facts which may be relevant, when the court is considering a matter, differ from case to case.

In a custody case, for instance, the range of facts which may properly be considered, are infinite. They include the history of the members of the family, parental attitudes, proposed changes within the family, the child or children's behaviour, parental behaviour, etc.

The question of relevance is, invariably, a matter of degree, to be arrived at by common sense and experience. Put differently, relevance is not a matter of black and white. Evidence may range all the way from being conclusive proof, of an issue, down to being of the slightest assistance. A judge need not be detained by the minutest of factual details; but should, rather, focus on the main contested factual issues.

Of all facts which are relevant, not all may be in dispute

Of all facts which are relevant, not all may be in dispute. On occasion, facts may be common cause and, therefore, not worth wasting time on; by requiring evidence to be led on same. Judges often save time by enquiring whether there is a dispute of fact on certain matters. If none exists, judges may ask if a set of agreed facts can be produced, to save on time. There is, therefore, nothing wrong with placing, before the court, an agreed statement of facts; and inviting the court to deal with the case on that basis. However, the courts must always be vigilant that they may be cases that may not be amenable to simple presentation of agreed facts.

Most jurisdictions have rules that provide for agreed statements of facts, and inviting the court to make a determination based on same. Courts must, however, be cautious in accepting agreed facts; where one of the parties is not legally represented. Care must be taken to ensure that the unrepresented party understands, and agrees with, the facts. The unrepresented litigant must be able to understand the significance of the facts included, and those excluded. Sometimes, the material tendered, in support of the agreed facts, may not be supportive. So, it is important that a judge must look out for this possible discrepancy.

It is important to bear in mind that a court is not obliged to accept evidence just because it is unchallenged. Similarly, a court should not, necessarily, accept all that is stated in an agreed statement of facts; especially where a consideration of other evidence, or the totality of evidence, points to factual findings contrary to those contained in the agreed statement of facts.

Where facts are in dispute, their resolution often depends on an 'unruly horse' called credibility, or simply put, the credibility of witnesses. Any judge will attest to the fact that assessing credibility is a difficult task. Credibility involves wider problems than mere 'demeanour'; which is mostly concerned with whether the witness appears to be telling the truth.

Credibility

The question of credibility elicits certain questions. The first is whether a witness is truthful or not. The second is whether the witness, although a truthful person, is telling something less than the truth on the issue or, conversely, whether the witness, although an untruthful person, is telling the truth on this particular issue. The third is whether the witness, although a truthful person, is telling the truth as he, or she sees it, that is to say, did the witness register the intentions of the conversation correctly and, if so, has the witness' memory correctly retained the intentions. There are many other questions that a trier of fact may ask, in addition to the above, for instance, 'could it be that a witness, although he, or she, is telling the truth, has had their recollection tainted by unconscious bias; or by over discussing it with others?'

It is important not to lose sight of the fact that the process of litigation subjects the memories of witnesses to powerful biases. It is in the nature of litigation that witnesses would, often, have a stake in a particular version of events. This is obvious where the witness is a party, or has a tie of loyalty, to a party to the proceedings. Some other, more subtle, influences include allegiances created by the process of preparing a witness statement, and of coming to court to give evidence to one side of the dispute. Sometimes, the desire to assist, or at least not prejudice, the party who called the witness, or that party's lawyers, as well as a natural desire to give a good impression, in a public forum, can adversely impact on truth telling. It is also important that judges should not be too quick to equate confidence with truth telling. Some conmen are known to be extremely confident; and judges must always be on their guard against such witnesses.

It is often said that, with every day that passes, the memory becomes fainter, and the imagination becomes more active. Credibility also embraces not only the concept of a witness's truthfulness, but also the objective reality of the witness, that is to say, his, or her, ability to observe, or remember, events about which the witness is giving evidence.

When they are faced with the task of assessing evidence, judges will only place weight on evidence which they consider to be reliable. The only snag, to this, is that assessing reliability can be problematic. In the ordinary course of events, evidence which is self-contradictory is less likely to be reliable. As is often the case, a witness may make contradictory statements; both of which cannot be correct. However, on occasion, contradiction does not, necessarily, result in evidence being considered unreliable.

The anxious cases are those which arise, not infrequently, where the testimonies of two crucial witnesses are in direct conflict, in such a way that one must be lying; and yet both appear to be equally plausible, or implausible. In a situation such as this, a judge must give reasons as to why he, or she, prefers the evidence of one witness over the other. Difficult as this situation is, a judge cannot say that he, or she, does not know who to believe; and the judge cannot, therefore, make findings of fact. The judge has no choice but to reason his, or her, way through the contradictions.

In each case, that serves before them, judges must make an earnest evaluation, of the evidence, taking into account the nature of the contradiction; and whether, or not, it has a bearing on the issues being tried. It is said that in every contradiction, there resides two possibilities, namely deliberate falsehood and the possibility of honest mistake. The evidence of a witness must also be considered in light of the whole evidence tendered. It is always important, when considering the credibility of a witness, to test the veracity of same; with reference to the objective facts proved independently, of the testimony given, for instance, by reference to documents in the case.

Contradictions in evidence

It is all too common for witnesses to give such diametrically opposed versions that a finding of facts becomes difficult, or even impossible. Where it concerns witnesses of one party to the litigation, the court may, well, reject the testimony of both witnesses, or of one of them as being untruthful. A party whose witness has told a mixture of the truth and lies is, in all likelihood, likely to lose a case.

In summation, it is fair to say that credibility involves the following considerations:

- Truthfulness or honesty;

- Reliability;

- Understanding;

- Effect of other evidence;

- Non-verbal clues; for instance, a witness's conduct, manner, bearing, behaviour or delivery. In short, anything which characterises a witness' mode of giving evidence has a bearing on credibility.

In my experience, judges may find the following practical tips useful when assessing credibility:

- Do not make up your mind too quickly;

- Be suspicious, if you must, but do not show it;

- Let the witness repeat him/herself;

- Ask the witness to elaborate;

- Ask the witness temporal questions.

Demeanour

Earlier on, it was indicated that demeanour is not the same thing as credibility. The difference is that demeanour refers to a judge's ability to assess whether a witness is telling the truth; from the manner in which the witness testifies. A witness's demeanour includes varied mannerisms, and characteristics, such as the tone of voice in which a witness's statement is made, the hesitation or readiness with which answers are given, or the look of the witness.

Demeanour also includes things like the witness' carriage, or deportment, their evidence of surprise, gestures, general bearing, facial expression and yawns. Yet other aspects concerning the issue of demeanour are the use of the witness' eyes, the giving of furtive, or meaningful, glances or shrugs, the pitch of the witness' voice, self- possession or embarrassment, air of candour or seeming levity. The list is quite lengthy.

When all is said and done, demeanour is another unruly horse. Giving evidence in the artificial, not to mention stressful, circumstances of a court room may impact on the assessment of evidence; often leading to the wrong conclusion. For instance, the mere fact that a witness appears confused may not mean that he, or she, is not telling the truth. In reality, it is difficult to attribute, to judges, the ability to tell whether a witness is telling the truth; from the manner in which the witness is leading evidence. Some judges consider the following as indicative of a lying witness:

- They wait longer before giving an answer;

- They make more word and phrase repetitions;

- They make fewer hand and finger movements;

- Liars seem to include longer pauses, in their speech, than truth tellers;

In my experience, it does not always follow that any of the above may be a reliable indicator that a witness is not telling the truth. Judges need to be very careful before they conclude, for instance, that a trembling witness is, necessarily, lying. It could be stage fright, more than a motivation to lie, that could cause a witness to tremble when giving evidence. Similarly, it does not always follow that a witness who gives evidence looking down, or avoids eye contact, is telling a lie. There may well be a host of reasons as to why the witness is avoiding eye contact. It may be his nature or even his culture.

Human behaviour

Law, as a discipline, can benefit from other disciplines that explain human behaviour. For instance, psychologists have investigated whether demeanour can be used, effectively, to determine whether a person is lying. In an influential article, Professor Olin G. Wellborn has found that there is some evidence that the observation of demeanour diminishes, rather than enhances the accuracy of credibility during judgements. Under this view, the witness's credibility should be determined not on the witness's demeanour, but on the witness's accuracy of perception, memory, and ability to recount their story.

In an instructive reflection, which would resonate with the experience of many judges, an Australian barrister, Chester Porter QC, once pithily observed that: 'The best witness I ever saw, whose demeanour was 100 percent perfect, was Australia's top conman". In a paper delivered at University College, Dublin, in 1973, Judge MacKenna once described how he goes about finding facts. He stated the following:

> *"This is how I go about the business of finding facts. I start from the undisputed facts which both sides accept. I add to them such other facts as seem very likely to be true, as, for example, those recorded in contemporary documents or spoken to by independent witnesses like the policeman giving evidence in a running down case about the marks on the road. I judge a witness to be unreliable if his evidence is, in any serious respect, inconsistent with these undisputed or indisputable facts, or of course, if he contradicts himself on important points. I rely as little as possible on such deceptive matters as his demeanour. When I have done my best to separate the true from the false by these objective tests, I say which story seems to be the more probable, the plaintiff's or the defendant's?"*

Fact finding is complex

The process of finding facts is complex. Judges use countless mechanisms or factors in search of the truth. For instance, considering motive may be helpful. As a general rule, judges tend to place more weight on the evidence of uninterested persons. The requirement, though, is that even if a witness has a motive to lie, the court must still assess whether, and to what extent, motive affected the truthfulness of the witness's testimony. From time to time, judges are required to consider expert testimony. This requires that a judge be capable of understanding technical and scientific evidence. However, in law, expert testimony remains opinion; and should not be accepted 'willy-nilly' as the gospel truth. It is also important to assess expert evidence in the context of all the other evidence; and not in isolation.

It is part of judge's function to draw inferences from proven facts. For instance, the court is entitled to say 'because of the proven facts 'A' and 'B', a third fact, 'C,' is more probable than not. There are some very cardinal points to note if judges are to draw inferences. These are that:

- In making inferences, judges must distinguish between reasonable inference and conjecture.

- A conjecture is a mere guess, without any evidential basis.

- An inference is a deduction from the evidence and, if it is a reasonable deduction, it has the validity of legal proof.

- An inference is a process of reasoning by which a factual conclusion is deduced; as a logical consequence from other facts that are established by evidence.

- Documentary evidence is critical in judicial fact finding. Some judges find it more reliable than oral evidence, especially in commercial disputes.

- The disadvantage of documentary evidence is that there is always a danger that it may be forged.

- Factual findings are made by considering the totality of all relevant evidence.

- It is important for judges to keep an open mind until all evidence is led.

- No evidence can be properly assessed if it is divorced from the context.

This chapter has discussed, in some detail, the finding of facts. This topic cannot, however, be discussed in isolation of another related topic, that of standard of proof. In making findings of fact, the standard of proof is very relevant. It has been described as a special rule to protect the integrity of the judicial decision making process. In civil matters, the standard of proof is on a balance of probabilities while in criminal law, it is beyond reasonable doubt.

In the process of making findings of fact, judges are not at liberty to do so arbitrarily, such as by simply saying that they do not believe a particular witness; without saying why. In other words, judges must give reasons for any findings of facts they have made. This is so for two reasons. Firstly, those whose evidence has been rejected are entitled to an explanation as to why. Secondly, in assessing the adequacy of a fact finding exercise, any appellate court will expect the findings to be sufficiently reasoned.

Facts are the bedrock of judicial decision making. Admittedly, they can be difficult to determine but at the end of the day, fact finding must be done; as it is central to both criminal and civil trials. In making findings of fact, judges must be guided by logic, common sense and the standard of proof. Never should the finding of facts be made arbitrarily. In this regard, it is important for judges to develop self-awareness when embarking on the exercise of finding facts.

In my experience, it is a good idea to focus on probabilities and inconsistencies, rather than the unruly horse called demeanour. It helps to pay attention to contemporaneous documents. Many judges would agree that where oral testimony conflicts with contemporaneous documents, it is reasonable to prefer contemporaneous documents. It is of importance that judges should remember that the probabilities of a witness's testimony must always be measured against incontrovertible facts. At the end of the day, the probabilities, together with external and internal consistency, should always be the defining feature of factual findings.

It should be plain from the above narrative that I have some misgivings about demeanour. However, I should not be understood to be saying that it is a completely, and absolutely useless, tool in the search for the truth. All that I am trying to communicate is that if judges rely on demeanour, more than probabilities, they must give reasons for doing so. In choosing between witnesses' testimonies on the basis of probability, judges must always bear in mind that the improbable account may well be true. Sight must never be lost of the fact that the improbable, by definition, is that which may happen; and it would be unjust if an account, given by a witness, was rejected simply because it was bizarre, or unprecedented.

Chapter Thirteen

JUDGEMENT WRITING

Just like for the previous chapter, the topic under discussion, in this chapter, may be more relevant to adjudicators, than to other persons. However, there is no harm in giving the general readership an insight into the responsibility of judgement writing; a task which is at the very heart of judicial functions.

At the end of reading pleadings, listening to the testimonies of witnesses, or to the submissions of litigants and/or their lawyers, judges are required to write a judgement; setting out the reasons for the conclusions that they have reached. Preparation, audience and structure form a tri-part judgement writing process; developed by judges and used in courts throughout the international judicial community. Judges are, perhaps, the only public officials who are required to give reasons for their decisions; and to do so publicly.

Keep them brief

Anyone who has read my earlier judgements would not fail to notice that they read like academic treatise. Many ran into 100 pages or more. That was an error. With time my judgements shrunk in length and now my longest judgement, on average, is hardly 20 pages, and a majority around 12 pages. It is a sea change.

A question is often asked by judges, and jurists alike, as to whether judgement writing is an art or a science. It seems, to me, that the answer should be that it is both. It is also my view that a good judgement combines both an artistic and a scientific feature. Quite plainly, the artistic aspect relates to the structure, layout and flow of a particular judgement; while the scientific feature relates to the contents of the judgement which, in turn, will relate to the parties, the facts and the issues for resolution, or determination, in the case. The process of determination of a case is completed when the judge, after considering submissions by the parties' lawyers, determines the applicable law and arrives at a decision based on the evidence presented, in a case, and the applicable law.

Judgment writing is a skill that can be learned, practiced and refined. It is often said that practice makes perfect. I take no issue with this adage; as more than fifteen years on, as a judge, I still try to improve on writing judgements. I often ask myself if there is any value to an additional sentence that I just wrote. Judgement writing is about communicating well and clearly. A major weakness of judgements is rambling and not focusing on the real issues.

Clarity

At the heart of a good judgment is clarity of thought, which should translate into clarity of expression. Clarity, in a judgement is extremely important because, at the end of trial, the parties, whether the winning side, or the losing side, but more so the latter and their attorneys, would want to know why the case was decided in the way that it was. Clarity is also important for the purposes of informing the parties whether to appeal or not.

A judgement that is not easy to read or to be understood, even by an average newspaper reader, is probably a bad one. My personal experience is that a well-structured judgement enhances clarity. In addition to clarity, a judgement must endeavour to be brief and simple. A brief judgement is often achieved by a judge being able to make findings of fact, analyzing the crucial legal issues that arise, from the facts, and giving reasons for deciding in a particular way. A senior judicial colleague once told me that the longer the judgement, the greater likelihood that the losing party, who desires to take the matter on appeal, may not be able to identify the crucial matters that persuaded the judge to conclude the case in a particular way. This increases the chances of reversal, on appeal.

For reasons of pride, most judges do not like being upset on appeal. I know a number of judges who feel very emboldened by their judgement being upheld by the Court of Appeal. Again, although judges should not spend sleepless nights over being overturned on appeal, the fact is that most judges do not regard it as a happy experience. It would appear that some judges feel slighted, and even insulted, when their decisions are reversed on appeal. The reality, as I pointed out in the earlier chapters, of this book, is that it is perfectly acceptable for an apex court to differ with a decision of the High Court; and that the reversal of its decision does not, necessarily, mean that the High Court was wrong. There are times when apex decisions have gotten things wrong. It is all part of the adjudication process.

An average reader must follow a judgement

Returning to the main subject under discussion, a judgement must be lucid and must be such that an average reader must be able to discern why the losing party lost. It follows, therefore, that any judgement which is not easy to understand because it is not lucidly set out, or is difficult to comprehend because its reasoning is weak or flawed, cannot be a good judgement. In fact, such a decision runs the risk of alienating the losing side, and also faces the prospect of being overturned on appeal. In sum, a bad judgement is of little, if any, joy even to the winning side. If one wishes to be uncharitable, they could go so far as to say that a bad judgement is not worth the paper that it is written on.

Judgement should flow

On the artistic level, a good judgement should flow, and be easy to follow. An excellent command of the language, by the court, is a distinct advantage in the churning out of a good judgement. On the flip side of this, it must be acknowledged that it is not every judge who is a linguist, or a wordsmith. This notwithstanding, judges can improve, and complement, their given ability by reading extensively, and practicing language, so as to acquire the necessary faculty to be able to write a literate judgment.

I am compelled to mention that it is not a requirement, of the law, that judges should produce classics. But at the very least, the end product, namely their judgements, must, or should, be easy to understand and, if possible, to enjoy reading. It is worth reiterating that reading, widely, may help to improve one's writing skills. In my experience, it is a good idea to read the works of a judge who is an acknowledged authority in judgement writing; if one could be found.

Structure

On the scientific level, of judgement writing, content and the reasoning path are absolutely essential. To this extent, structure is very important. A good judgement must have an introduction and a conclusion, much like a good essay. The structure of a good judgement will often contain the following:

i.   An introduction; this will often refer to the parties;

ii.   The facts of the particular case;

iii. The law and the issues for resolution;

iv.   The application of the relevant law to the issues, and the evidence in the case;

v.   The determination of the case. This concerns the findings, of the judge, on the evidence; and in light of the applicable law;

vi.   The conclusion arrived at. This will include relief granted and costs, if any.

Preparation

A good judgement requires thorough preparation. In my experience, it helps to sketch a broad outline indicating the evidential facts, the ultimate facts, the legal principles and some observations on demeanour or credibility. All these are extremely useful for clarifying thought processes; in preparation to write judgements. It may also help, in writing judgements, to ask the question who the judgement is, primarily, intended for. Possible categories of audience include fellow judges, if sitting in as part of a panel, litigants and their lawyers, the public and courts of appeal.

For whom is judgement written?

As a general rule, judgements are written, primarily, for the litigants and their lawyers. Former Chief Justice of the Indian High Court, Justice Sunil Ambwani, was on point when he said:

> *"The winner is not much interested in the reason for success, as he is convinced of the righteousness of the cause. The loser, however, in expensive litigation is entitled to have a candid explanation of the reasons for the decision. It is not only for exercise of any appellate right but also to uphold the intellectual integrity of the system of law … and logical reasoning."*

Some decisions are of national importance and where this is so, the court may have, as its primary target, the parties and the public. It seems logical that if the primary target is the public, then the judgement must be written in such a way that the public may easily understand it.

Judges of the lower courts may be, justifiably, keen that their decisions and reasoning must be understood by the appellate court. The lack of clarity in a written judgement can bestow upon the appeals court, the unduly burdensome task of guessing how the lower court came to the decision reached. For all that may be said about judgements, what holds true is that there is no single structure, of a judgement, which is, generally, recommended; although judgements often follow similar structure, in that they, typically, have an introduction that sets out the facts of the matter, they discuss the law and apply it to the facts; after which they make a conclusion that is clear.

The above approach, which is associated with Justice Roslyn Atkinson of the Supreme Court of Queensland, in Australia, often goes under the acronym FLAC, meaning 'F' for facts, 'L' for Law, 'A' for application and 'C' for conclusion. The famous Lord Denning said that just like a short story, or play, a judgement requires an introduction, a middle and an end. He described the structure as follows:

> *"I try to make judgments live... I start my judgment, as it were, with a prologue - as the chorus does in one of Shakespeare's plays-to introduce the story. Then I go from act to act as Shakespeare does-each with its scenes drawn from real-life...I finish with a conclusion-an epilogue again as the chorus does in Shakespeare. In it I gather the threads together and give the result..."*

In South Africa, the Honourable Mr. Justice M.M. Corbett, Former Chief Justice of the Supreme Court of South Africa, goes into more detail, on judgement writing. He recommends a basic structural form, for judgement writing, as the following:

i.   Introduction;

ii. Setting out of the facts;

iii. The law and the issues;

iv. Applying the law to the facts;

v.   Determining the relief, including costs and;

vi. The Order of the Court.

The United States of America Judicial Writing Manual lists five key structure elements:

1. Introductory statement of the nature, procedural posture and result of the case;

2. Statement of the issues to be decided;

3. Statement of the material facts;

4. Discussion of the governing legal principles and resolution of the issues; and

5. Disposition and necessary instructions.

The style and organization of written opinions will, inevitably, vary; regardless of the chosen framework. Consistent logical structure is helpful for both the judge and the audience.

A structure provides the essential pillars of a judgement. It ensures that issues are clearly stated; and that the relevant facts, and law, are set out in a clear fashion. That helps the reader to understand the judgement. The use of headings and sub-headings, Roman numerals, or other means of disclosing the organizational structure, of a judgement, to the reader, is always helpful; particularly when the opinion is long and the subject matter complex. Headings, sub-headings and sub-divisions not only provide road signs for the reader, but they also help the writer to organize his, or her, thoughts; and to test the logic of the opinion.

Each of the above examples highlights the fact that while structures, in judgement writing do vary, key elements remain constant. These can be summarized as the following four points:

1.   The facts;

2.   The law;

3.   The application of that law;

4.   The judge's conclusion.

It is not realistic to expect that every judgement will be understood by everyone; but no effort should be spared in ensuring that a judgement can be understood by as many ordinary readers as possible. This can be achieved by eliminating unnecessary words and sentences; which do not add any value to the text of the judgement.

As indicated earlier, justice requires clarity. This means that judges must try, as much as possible, to write in plain and simple English. They must be considerate, in their language, and should refrain from disparaging parties that appear before them. Judges need not label witnesses, or lawyers, as liars; unless such a finding is material to the issues before the court.

The language of the court must be kind and neutral. It may be recalled that one of the attributes of judgeship, which was listed, in the earlier chapter of this book, is kindness. This should be lived out; even in judgement writing; and hence the requirement for the language of the court to be kind, considerate and neutral. Aside this, it should be remembered that a judge, too, is a human being; who may find himself, or herself, in the witness box, one day, and would, almost certainly, not like it if any person used disparaging remarks against him, or her.

The entire trial, or courtroom, process is designed to elicit evidence and information which will be applied to the existing governing law; resulting in a judicial decision. As has been repeatedly stated, in the pages of this book, a judicial decision should rest upon legal grounds alone. Neither findings of fact, nor the decision, itself, should be based upon suspicion, surmises or conjectures.

Just as it has been pointed out that not every judge is a linguist, or wordsmith, it, similarly, needs to be mentioned that judges differ both in their writing styles, and in the prose that they employ. Signature writing methods, or practices, can enliven written opinions and judgements, and they should, thus, be welcomed; so long as the written product remains clear and structured. The excerpts below are two opening paragraphs on the same case. They illustrate the flexibility of writing best practice; within an individual judge's own writing style. Writing styles are as unique as individual judges' writing. Consistent adherence to the best practices, which have been discussed above, provides clarity to judgements; regardless of audience. Below is, produced, a possible template of a judgment (Criminal) to guide judicial officers.

Template

Sample judgement template (criminal)

Cr/Cv/ App [Number]

IN THE [NAME COURT]

IN THE MATTER OF

BETWEEN:

[NAME]

AND

[NAME] OR STATE

COUNSEL:

[NAME] xxxx for the Applicant

[NAME] xxxx for the Respondent

CORAM:

JUDGEMENT DELIVERED [DATE]

Introduction

1. Preliminary Issues;

2. Summary of Prosecution/Plaintiff's case;

3. Summary of Defence/Defendant's case;

4. Issues to be determined.

Evidence and Factual Findings

5. Prosecution/Plaintiff's Allegation on Issue A

   a) Prosecution/Plaintiff's evidence in support of the allegation;

   b) Defence evidence on the allegation;

   c) The judge's evaluation of the evidence;

   d) Applicable Law.

6. Prosecution/Plaintiff's Allegation on Issue B

   a) Prosecution/Plaintiff's evidence in support of the allegation;

   b) Defence evidence on the allegation;

   c) The judge's evaluation of the evidence;

   d) Applicable Law.

7. Prosecution/Plaintiff's Allegation on Issue C;

   a) Prosecution/Plaintiff's evidence in support of the allegation;

b) Defence evidence on the allegation;

c) The judge's evaluation of the evidence;

d) Applicable Law.

8. Statement of the Law on the Issue A

   a) Statutory Law;

   b) Case Law.

   c) Deliberations.

9. Statement of the Law on Issue B

   a) Statutory Law;

   b) Case Law.

   c) Deliberations.

10. Statement of the Law on Issue C

   a) Statutory Law;

   b) Case Law;

   c) Deliberations.

11. Applying the Law to the Facts

   a) These facts [In Issues A, B or C]…

   b) When viewed in the context of this section of the Constitution/Law/Regulation/Contract/Precedent/ Principle of equity [choose one]…

Conclusion

1. Finding of guilt (or acquittal) or liability

2. Aggravating or mitigating circumstances

3. Sentence

4. Order, Decision/Findings (Civil)

Although judgement writing can be learned, practiced and refined, it is ultimately a matter of individual choice how one approaches the task. However, and speaking for myself, I can offer certain practical tips born from experience. Writing a judgement may, well, start after reading pleadings and the evidence, in an appropriate case, and before submissions by the parties or their lawyers. A rough outline that is generated, at this stage, may change after considering written and oral submissions.

A judge's note taking in court is also useful in terms of recording the live issues, and what point the parties differed on; and why. Once the judge has all the raw materials needed to write a judgement, the next important stage is, usually, the opening paragraph. Many judges would testify that the opening paragraph is crucial. It can take days to construct and, on rare occasions, it can take seconds or minutes.

Experienced judges say that the first page of a judgement must, ideally, say it all. It sets the foundation and paints, in broad strokes, the course that the judgement is likely to take. Most judgements notoriously start with the usual: 'This is an application for…' There is nothing wrong, in principle, with this line; but is not, necessarily, interesting or, indeed, the best way of starting a judgement. Those familiar with how Lord Denning started, and wrote, his judgements would agree that he was very skilled and artistic, and yet very clear. A good example is his introductory remarks in his famous 'Bluebell time in Kent' judgement. This is what he wrote:

> *"It happened on April 19, 1964. It was bluebell time in Kent. Mr. and Mrs. Hinz had been married some 10 years, and they had four children, all aged nine and under. The youngest was one. Mrs. Hinz was a remarkable woman. In addition to her own four, she was foster-mother to four other children. To add to it, she was two months pregnant with her fifth child.*
>
> *On this day they drove out in a Bedford Dormobile van from Tonbridge to Canvey Island. They took all eight children with them. As they were coming back, they turned into a lay-by at Thumham to have a picnic tea. The husband, Mr. Hinz, was at the back of the Dornmobile making tea. Mrs. Hinz had taken Stephanie, her third child, aged three, across the road to pick bluebells on the opposite side. There came along a Jaguar car driven by Mr. Berry, out of control. A tyre had burst. The Jaguar rushed into this lay-by and crashed into Mr. Hinz and the children. Mr. Hinz was frightfully injured and died a little later. Nearly all the children were hurt. Blood was streaming from their heads. Mrs. Hinz, hearing the crash, turning around saw this disaster. She ran across the road and did all she*

could. Her husband was beyond recall. But the children recovered.

An action has been brought on her behalf and on behalf of the children for damages against Mr. Berry, the defendant. The injuries to the children have been settled by various sums being paid. The pecuniary loss to Mrs. Hinz, by reason of the loss of her husband, has been found by the judge to be some £115, 000; but there remains the question of the damages payable to her for nervous shock – the shock which, she suffered seeing her husband lying in the road dying, and the children strewn about."

It is not every judge who can write like Lord Denning. Besides we don't need to be a Lord Denning, but just ourselves. The idea, behind the above example, is to learn that it is possible to communicate simply in a judgement.

Practical tips

To continue with practical tips on how to write a judgement, after introducing the issue, the next step is to deal with the main body of the judgement; and discuss the facts. Some judges reproduce the pleadings of both parties, in their judgements, which is not a good practice. The idea is to summarize the facts as found by the judges, and avoid reproducing pleadings which makes reading difficult and unpleasant. When summarizing facts, care must be taken to set out all the facts. As was stated earlier, only relevant facts matter; and weaving irrelevant facts into a judgement compromises its credibility.

In summarizing relevant facts, it may be necessary to highlight the findings of credibility. As such, and as has already been pointed out, judges must not be too quick to label witnesses as liars; unless such a finding is relevant to the issues in dispute. Once the findings of fact have been summarized, it becomes essential to set out the law in a clear fashion. A word of caution, here, is that one need not discuss the law any more than is necessary to the facts, and circumstances, of each case. It is, however, very important to set out, and apply, the law in a judgement; because the failure to do so raises legitimate doubts as to whether the judge knew, let alone applied, the correct law. It is always better to paraphrase the law than to quote it. Quotations must be done sparingly; and only where necessary.

After applying the law to the facts, a judge must conclude his, or her, judgement; and the conclusion must resolve each of the issues identified in the case. It is important that the conclusion should not contain any new material, or law, that was not discussed in the body of the judgement. Traditionally, most judges announced their decision at the end of the judgement; and not at the beginning. The conclusion must show how the decision is reached. It must be consistent with the introduction, and body, of the judgement. At the end of it all, readers must be able to tell, from the judgement, the reason for the conclusion reached by the judge.

Language

Judges must endeavour, at all times to use moderate language. They must be careful in the manner that they criticize participants to the litigation; such as lawyers or witnesses. This is important because adverse criticism may have unpleasant reputational consequences. Judges should not lightly cast aspersions on the professional competence of a lawyer, or a witness. While adverse criticism may be warranted, in some cases, it is also true that praise may, also, be warranted at times. But criticism and praise must be used sparingly; and only in deserving cases. Calm detachment in thinking, and moderation in expression, is what defines a good judge.

Judges must always bear in mind that, by their decision, they may end people's lives, reputations or careers; and it is for this reason that they should avoid shortcuts. A lazy, and distracted, judge is inimical to justice. The realization that one's future has been determined by a lazy, or distracted, judge can be a truly chilling experience.

In his novel 'Resurrection', the great Russian author, Tolstoy, evokes the chilling feeling; when describing the three judge trial court that was to decide the fate of an innocent woman who was charged with murder. He wrote: 'The President of the Court was anxious to begin the sitting and get through with it as early as possible, in time to call, before six o'clock, on the red-haired woman with whom he had begun a romance, in the country, last summer. The second judge was feeling gloomy; having just been told that his wife would not be making any dinner that evening. The third member of the court was suffering from gastric catarrh'.

In summation, it is important to say that a judgement must flow with the beginning that has a logical connection to the end. The judge should set the scene, simply and clearly, as a prelude to other scenes of the story. The first page should be the prime of a judgement; it must say it all. The first page sets the foundation, and maps out the course, of a judgement. The conclusion must include the orders, and relief, granted by the court; with the relief being as precise as possible, and not subject to interpretation.

It is good practice not to hurry to deliver judgement; unless the matter is urgent. It is also good to read, and re-read, one's judgement and edit it carefully so that it reads well; and is as clear as it can be. Editing a judgement is very important, because it can identify wrong references, inappropriate language, irrelevant findings, inappropriate punctuations, and can eliminate repetition; so that one is left with a lucid judgement that reads well.

As has been stated, a good judgement must be clear, simple and brief; and must give reasons for the decision that the judge has taken. The reasons, for the judgement, must, clearly, demonstrate that the judge understood the issues for determination and the arguments, of the parties; and also that the judge has considered the authorities placed before him, or her. A good judgement is one in which the judge has understood the relevant law, and has applied the law to the facts. If this is not apparent, on the face of the judgement, then it is doubtful whether judicial duty has been discharged; as required.

Chapter Fourteen

SENTENCING

In a criminal trial, after an accused is found guilty, then comes sentencing. The purpose of this chapter is to shed light on some judicial approaches to sentencing offenders, who have been convicted of serious crimes. The chapter discusses various theories of punishment.

Quite often, when sentencing, the approach of judicial officers, will be informed by the nature, circumstances and gravity of the crime. The approach includes, necessarily, which penal philosophy, the judicial officer would want to embrace. This chapter also seeks to identify the factors that determine the choice of sentence.

It is often said that although it is difficult to identify and put any value to common factors that are considered, when sentencing, the seriousness of the crime seems to carry more weight than the previous record, and age factor, in the selection of a sentence.

Sentencing and punishment are as old as society. This suggests that the use of punishment in society is inevitable; hence it requires to be balanced, appropriately, in order to guard against excessive sentences. The history of most societies suggests that criminal law originates in the sense of retribution at a personal level, when one party has been violated and desires to retaliate. But as society develops, these feelings are replaced by state-led punishment against those who commit wrongs.

The philosophical basis of punishment has undergone some reforms over the years, so that punishment can be perceived as less harsh, or punitive, due to the historical penological developments, at specific times. At the end of the day, the idea that punishment, as a social phenomenon takes different forms in different societies, jurisdictions and stages, in history, and that it is informed by social forces, with the aim to enhance social order and rules, cannot be faulted.

Sentence must be appropriate

Sentencing that comes at the end of the trial process is a very important stage; where the court must determine the appropriate punishment. It is generally accepted that an appropriate sentence must consider three factors, namely the crime, the offender and the interests of society. In this approach, the punishment should fit the offender, the gravity of the crime and should be fair to the community, or state. Additionally, punishment should contain a certain amount of mercy.

Judicial sentencing takes place within a legal and social framework; which imposes certain limitations on the discretion of the court. In this regard, judicial decisions are not immune from the broader influence of social factors. It is noteworthy that it is possible for sentencing approaches to be determined by various factors, and dimensions.

The judicial sentencing of convicted persons remains a complex process; which is characterized by inconsistencies in approach. Sentencing approaches become even more complex when they are applied to different offenders; who are convicted of similar serious crimes. It is for that reason that it is important to understand the factors that underlie the differences in the sentences imposed over the years, and currently.

It seems proper for judicial sentencing approaches to be analyzed in accordance with the demands of changing times and contexts. The assessment of, or engagement with, judicial approaches should not be seen as a matter of obstruction but should, rather, be viewed as an attempt to enhance appropriate judicial leadership; as expected by society. This implies that judicial approaches might be shaped by the public interest, and the mood of the time. Different courts seem to hold divergent approaches in their sentencing decisions; in respect of both young and adult offenders. It appears that, as the result of sentencing discretion and different gravity of crimes, these divergences are inevitable, even if courts have the same penal philosophy.

Disparity

Disparity in sentencing is a serious concern for many jurisdictions. It tends to undermine the integrity, and fairness, of the criminal justice system. It is, therefore, proper to put in place some guidelines that ensure that the courts are consistent. It cannot be correct that sentencing should be a matter of the individual preferences of judicial officers. However, in evaluating variations in sentencing, it must always be borne in mind that all cases are unique; and that they reflect variations in the nature of the crimes and offenders that serve before the courts. Similarly, it must be remembered that the conditions in one case are different from the conditions in another. In this respect, the term 'equal approaches' appears to refer to 'equality of consideration', when it comes to the factors to be taken into account, in sentencing decisions.

Disparity, in sentencing, has tended to focus on the custodial part of the sentencing. If the truth be told, this is one of the most difficult decisions that a court has to make. Custodial sentencing is a task that must be approached with extreme care, sensitivity and humanity. Speaking for myself, in my over fifteen years on the bench, and even at the time of writing this book, I have seen many disconcerting, and in some cases plainly alarming, disparities in sentencing, with respect to cases that are almost identical. In fact, some have been so glaring as to damage, or potentially damage, the reputation of the judiciary.

The question that courts often have to answer is how should they punish those who break the law; and what is hoped to be achieved by the punishment. This, seemingly, simple question has no easy, or universally agreed, answer; and it continues to be a source of tension amongst lawyers, judges and scholars. Determining a sentence is an extremely complex exercise that includes elements of personality, humanity, moral philosophy, behavioural psychology and evidential assessment.

Purpose of sentencing

The literature on sentencing is littered with diverse opinions as to, precisely, what the purpose of sentencing is; and, exactly, how to go about it. In years past, the predominant view used to be that the object of appropriate sentencing was crime deterrence; through retribution. The prevailing logic, then, was that through harsh punitive measures, and the loss of individual liberty, precedents could be set; to deter others from committing the same offences. This view rested on the simplistic notion that the 'an eye for an eye' approach induced the kind of pain, or inconvenience, which those who were appropriately punished would not dare to repeat.

In terms of this view, individuals who commit offences are breaching rules that bind society together, and are responsible for disrupting the peace and order that society needs to prosper. This logic was derived from the Social Contact Theory, which is the hallmark of political philosophers such Thomas Hobbes, John Locke and Jean Jacques Rousseau.

As already indicated, the Social Contract Theory refers to the idea that a citizen's moral and/or political obligations depend on an implicit agreement between them to form the society, in which they live, by accepting the same behavioural values. The essence of this theoretical perspective is that, as part of the obligations of citizenship, citizens must refrain from wrong doing; in order to gain the benefit of the security that is provided by the executive, legislative and judicial arms of the government who, collectively, balance the needs and interests of all; through administering and managing a society that is underpinned by a common rule of law.

Under the Social Contract Theory, it was believed that by imposing custodial sentences, which restricted individual liberties and freedoms, the offenders would lose their ability to criminally influence other citizens; and would be unable to take advantage of the apparatus of the state. It was also believed that the resulting precedent sent a message of deterrence; that would prevent others from committing crimes.

It follows, from the observations that have been made, so far, on sentencing, that those who engage in 'self-help' and break the law, thereby breaching the societal code of conduct that exists, in order to guarantee the security of all, ought to be appropriately punished; so that they don't repeat the offensive conduct. It also follows that those who are minded to do so would refrain from breaching the law; for fear of punitive consequences, which for serious offences, include a custodial sentence. In punishing wrong doers, the state is considered to be protecting the entire society by preserving the rule of law, and maintaining an orderly society.

There are variations in approach to sentencing, between the courts and among judges, which require to be justified in the light of the divergences in crime and its seriousness; and offenders alike. Sentencing is a complex and multi-faceted phenomenon, involving history, law and sociology. Judges not only differ in their penal philosophies, and attitudes but also in ways in which they define what the law is. They also differ on what the social system expects of them, in terms of how they use information and in the sentences that they impose.

Sentencing should not reflect personal revulsion

Sometimes, and regrettably so, judges impose sentences that may reflect their personal revulsion to a particular offence or interpret the world, selectively, in ways that are consistent with their personal motivations and subjective ends. Regardless of what position one takes, with regard to the social purposes that sentencing should serve, it is likely to be repugnant, to the average man's sense of justice, if such differences are allowed to persist.

It is apparent, from a cursory reading of sentencing rulings, that sentencing approaches are not as simplistic as one would think. In some jurisdictions, the disparity in sentencing offenders who committed a similar offence, under similar circumstances and sharing common features, is difficult to justify. Inconsistencies are evident not just among the individual sentences, of the same court, but also between areas of the same jurisdiction; and between the different sentencing jurisdictions.

The worst type of inconsistency concerns the way in which judicial officers decide on which approach to adopt when making the sentencing decision; that is to say where one judicial officer decides that a particular offender should receive a short sentence, on the grounds of rehabilitation, while another judge decides that the same offender should receive a lengthy sentence, on the grounds of deterrence.

These divergent approaches may lead to the unequal treatment of offenders by the criminal justice system.

Rather unfortunately, in my view, not many countries have bothered to assess sentencing disparities.

In Botswana, a claim has often been made, as I imagine is the case in many other countries, that sentencing patterns are often arbitrary and unjustifiable. In recent years, there have been conflicting claims that sentences are influenced by a wide range of factors, which often defy scientific evaluation. It is also claimed, quite frequently, that the leniency, or severity of sentences, is linked to over-population in prisons; while the opposing view contends that lenient sentencing approaches mean that appropriate sentences are not imposed on offenders who are convicted of serious crimes.

It is indisputable that the levels of crime differ for each locality, at a particular moment, and that public opinion, and judges, could interpret these patterns differently. In other words, it is contended that judicial officers could adjust their sentences to be commensurate with a perceived increase in crime and, similarly, when there is a decrease in crime, penalties could be more lenient.

Explanations for the existence of sentencing disparities differ widely; with some suggesting that harsher sentences are on account of escalating crime rates; and others contending that some judicial officers are simply soft on crime. Yet others suggest that judicial approaches must be in accordance with the proportionality principle; which is one that requires judicial officers to strike a balance between the gravity of the crime, the age factor, a prior record, the severity of punishment and the individual circumstances of the offender.

In passing an appropriate sentence, judicial officers must have regard to the overall social context. As indicated earlier, sentencing does not take place in a sociological and politico historical vacuum; rather the changing context tends to shape, and influence, sentencing approaches. Judicial officers, being part of society, are also affected by crime in one way or the other, and this might influence how they think; and their sentencing patterns. This means that judicial officers must always be careful to ensure that sentencing remains as objective as it can be; and must also avoid a knee-jerk reaction, to crime, by imposing harsher sentences on offenders, simply because levels of crime are high.

There can be no doubt that choices, in favour of specific theories of punishment, might depend on the specific circumstances of each country. Societies have choices with regard to competing models of criminal justice, at particular moments. An orderly society, which is based on the rule of law, should not be too keen to convict without due regard to the rights of suspects. The central assumption, in a society based on the rule of law and respect for human rights, is that entrenching rights and procedures could lead to appropriate sentences, and community confidence in state penal organs.

Sentencing involves moral judgments pertaining to the gravity of crimes; and the appropriate levels of punishment which are of vital importance both to criminal accused and to society. In penal discourse, the court has the right, and power, to make a judgment. However, it is important not to view sentencing, and punishment, purely as a matter of personality, or individual attitude. There is need to infuse rationality and fairness to the sentencing process. In punishing those convicted of a crime, there may be room, depending on the circumstances of each case, to reflect on the underlying causes of crime. This is so because individuals behave within a social context.

Quite often an accused person's behaviour tends to emanate from social relationships that involve the state and the broader society. This explains why any punishment must, appropriately, take into account the interests of the accused and society, as represented by the state. It follows, in my view, that an individual offender is likely to view punishment as being connected to a broader context of what is right and wrong, at a particular point in time. This idea implies that moral reasoning tends to be shaped by general attitudes. It calls for broader sentencing approaches, in terms of psychology, the criminal's social background, criminal law and social science knowledge. This perspective demonstrates that punishment is not a simplistic phenomenon that can be viewed from a one-sided position; particularly in plural societies. Sentencing trends, and shifts, are likely to be influenced by various movements of thought; in different specific societal contexts.

It is the duty of the courts, to embrace approaches, or theories, that would ensure fair sentences; having regard to all the circumstances of a case. The courts must, of necessity, look at the harmfulness of the crime, the conduct and the degree of culpability of the offender, in order to gauge the measure of punishment, and to prescribe a deserved sentence; with the aim of prevention of crime and fairness to the convicted criminal. To this extent, the seriousness of the offence may be a relevant factor. It is quite common for the courts to explain higher sentences on the basis that the offence committed is a serious one. The moral culpability, of the offender, provides the sentencing court with the right, and duty, to punish. The reasoning for this is that the offender deserved the punishment; which he brought unto himself.

As it often happens, where the offender is a habitual offender, he or she, may deserve a more severe sentence, as compared to a similar offender who has not offended in the past. By this differential punishment, for subsequent offenders, it is hoped that a harsher sentence will drive the message home to the offender, and the broader community, that crime does not pay. In this regard, serious offences, committed by responsible persons, should justify severe censure. Significantly, even deserved censure should be proportionate to the seriousness of the crime; and the degree of guilt.

Severe sentences

Generally, and often instinctively, severe sentences are viewed as unfair. This view calls for a less mechanical conception of the principle of proportionality in sentencing; in other words, not equating proportionality with the notion of revenge, mere retribution and biblical notions of an eye for an eye. Few people can contest that, as a general rule, the seriousness of the offence should matter; in considering the appropriate sentence. For instance, murder is more serious than aggravated assault; hence the injury is greater, and more serious than manslaughter, because the offender's culpability is greater.

Broadly speaking, factors of prior record, which seem to be considered in sentencing decisions include the number of previous convictions, similarity of previous crimes to the present crime, frequency of re-offending, seriousness of previous offences, age of the accused, when he, or she, received previous convictions, and previous sentences. In this regard, the degree of gravity of harm and the extent of prior convictions, tend to give weight to the meaning of 'seriousness of crime' in sentencing approaches, to a varying degree, between different courts.

In modern plural societies judicial sentencing decisions should not, simply, be a matter of penal philosophy; rather there are other factors, for consideration, including the accused person's social background, age and other relevant circumstances. Sentencing is a matter for the trial judge, and appellate courts will hardly, ever, interfere; unless the trial court, plainly, misdirected itself on the law and fact.

Deterrence

The theory of deterrence, as explained above, no longer holds sway in contemporary society. It is, increasingly, accepted that the perceived benefits of such retributive sentencing measures do not, necessarily, achieve the desired outcomes; namely a reduction in crime and a safer society. On the contrary, research has demonstrated the futility of the theory of deterrence; as it has been shown that deterrent sentencing has failed to reduce crime and make society safer. In fact, one thing that may safely be said about punitive sentencing is that not only has it failed to reduce crime, and make society safer, but it tends to create huge financial costs to government, and produces cycles of criminality that fail to protect the public.

Several studies have demonstrated that the threat of imprisonment has minimal deterrent effect. Research has also shown that harsher sentences, such as long prison sentences, do not have a corresponding deterrent effect. On what I consider to be a positive note, the theory of deterrence is slowly giving way to the rehabilitative theory. The main focus, of the rehabilitative approach, is on rehabilitating the offender; so that he, or she, becomes a responsible member of society. It is the anti-thesis of the deterrence approach; as it focuses on making sure that the offender is assisted, by the society, to be a law abiding citizen; and to refrain from hurting the society, in which the offender is a member. It must be noted that the rehabilitative approach may not sit well with proponents of the retributive approach. However, and speaking for myself, the rehabilitative approach is very progressive and is what contemporary society needs; especially in view of the research that shows that deterrent sentencing has little, if any effect at all, on deterring would be offenders.

The rehabilitative approach emphasizes on the importance of the individual offender and proportionality of penalties; to fit the specific needs and circumstances of the individual offender, so as to achieve a more meaningful, and specific, form of justice. It is, therefore, absolutely important that judges must be exposed to literature on punishment and also to empirical data, so that when they consider what sentence is appropriate, they can also be guided by research.

Rehabilitation has, now, firmly become the most accepted normative, and utilitarian, response to crime in the twenty-first century. A proper rehabilitation framework includes a broad array of programmes; including mental health, substance abuse, and educational services. The idea is to build and not to destroy. The rehabilitative approach is geared towards empowering offenders with the skills, and other competencies, to enable them to be responsible members of society.

As has already been observed, the rehabilitative approach is progressive in that it aims to reduce the re-occurrence of crime; as opposed to a reactive response to a crime which has already been committed. The rehabilitative approach is pursued in realization of the fact that most offenders will still be released, from custody, at some point during their lifetimes.

While there are some who do not subscribe to it, the rehabilitative approach is more comprehensive and forward looking than the retributive approach. It is more comprehensive in the sense that it takes into account a number of factors and/or variables. The approach does not look at the offender, and the offence committed, in isolation. It ensures that, at the end of the day, the interests of society are served; by ensuring that the punishment fits the crime, and takes into account the interests of both the offender and the society. It behooves the judges, whenever they are passing sentence, to be comprehensive and broad, in order to ensure that the best and most socially beneficial sentence in administered.

I appreciate that it may seem to some, especially those who have been victims of crime, or have relations and friends who may have suffered terribly at the hands of criminals, that the rehabilitative approach is too soft on criminals, and has no regard for the victims of crime.

Public opinion in sentencing

In determining appropriate sentences, judges must not pander to public opinion. They are the professionals, and are the experts. They must, thus, approach sentencing objectively and fairly, ensuring that they don't succumb to mob justice. Judges must ask themselves important questions such as does the prison system actually facilitate the effective rehabilitation of offenders and does it help reduce crime, secure justice and positively transform communities affected by crime? In under-resourced settings, such as those that prevail in most African jurisdictions, this is even less likely to be the case; as the defendant's mental and physical health is, in fact, likely to suffer further; in custody.

In most parts of Africa prisons are a living hell. They are sites of grotesque violation of the right to human dignity.

Overcrowding is all too common. The over-crowded and poor conditions of the prisons jeopardize the lives of those who are in custody, by forcing them to live in conditions where they are more likely to contract serious mental and physical health diseases; with limited access to treatment or care. The conditions in the prisons, across a number of African jurisdictions, result in many convicted, non-violent individuals living in a state of constant fear; due to the close proximity of potentially violent criminals and murderers. The over-crowding is exacerbated by prolonged periods of pre-trial detentions. In some countries, in Africa, pre-trial detention can run for close to a decade; which is a total travesty of justice!

Judges must not resort to custodial sentences where, having regard to all the circumstancing of the case, such as over-crowding, a non-custodial sentence may best promote the interests of justice. Judges must also bear in mind that custodial sentences usually result in stigmatization that will affect convicted prisoners' ability to find gainful employment, and re-integrate into society, upon their release. This, in fact, leads to a perpetual cycle of criminality; and an increased cost to the state.

It is also worth considering the indirect socio-economic impact of custodial sentencing. The cost, to the state, of feeding a prisoner, is very high. The cost of custodial sentence also manifests itself in the fortunes of the family members of those that are imprisoned, especially the dependents; who may be denied schooling, and medical opportunities, on account of the needless imprisonment of bread winners.

In a number of African societies, where patriarchy still holds sway and men are the breadwinners of their families, imprisonment usually translates into condemning their wives and children to poverty. It follows, therefore, that care must be taken not to unjustifiably deprive family bread winners from providing for their families, communities and society. The crucial consideration for judges is always to ensure that custodial detention is only used when necessary, and is based on fairness and due process of the law. In countries where resources are scarce, a fundamental issue is how to implement non-custodial measures which are inexpensive, or free, implementable and effective.

Fines, as punishment, commend themselves in certain cases; especially for economic crimes. Fines and compensation orders are easy to make, and ought to be made, in appropriate cases. It is generally accepted that the use of fines is more progressive, as compared to the imposition of custodial sentences; especially in instances where a victim has been deprived of their property. Ordering the return of property may meet the expectations of a victim; more than a custodial sentence that is not accompanied by a restitution order.

More significantly, fines are more appropriate for asset recovery in corruption cases. Fines, as a form of victim compensation, are often successfully used as a form of reparative justice. The problem with the imposition of fines, however, is when the offenders default; leading to possible imprisonment. In order to minimize possible default, the courts must consider imposing realistic terms relating to amounts, and time-lines, that suit the circumstances of the offender.

Judges must approach sentencing with extreme care. They should be careful not to impose sentences that destroy, rather than build, an individual to be a responsible member of society. As has been pointed out, the 'an eye for an eye' approach, which is premised on the erroneous assumption that harsher sentences reduce the crime rate, and make society safer, is not supported by empirical studies. It is important that criminal justice agencies must work, together, more closely, to make less use of imprisonment.

The authorities in charge of the criminal justice system must invest in finding suitable alternatives to imprisonment. A criminal justice system that respects the values of fair trial must avoid prolonged periods of pre-trial detention; and judges should refuse to lend their authority to prolonged periods of pre-trial detention. I am aware that saying this may leave a sour taste in the mouths of some, but there is also merit in the decriminalization of some offences, such as being a rogue and vagabond, loitering, prostitution, and failure to pay debts. If this is done, it may contribute to reducing overcrowding in prisons.

International principles

Judges may also be properly guided on how best to approach sentencing, by following international principles. According to international principles and best practice, on sentencing, custodial sentencing must be a last resort; and must only be imposed where the seriousness of the offence so requires, and it would not be appropriate to impose any punishment other than imprisonment.

Judges must embrace a scientific, and rational, approach to sentencing; that undertakes the following:

- A risk assessment, that takes into account the likelihood of recidivism;

- An assessment of factors that decrease the likelihood of recidivism;

- An identification of the most effective sentencing options.

There is a growing body of research, in psychology and criminology, that identifies the risk factors for criminal behaviour generally, especially for particular offences, such as rape, robbery and murder; that judges need to familiarize themselves with, so that the sentences they impose are more rational and consistent with science and evidence.

Chapter Fifteen

REMOVAL OF JUDGES
. . . .

The process of removing judges is as important as the process of appointing them. It is a process that must not be susceptible to any form of manipulation. Often, a myriad of tricks are deployed to mud- smear and defame a judge; with the hope that the judge will either resign of his, or her own accord, or that an opportunity will be created; to remove an 'inconvenient' judge. As one prominent politician once, said to me, "When we come to power, we shall remove that Chief Justice, by simply finding an offence for him". I will not dwell on how alarmed I was by that statement. It suffices to say that those words were most unfortunate and uncalled for and such conduct is the reason why it is absolutely important that the process of removal, of judges, be insulated completely from political interest and manipulation.

International law

In terms of international law and best practice, judges are entitled to a fair hearing; prior to any contemplated impeachment process.

The judiciary, as an independent arm of government in the democratic world, is one of the structures that must exercise, and promote, the rule of law. The rule of law, itself, cannot be accessed, promoted and protected, where the appointment and removal of judges is politicized; and removal is a matter of political convenience. Judges must only be removed in accordance with the letter, and spirit, of the constitution; and not for extraneous reasons.

Judges may be removed for misbehaviour; of the nature that is grave, or gross, and makes the continuance of judicial office untenable. Judges may also be dismissed for gross incompetence, or they can be removed, from office, for reasons infirmity of mind or body; following due process. In the event of removal and/or dismissal of a judge, the law must be clear as to the criteria for the removal.

Decision to remove a judge is a grave one

The decision to remove a judge is a grave one. It is often preceded by suspension. It is good practice that before a judge is dismissed, he, or she, must be afforded an opportunity to show cause why suspension cannot be effected; and an impeachment tribunal established. This is done in a number of democratic countries; and it accords with the principles of international law. Article 10 of the Universal Declaration on Human Rights, provides that everyone is entitled to a fair, and public, hearing; by an impartial tribunal.

The independence of the Judiciary has in recent years come under the spotlight, particularly in Africa. In 2015, Botswana joined a list of countries that suspended judges; following a petition that the said judges wrote, expressing no confidence in the then Chief Justice. The judges were not afforded a hearing, before being suspended, and, in a surprising turn of events, the High Court held that their suspension was in order; as they would be afforded a hearing during the impeachment process. Botswana's Constitution says that 'judges may be removed, among other things, for 'misbehaviour'. Interestingly, the term 'misbehaviour is neither defined, nor qualified and is, therefore, ambiguous and liable to abuse. The threshold falls below the more appropriate, and exacting, standard of 'gross misconduct'. Significantly, nowhere does the Constitution, of Botswana, or any other law, prescribe the procedure on how any disciplinary process, against a judge, should be carried out. The law is also silent on the role of the Judicial Service Commission.

Ghana

In Ghana, the removal of Judges and/or the Chief Justice is enshrined in the country's constitution. Article 146 (1) provides for misbehaviour and incompetence, or the inability to perform the functions of his, or her, office arising from infirmity of body or mind; as grounds for removal of a judge. The procedure is that a petition, for the removal of a judge, is received by the Chief Justice, who then must set up an Ad hoc Council to determine if there is a *prima facie*, or tentative, case against the accused judge. Where the petition is against the Chief Justice, the Republican President will, instead, receive the petition.

The Ad hoc Council comprises three judicial members, who are appointed by the Chief Justice, and two other persons who are not members of the Council of the State, or members of Parliament, or lawyers. In terms of the removal of the Chief Justice, the Ad hoc Committee varies only to the extent that it includes two Justices of the Supreme Court of Ghana. The other members remain the same as for the removal of a judge. During the process of removal of a judge, the President is at liberty to suspend the judge, concerned, based on the advice and recommendation of the Chief Justice, or of the Council of State; if it is the removal of the Chief Justice that is under consideration.

According to Article 146 (8) of Ghana's Constitution, the hearing for removal of a judge, or the Chief Justice, is to be heard in camera; and the subject of the proceedings is entitled to be heard in his, or her, defence; led by herself/himself, or a lawyer or an expert of the judge's choice. At the end of the hearing, the Republican President must act according to the recommendations made by the Ad hoc Committee, as to whether, or not, the judge should be removed from office.

In the recent impeachment of twenty (20) judges, in Ghana, between 2015 and 2016, an investigative journalist, Anas, petitioned for the removal of judges who, it was alleged, had been involved in bribery and corruption. The petition is referred to as the Tiger Eye PI. Notably, the case of Justice Koffi Essel Mensah is discussed therein.

Judge Mensah, who was one of the leading judges in Ghana, was implicated to have accepted bribes from people. Anas petitioned the Council, in accordance with Article 146 of the constitution, for the removal of Judge Mensah. The judge was served with the petition on 9th September 2015, and asked to respond by 14th September 2015. Although he was given the details, of the alleged misconduct, there was insufficient evidence attached. His legal representatives requested that the same be provided, and that sufficient time be given for him to respond.

In an interesting twist to the matter, some judges, namely Mustapha Habib Logoh, Paul Uuter Dery and Gilbert Ayisi Addo, petitioned the legal status of the petitioner. The Supreme Court ruled against them, and proceeded on the basis that, there were reasons to conclude that the contents of the petition were true, and that the legal status of the petitioner was immaterial. The judges complained about the court's breach of the right to administrative action; and the right to a fair trial.

In the case of **His Lordship Justice Paul Uuter Dery v Tiger Eye PI and the Chief Justice of the Republic of Ghana and the Attorney General,** the Plaintiff, Judge Dery, petitioned that due process had not been followed in the process of removing him. He made out a case that, contrary to the provisions of the law and before a prima facie case could be established, by the Chief Justice, the Chief Justice made publication, in newspapers, of the petition, which fully published the Plaintiff's names. He, successfully, asked the Court that the Petition be declared null and void; as it went beyond the restriction of the President, and into the public space, before conclusion of the matter. The Plaintiff also prayed that any future processes that might be taken, against him, be made in private. The court held that it was, indeed, unconstitutional that the petition was made public; before a *prima facie* case was established. It, further, held that the second Defendant acted unconstitutionally, by publicizing the petition on his personal social media platforms, and in newspapers. Lastly, court held that that naming the Plaintiff (judge) in the media was also unconstitutional. However, it was also the court's holding that, despite its findings, the petition against the judge remained valid; and the due processes of investigation were to continue.

Kenya

Article 168(1) of the Kenyan Constitution, provides that a judge may be removed from the office for the following reasons;

a) Inability to perform the functions of the office arising from mental; or

b) physical incapacity.

c) A breach of the code of conduct prescribed for judges of the superior.

d) courts, by an Act of Parliament.

e) Bankruptcy.

f) Incompetence.

g) Gross misconduct or misbehaviour.

The Republican President, or any individual, may petition for the removal of a judge from her/his office. Within fourteen (14) days of receipt of the petition, a judge is placed on suspension, with half salary, on the recommendation of the Chief Justice and the Ad hoc Tribunal. In Kenya, unlike in the other countries already discussed, the Tribunal, for removal of a judge, comprises the Speaker of the National Assembly, three judges from common law jurisdictions, one advocate, with fifteen years' experience, and two persons with experience in public affairs. Within fourteen days of the notice of removal process, the judge must be furnished with a notice detailing the allegations, the charges, and the summary of the evidence in support of the allegations. The process is that the hearing must be conducted in camera; but the judge is allowed to request that the hearing be held in public.

The judge, under investigation, is allowed to choose her/ his representative and to call witnesses and cross-examine them. The judge is also at liberty to make final submissions at the end of the hearing. The rules of natural justice must be complied with. At the end of the process, the Tribunal is obliged to write the reasons for its decision; and the Republican President must act in accordance with the recommendations made by the Tribunal.

It was held, in the matter of **Judicial Service Commission v Mbalu Mutara & Another,** that a judge, who was removed from his position, had the right to fair administrative act; and that due process, in accordance with the law, must be followed. The Judicial Service Commission appealed the case in which Mutara was petitioned for thirteen (13) complaints against him, for gross misconduct, incompetence and misbehaviour. The complaints were, mainly, from Advocates. The Judicial Service Commission began the process of investigation, and Mutara was notified of the complaints. He chose his legal representative, who made submissions on his behalf, and at the end of the process, Mutara was made aware of the outcome of the investigation.

The outcome of the Judicial Service Commission proceedings was that only three of the complaints, against Mutara, were found to have some substance. A recommendation was made for his removal and suspension; and a Tribunal was also set up to investigate him. Mutara then petitioned the High Court, citing that he was denied the right to a fair administrative act; as he was not afforded a fair hearing. He also complained that the Tribunal, which was set up, was unconstitutional and incompetent. Mutara argued that he was not given the reasons for his removal; and that the outcome, of his hearing, was sent to the media, before him. The High Court found for Mutara.

On appeal, the Judicial Service Commission wanted the Supreme Court to determine two issues; namely:

a) Whether in the removal of a judge, the Judicial Service Commission must afford the judge fair administrative action;

b) Whether the Republican President can, after receiving a petition for removal of a judge, suspend the judge and set up a Tribunal, at the same time, within 14 days.

The Appeal Court found for the Judicial Service Commission, and held that it had the administrative powers to call and cross- examine witness. The Appeal Court held that the judge was afforded a fair hearing. On the issue of a Tribunal, the court held that the Tribunal was properly established. The Judicial Service commission won, on appeal, and the High Court judgement was dismissed.

Swaziland

Swaziland has, for a long time, been marred by issues of lack of respect for the independence of the judiciary. As is the case for Kenya, the reasons that are often stated, as grounds for removal of a judge from office, are serious misbehaviour or inability to perform the function of the office; arising from infirmity of body or mind. The process of removing a judge provides for the setting up of an Ad hoc Committee. The Committee should comprise the Minister responsible for Justice, as the Chairman of the Civil Service Commission, and the President of the Law Society of Swaziland.

The Judicial Services Commission is mandated to investigate any allegations against a judge. During the process of the investigation, the King of Swaziland, may suspend the judge, in question, until the proceedings are concluded. The recommendation made by the Judicial Service Commission, entitles the King to act in accordance with that recommendation, on whether, or not, to remove the judge.

The case of Judge Masuku is a classic one, which had been ongoing from 2002 to 2004, when he was appointed to the High Court; and then demoted to the Industrial Court. The judge only learnt about his transfer from the media; as no formal communication was directed to him. In

2011, the then Chief Justice Ramodibedi, yet again, issued a petition, against Justice Masuku, for his removal. As the Petitioner, Chief Justice Ramodibedi did not recuse himself from the hearing, wherein he accused Justice Masuku of thirteen (13) charges; which included insulting the King of Swaziland. International and regional bodies spoke out strongly against the lack of due process, in the proceedings that led to Masuku's hearing. At the hearing, Justice Masuku was not given any evidence, to be able to defend himself. His colleagues, family and interested people and organizations, were not allowed to enter the venue of the hearing, at all.

Zambia

Zambia, too, has had its share of attempts to remove inconvenient judges. Article 98 (2) of the Constitution of Zambia provides for the removal of a judge. The reason provided, for the removal, is for the inability to perform the functions of the office, whether arising from infirmity of body or mind, incompetence or misbehaviour. The Republican President is the person who is allowed to initiate the process of removing a judge. The investigations, into allegations against a judge, are carried out by the Judicial Complaints Authority. The Authority makes recommendations to the Republican President, or to the Chief Justice; depending on whether it is Chief Justice, or a judge, who is being sought to removed.

The Judicial Complaints Authority comprises five people who are serving, or retired judges, or qualified for judicial office; and are appointed by the Republican

President, with the approval of the National Assembly. The President is at liberty to suspend a judge or the Chief Justice; pending the outcome of the investigations. Should the Ad hoc Committee, which is set up by the Judicial Complaints Authority, recommend removal, the President must act in accordance with the recommendation.

Latimer House Principles on removal of a judge

International law has defined best practices in terms of removal of judges. The principles for the removal of judges are developed regionally and internationally. The most commonly known principles, of the independence of the judiciary and judges, are, already alluded to, the Commonwealth Latimer House Principles; which are, mainly, applicable to the Commonwealth countries. They are, however, cited extensively by scholars; as precedents in upholding the independence of the judiciary.

The Latimer House principles, and, indeed other principles, are clear that the removal of judges should not be used to penalize them, or for their intimidation. The principles, further, provide that the procedure to be adopted, in the removal of judges, from office, must include appropriate safeguards, and must be open and fair. This is to protect the judiciary, judges and their integrity. A judge who is the subject of removal proceedings must be made fully aware of the charges, within a reasonable time, and as per the dictates of the constitution; on the provision of the removal of judges.

During the impeachment process a judge, having been served with charges, must be able to make a defence, by himself, or herself, or through a chosen lawyer or a representative. There is greater emphasis that the Tribunal, which is set up to conduct investigations and hear the matter, against a judge, must be independent and impartial.

The applicable principles, highlighted by many international legal instruments, emphasize that a judge must be presumed innocent; until the final outcome of the investigation and hearing. A judge, under investigation, has the right to present evidence, to cross- examine witnesses and also to secure legal representation. The judge should have the right to review the proceedings, in order to ensure that all the processes that were undertaken were done in accordance with the due process of the law. Critically, the process must allow a judge to appeal the removal, where they believe it did not proceed appropriately.

The International Bar Association Minimum Standards of Judicial Independence provide that the grounds for removal of judges shall be fixed by law, and shall be clearly defined. This is to narrow down the interpretation of the grounds for removal; which may give room for removal, even where it is not necessary. Article 30 of the International Bar Association Minimum Standards of Judicial Independence provides that removal must be by reason of a criminal act or through gross, or repeated, neglect; which has shown that the judge has manifestly held himself, or herself, to be unfit for the position of a judge.

Bangalore Principles

The Bangalore Principles set the standard for removal of judges very high; so that judges are not easily removed from their office. The Principles acknowledge that there is, indeed, need to evaluate the conduct of the judiciary; but it should be limited so as to protect the judges and the office that they hold. While the highest standards are expected, of a judge, failure to meet those standards will not be enough justification to remove a judge from office. The removal of a judge would only be justified where his, or her, short comings are so serious; as to destroy confidence, in the judicial system, and the judges' ability to, properly, perform judicial functions. The Bangalore Principles also emphasize that not every breach necessitates a removal. Removal must be weighed alongside public confidence, the integrity of the judiciary and the incapacity of a judge.

The United Nations Basic Principles on the Independence of the Judiciary, Lawyers and Judges, provide for the interrelation of removal and the capacity to hold office, and diligently so. Article 18 provides that removal must be based on incapacity or misbehaviour or failure to discharge the role of the office of a judge; which is held in high esteem, across the world. The UN Principles state that substantive grounds of removal must be discernible; and the process for removal must be determined in accordance with established standards of judicial conduct.

The Principles and Guidelines on the Right to a Fair Trial and Legal Assistance in Africa provide, as do the Latimer and

United Nations Basic Principles, that the removal of a judge must be based on gross misconduct; which is incompatible with judicial office. Removal should never be based on the simple fact that the authorities do not like the decision that a judge gave in a particular case. The United Nations Special Rapporteur has, categorically, also added to the measures that should be taken in removing judges. In line with the International Bar Association Principles and the Latimer House Principles, the Rapporteur, in his 2014 Report, stated that instances of professional misconduct, which are gross, inexcusable and bring the judiciary into disrepute, warrant removal.

It may be helpful to comment, briefly, on whether some of the procedures prescribed by international legal instruments were complied with in some of the case studies discussed earlier. In Swaziland, the process of removal has become blurred, over the years. It is apparent that there had been a target on Justice Masuku, from the early 2000's, until he left the judiciary. The process for his removal flouted every fundamental rule prescribed by the Latimer and United Nations Basic Principles on the removal of a judge.

The International Bar Association, and the Latimer, Principles prescribe that in removing a judge, the test should be based on whether the judge is so incapacitated that he, or she, cannot exercise his, or her, role, or that the judge's conduct is extremely gross; and he, or she, cannot be expected to perform their judicial duties. The apparent role of the then Chief Justice Ramodibedi, in meddling in his judicial functions, and then the proceedings against Justice

Masuku, also point to the lack of constitutional structures to protect those who will be persecuted for their efforts; as meticulous judges who want nothing but to dispense justice. Swaziland needs to put in place appropriate laws, and systems, to avoid turmoil in the judiciary; which also shows lack of effective rule of law.

The removal of judges in Kenya has, in the main, followed the due process of law; partly because the judiciary, itself, was equally determined that constitutional prescriptions, and international standards, be followed, in the process, and that politicians should, simply, not be allowed to remove inconvenient judges.

In concluding the discussion, on the removal of judges, it is important to emphasize that international law provides that a strict, and narrow, interpretation of misconduct, and capacity, must be employed in the process of removal of judges. Authorities who are considering the removal of a judge are enjoined to take into account relevant considerations, such as the integrity of the judiciary, the personal integrity of the judge, the public interest and, also, the confidence, of the public, in the judiciary. This should be balanced before taking the drastic step to remove a judge.

In a number of cases, internal administrative and/or disciplinary measures may be taken, against a judge, without the need to invoke impeachment proceedings under the constitution. There a number of minor offences that judges may commit, that fall short of the required constitutional threshold of 'misbehaviour' or 'gross misconduct'. For instance, a judge who is consistently rude to lawyers, or other judges, or one who does not deliver judgments, in time, may be dealt with internally, first, before the issue is escalated to an impeachment offence.

It has become apparent that, as with the cases discussed earlier, there are times when judicial interference is clouded by serving the executive, and bowing to political climates; rather than application of the expected standards of high adherence to the relevant international principles, that are meant to safeguard the independence of the judiciary. Such political pressures taint and destroy the public view of the judiciary, as in the case of Swaziland; which has a checkered history of judicial interference by the Monarchy, and weak judicial structures regarding the protection and removal of judges.

Where local structures are weak, and there is no provision for comprehensive processes, countries must align their processes with international law; so as to safe guard, and promote, the independence of the judiciary. It does not need any emphasis that a judiciary which serves the executive is non deserving of public confidence, as it breaches the principles of the rule of law. Modern democracies must be at the fore-front, to protect and promote the independence of the judiciary.

CONCLUSION

It seems appropriate to end this book by reflecting broadly on the changing role of judges. The role of judges has changed dramatically since the day I was first called to the bar in 1990. At that time judges would frown upon any suggestion that they could be required to manage the files and even encourage parties to settle their matters. Management of files was the job of registrars. Encouraging parties to settle their matters was considered risky as it may compromise the impartiality of judges.

Nowadays, judges accept that they have to manage cases and encourage parties to settle if that is considered desirable and appropriate. In some jurisdictions judges are actively involved in mediation with excellent results for the speedy dispensation of justice. In other jurisdictions the idea of judges mediating has not struck a chord.

I also tend to think that in the olden days, at least in my jurisdiction, judges tended to be less friendly than now, and appearing before a judge was filled with intense anxiety – and sometimes fear. Judges tended to be stricter on time keeping and dressing code. I speak from experience with respect to appropriate dressing code. Once, soon after law school, in one of my earlier appearances, a judge refused to allow me to argue because, as he put it, he, "didn't see" me. I was dressed in an immaculate dark, pierre cardin brownish suit; that the judge considered inappropriate. I served in a time when a failure by a lawyer to turn up in court in time may result in contempt of court proceedings and which in turn may lead to imprisonment.

Authority of the judge

Nothing much has changed in terms of the authority of the judge. Litigants still, by and large, hold judges in high regard, and trust their sense of fairness. But, given the sheer change in technological advancement in the last few years, and social changes, today's judges are required to be more versatile and dynamic. It seems to me that in this era, subject to the level of telecommunication infrastructure and network reliability, it is no longer necessary to have hard copies of files in court. It should be sufficient for judges to just walk into court with their computers. I admit that they may well be exceptional circumstances where hard copies may still be necessary. Depending of course on the level of technological development, and network reliability, it seems to me that activities such as roll call or status conferences should now be conducted through video link or such other similar devices.

A judge in the digital era

I know that many of us, judges, still under-utilize the tools that we have been given to improve the services that we render to litigants, such as smart phones and laptops. Many of us still use, at best, our lap tops to send personal emails, and not on work related matters. We need to pay attention to the need to upgrade judges' computer skills in order to enhance efficiency and improve their capacity to conduct research.

I know from experience that we utilize just a tiny fraction of the gadgets that we are given. Once, I had a printer in my chambers that I could hardly use. It was gathering dust. Sometime this is due to misplaced phobia arising out of habit. But once one makes a personal commitment to put these tools to good use the results are usually quite pleasing.

Judges' primary role is to resolve disputes that arise between citizen and citizen and citizen and the state. This can be seen every day in many jurisdictions. Judges start their courts in the morning and sit all day long, listening to litigants or lawyers present their clients' cases. This involves listening to witnesses, deciding disputed questions of fact, and applying legal principles to those facts to resolve the dispute.

As it always happens lawyers would be presenting different versions of what is alleged to have happened and proffering different interpretations of the law and asking the judge to rule in their favour; and every once in a while, a really new question arises that touches on social policy, and to which the law offers no ready answer.

Law is everywhere

The above routine in the life of a judge notwithstanding, a lot has really changed. The influence of the law is pervasive. Law is found everywhere. The rate at which legislation is being passed to regulate human affairs is simply staggering. The number of regulations passed by local authorities is difficult to enumerate. This means more work for the judges who are called upon to give meaning to all these laws and or regulations. The result is that more and more legal questions of an intricate nature are brought before the courts to resolve.

Our societies have become more conscious of their rights and those with some resources are prepared to litigate if need be to enforce their rights. In order to ensure that as many people as possible access justice some jurisdictions have in place a system of legal aid that allows even the poor to access justice. All these increases the work of judges. As every judge would probably confirm, one of the big challenges in court is to deal with unrepresented litigants. On many occasions they have a genuine and justiciable complaint but the form in which they present their cases may not be as required.

A few examples on how the law has expanded in the last century and the present would illuminate the point I am at pains to make on the phenomenal growth of law in every facet of our lives:

- The criminal law has expanded phenomenally, to include crimes hitherto not known such as cybercrime and a host of new offences, from drug laws to acts of terrorism.

- The law of delict has also grown spectacularly beyond the boundaries first painted by the House of Lords in the now famous case of *Donoghue v. Stevenson* - where the court explained that an injury that results in loss that is not foreseeable is not actionable. Now new boundaries of negligence are being fashioned in the crucible of litigation.

- The boundaries of the law of contract are also being re-drawn and expanded, to embrace lesser known cause of actions that seek to impose liability for non-economic, intangible losses in appropriate circumstances.

- Constitutional law is has taken over the space that used to be occupied by politics. These days matters that used to be the prerogative of executive power are subjected to judicial review and increasingly the courts are entertaining such litigation.

- In the field of human rights, there has been a big push to render socio-economic rights as justiciable as civil and political rights. Increasingly the courts are dismantling the walls of discrimination and prejudice based on sexual orientation and gender. We are now seeing many jurisdictions that have declared same sex marriages constitutional. In the recent past countries such as USA, India, Cayman Islands and Botswana have declared different forms of same sex relationships constitutional. It is indeed worth celebrating the fact that we now live in a world that takes the rights of minorities and the disempowered seriously, and does so through the law.

These changes could hardly be imagined a few decades ago when I was called to the bar. The time dynamic has infused new thinking and yielded jurisprudential out put that in the years past would have been frowned upon or simply regarded as a taboo. Judges are rational beings who must be driven only by evidence, rationality and fairness, even against the wishes of the majority.

One may ask what has contributed to the complexity of the law and made the job of judges more onerous. The list of the matters that judges are called upon to adjudicate are so many that it would be pointless to attempt to enumerate them. These include:

- Equality and equal protection of the law issues
- The right to liberty
- Terrorism and human rights
- Freedom of religion
- Freedom of expression
- Complex commercial litigation involving octopus-like multi-national companies

Public law

In the sphere of public law the issues that have really been difficult to resolve are those that involve weighing one value against another or others, or those that involve individual rights and the collective. These require judges to engage in fine balancing act. The issues of balancing individual human rights and collective security in cases of alleged terrorism act is particularly difficult; and so are some issues involving medical opinion on some complex medical procedures and related matters.

The case of a child with a rare genetic condition in the UK in 2017 or thereabout comes to mind. This was the case of Charlie Gad, who was born with a rare and fatal genetic disease. The doctors thought there were no chances of improvement and they applied to the High Court to authorize withdrawal of treatment which they considered futile, and allow the baby to die.

Charlie's parents, like most parents would have done rejected the advise. They had information that there is a chance the baby could be helped in the USA. The doctors in the USA had said chances of effective treatment were low but better than zero. The courts after much reflection authorized the withdrawal of treatment.

There are one or two features of this case worth noting. Firstly, it seems that although the decision whether to withdraw treatment or not was fundamentally clinical, the clinicians were unwilling to make judgment on their own, possibly for their own protection, and wanted the court to pronounce on the matter. This made perfect sense. In law, as the case of *Stump v Sparkman* in the USA demonstrated, judges are immune from liability on such matters. Secondly, the court relying on the evidence that to take the baby to the USA may worsen her situation refused to allow the parents to take her to the USA.

Then came the case of Alfie in the UK again. Alfie had a degenerative neurological condition. Her parents lost a court bid to reverse a clinical decision that it is in her interest to remove him from life support and allow him to die. The court agreed with the doctors that there is no hope that the child would get better.

There are other challenges in other sectors too. Information technology presents challenges similar to those posed above. It has been suggested by some authorities that we are currently living a revolution in communications as profound and important as the one sparked by Gutenberg's invention of the printing press in the 15th century - the revolution of interactive electronic communication.

It is far reaching changes like Gutenberg's invention that inevitably bring about an overhaul of the legal system as we know it and bring new legal norms to the fore. When developments of this nature take place judges cannot afford to lag behind societal changes. They too must innovate to keep pace with whatever changes may be taking place. Otherwise they risk being irrelevant as an institution meant to serve society and interpret the constitution as a living document and not a museum piece.

It is on account of the above breath taking developments that it has often been observed that our societies face the challenge of three revolutions - a rights revolution, a technological revolution and a demographic and social revolution created by populations that are increasingly mobile and ethnically and religiously diverse. All three of these revolutions collide and collude to shape each other and generate new legal norms.

The developments I have highlighted above have not really challenged the fundamentals of a judges' work. However, what they have done is to require judges to acquire some knowledge and skills that perhaps were not required in the yesteryear. Fundamentally, the judges' core mandate remains the same, namely, to decide cases in independently, impartially, based on law and facts only.

Judges must embrace continuous legal education

To remain effective and relevant in the modern world judges must have just more than elementary knowledge of the law and its logic. The judges must be willing to learn and familiarise themselves with jurisprudential developments in diverse areas of the law.

SELECTED REFERENCES

case

Attorney General v Unity Dow 1992 blr 119

Attorney General v Thuto Rammoge & Others 2016 CACGB-128-14

brown v board of education of Topeka, 347, US 483 (1954)

Donoghue v Stevenson [1932] ukhl 100

Dykes v Hosemann 743 f. 2d 1488

His Lordship Justice Paul Uuter Dery v tiger eye pi and the chief justice of the republic of Ghana and the attorney general (j1/92016) [2016] ghasc 80 (27 October 201)

Mafeelela v The State 1996 blr 15 (ca)

Mmusi & others v Ramantele And another 2012 (2) blr 590

Obergefell V Hodges 576 US (2015)

Penrice V Dickinson 1945 AD 6 at 14

President of the Republic of South Africa and Others v South African rugby football union and others CCT 16/98 [1999] ZACC 11; 2000 (1) SA 1 10 1999 (10) BLLR 1059 10 September 1999

R v Oak 1986 1 SCR 103

R v Sussex justices (1924) 1 KB 256 at 259

R v Valente [1985] 2 SCR 673

Regional Magistrate Du Preez v Walker 1976 4 SA 849 (a)

S V Roberts and others (CC 20/2011) [2012] ZAECPEHC 72; 2013 (1) sacr 369 (ecp) (27 September 2012)

Sirrors v Moore 375 US 335 (1964)

Stump V Sparkman 435 US 349 (1978)

Valente V the queen [1985] 2 S.C.R 673

International/ legal instruments

The Universal Declaration of Human Rights (UDHR)

The African Charter on Human and People's Rights

Books

Andrew Ashworth, Sentencing and criminal justice 151 (3d ed. 2000)

David Dyzenhaus, Judging the judges, judging ourselves (Hart publishing, 1998)

Dyzenhaus, Judging the Judges, Judging ourselves (Hart Publishing, 1998)

Edward Lazarus, Closed chambers (Penguin books, 1999)

Justice J B Thomas, Judicial ethics in Australia (2nd Ed, lbc, 1997)

R dworkin, Taking rights seriously (Cambridge: Harvard university press, 1978)

The American Bar Association: Rule of Law Initiative (2010) Handbook of International Standards of Sentencing Procedure

Articles/Papers

Aharon Barak, "The judge in a democracy" (Princeton University Press, Princeton, 2006)

Alvin b. Rubin ET. Al (2013), "Judicial Writing Manual: a Pocketbook Guide for Judges",(2nd Ed), Federal Judicial Center

Chief Justice M Gleeson, "Aspects of Judicial Performance", revised version of a paper "the role of the Judge and becoming a Judge" Delivered to The National Judicial Orientation Programme, 16 august 1998, Sydney

Collins, "Democracy and Adjudication" in Maccormick and Birks (Eds), (Claredon press, 1997)

Dworkin, R, "Law's empire", the Belknap press of Harvard University Press Cambridge (1986)

Honourable Justice Roselyn Atkinson, Supreme Court of Queensland, "Judgement writing" delivered to the Aija conference, Brisbane, 13 September 2002.

Mackena J, the Judge as Juror: "The Judicial Determination of Factual issues", (19850) 38 Current Legal Problems

The Right Honorable Lord Wright of Durley, "Legal essays and addresses" (1939) Cambridge University Press

Law Journals

Allison J R, (1994), "Ideology, prejudgment and process values", 28 New Eng L Rev 657

B.l Shientag, "The virtue of impartiality"in G.R. Winters ed., handbook for Judges (American Judicature Society,

1975) cited in B. Wilson, "Will women Judges really make a difference?") (1990) 28 Osgood Hall L.J 507

Hon. Danielle E Wathen, "When the Court speaks: Effective Communication as part of Judging" (2005) 47 ME LR 449 at 451

Judge C G Douglas iii, "How to write a concise opinion" (1983) 22 Judge's Journal 4 at 7

JA, "Judicial Intervention in the trial process" (1985) 69 ALJ 365

Justice B N Cardozo, The Nature of the Judicial Process (Yale University Press, 1921)

Justice J D Heydon, "Judicial Activism and the death of the rule of law" [2003] Aust Bar Rev 110

L'hereux-Dube J, "Reflections on judicial independence. Impartiality and the foundations of equality", CIJL Year Book Vol. vii

Lord Reid, "The Judge as Lawmaker" (1972) 12 JSPTL 22

Mason K, "Unconscious Judicial Prejudice", (2001) 75 ALJ 676 at 684

Sir Frank Kitto, "Why write judgments" (1992) 66 ALJ 787 (at 789)

Sir Anthony Mason, "The role of the courts at the turn of the century" (1993) 3 JJA 156 at 166

Reports

Australian Law Reform Commission, Equality before the Law: Women's equality, Report no. 69, 1994

INDEX